KU-256-791

Scapegoats and Social Actors

The Exclusion and Integration of Minorities in Western and Eastern Europe

Danièle Joly
Director Designate
Centre for Research in Ethnic Relations
University of Warwick

© Danièle Joly 1998

All rights reserved. No reproduction, copy or transmission of this publication may be made without written permission.

No paragraph of this publication may be reproduced, copied or transmitted save with written permission or in accordance with the provisions of the Copyright, Designs and Patents Act 1988, or under the terms of any licence permitting limited copying issued by the Copyright Licensing Agency, 90 Tottenham Court Road, London W1P 0LP.

Any person who does any unauthorised act in relation to this publication may be liable to criminal prosecution and civil claims for damages.

The author has asserted her right to be identified as the author of this work in accordance with the Copyright, Designs and Patents Act 1988.

Published by
PALGRAVE
Houndmills, Basingstoke, Hampshire RG21 6XS and
175 Fifth Avenue, New York, N. Y. 10010
Companies and representatives throughout the world

PALGRAVE is the new global academic imprint of
St. Martin's Press LLC Scholarly and Reference Division and
Palgrave Publishers Ltd (formerly Macmillan Press Ltd).

ISBN 0–333–71418–0

This book is printed on paper suitable for recycling and made from fully managed and sustained forest sources.

A catalogue record for this book is available from the British Library.

Transferred to digital printing 2001

Printed and bound in Great Britain by
Antony Rowe Ltd, Chippenham, Wiltshire

QM LIBRARY
(MILE END)

For Gustavo and Nicolas

Contents

Acknowledgements

This volume developed from a selection of papers presented at a symposium held at the University of Warwick, 5–8 November 1993, under the auspices of UNESCO, entitled 'Emerging trends and major issues in migration and ethnic relations in Western and Eastern Europe'.

Our warm thanks go to Serim Timur, from the Population Division of the Sector of Social and Human Sciences of UNESCO for her valuable collaboration in the organization of the joint UNESCO-University of Warwick Symposium.

Our thanks also to Rose Goodwin for a masterly preparation of this manuscript for publication.

Notes on the Contributors

Jorg Alt, Jesuit Refugee Service, Leipzig, Germany

Ioan Aluas, (late Professor) Babes-Bolyai University, Romania

Floya Anthias, Professor, University of Greenwich, London

Jochen Blaschke, Director, Berlin Institute for Social Research, Germany

Giovanna Campani, Lecturer, University of Florence, Italy

Asbjørn Eide, Director, Norwegian Institute of Human Rights, Oslo, Norway

Zdenka Jarabová, Lecturer, Palacký University, Olomouc, Czech Republic

Danièle Joly, Principal Research Fellow, Centre for Research in Ethnic Relations, University of Warwick

Cathie Lloyd, Research Fellow, Centre for Research in Ethnic Relations, University of Warwick

Liviu Matei, Lecturer, Babes-Bolyai University, Romania

Alan Phillips, Director, Minority Rights Group, London

John Rex, Professor Emeritus, Centre for Research in Ethnic Relations, University of Warwick

Ana Vasquez, Research Fellow, CNRS – University of Paris V, France

Angela Xavier de Brito, Research Fellow, CNRS – University of Paris V, France

Introduction

The European continent of the 1990s is characterized by upheavals and crises stretching over the whole span of economic, social and ideological assumptions which underpin the stability and integration of society. This is true in both Western and Eastern Europe, which have been brought together into one whole with the collapse of the Berlin Wall and the sudden demise of communist regimes. While conflicts and dislocation have dominated the Eastern part, Western Europe has found itself in the throes of a profound crisis, accelerated by European unification.

Throughout Europe the issue of ethnic minorities and the racism they experience have come to the fore. These minorities are mostly of recent immigrant origin in Western Europe and of ancestral origin in the East, sometimes with a clearly defined territory. This book shows that the position of immigrant and minority groups within the majority society and the increased prejudices they encounter appear to share many similarities. This chapter starts by examining some theoretical tools which may contribute to a better understanding of the contemporary interaction between majority and minority populations.

The term 'minority' does not imply a numerical notion but a group 'singled out from the others in the society in which they live for differential and unequal treatment' because of their specific cultural or physical characteristics (Wirth, 1945 p. 347). Other authors have stressed the situation of 'domination, dependence and exclusion' which is that of minorities, focusing on an interpretation of the term 'minor' to mean 'under tutelage' (Simon-Barouh, 1982). For Wieviorka (1994), the concept of ethnic minorities tends to convey a twofold principle of inferiorization and differentiation concomitant with segregation, repression, stigmatization and racism. We shall now examine the factors which are deemed to bring about or exacerbate this 'minorization' of certain groups and the prejudice, discrimination and racism which they suffer.

EXPLOITATION AND POWER RELATIONS

It has been argued that 'malign' ethnicity leading to such ideology as racism develops when relations of exploitation and power are involved (Rex, 1986).

One typical example is that of slavery at the time of European expansion into its colonies. Humans were herded like cattle and owned like objects, the instruments of production. Their whole beings were bought and sold, not just their labour power (Cohen, 1976). This was the ultimate case of discrimination, rooted in relations to the means of production and implemented thanks to maximum legal rights at the disposal of the owners, including the right to kill slaves. As a consequence, slaves acquired, in the eyes of the owners and other free labourers, the attributes of their position: they were seen as a group of non-humans or sub-humans, devoid of thoughts and feelings and incapable of human behaviour.

Colonial subjects underwent a similar reification – although distinct from the above, as they were not slaves. Their subordination and form of exploitation were accompanied by differential treatment enforced through legal violence and specific penal codes. Prejudices developed about them which reflected their situation, turning on its head the cause and effect relationship, such as those finely analysed by Albert Memmi (1972); in this thinking, for instance, colonized people do not have the same needs as 'we' do, and therefore should be paid less (unequal pay), they are lazy and thus must be made to work through force (the institutionalization of forced labour).

In post-war Europe, when migrant labour was recruited to meet the needs of an expanding economy, migrants broadly occupied the jobs which were badly paid and involved unsocial hours – often unskilled labourers' jobs, considered too dirty and too taxing for the host population. Migrant workers occupied the lower strata of the working class and also constituted a reserve army of labour. In this framework racism and discrimination are related to capitalist accumulation as expounded by Castles and Kosack (1973). The *de facto* differential incorporation of immigrants and ethnic minorities made them suffer from discrimination in housing, education and employment. Theories of the split, dual and segmented labour market were put forward to explain the discrimination suffered by ethnic minorities (Bonacich, 1972, 1976). The gravitation of migrant workers into such economic activities also determined the images and prejudices which arose in the majority society; in countries such as France and Britain, where many of the immigrants were drawn from ex-colonies, this process was compounded by a prior prejudice towards the colonials. The concept of internal colonialism (Blauner, 1969, 1972) was developed to deal with ethnic minority oppression and exploitation, but more particularly to differentiate European immigrants from non-European workers who were originally slaves, peons or indentured labourers in the USA; this was not taken up in any significant manner to analyse the European scene, however. Another concept – that of underclass – was also used, initially in the USA, to characterize blacks doomed to permanent unemployment (Myrdal, 1964) and later in the UK for ethnic minorities excluded from fully sharing in the welfare state (Rex, 1979). If an underclass exists in the 1990s, it must include asylum seekers. The new in-migrant populations which are asylum-seekers suffer both discrimination and differential incorporation, as the rights they used to enjoy have been drastically eroded; in the eyes of the press and public, the notion of asylum seeking is inseparable from notions of bogus claims and scrounging.

IDEOLOGICAL FOUNDATIONS

It has been argued that racism results from the contradiction between the values and practices of a society; Myrdal (1944) explains racism in the USA as arising from the discrepancy between an American ethic of equality and the practice of discrimination. The only manner in which these can be reconciled is through a racialized other. In the same vein, Lapeyronnie (1993) establishes the relationship between racism and assimilation in France in the 1980s and 1990s, racism increasing in virulence as the distance decreases between the racist and the racialized. In the context of slavery, it is clear that the prevailing ideology of the time, which bounded Christians to treat all humans in a Christian manner, could not allow the enslavement of other humans. The answer to this dilemma was to dehumanize them; it was even posited that black people did not have souls. Within the discourse of Republican ideals in nineteenth-century France, colonial conquest was justified by the need to civilize 'barbarian, backward races'. This cut across the political spectrum, including most socialists such as Jean Jaurès in France and the Fabians in Britain, who for those reasons did not disavow colonialism but only its methods. The destruction of their culture and social organization was thus justified as pertaining to the 'races' which needed to be 'civilized'. It was at the same time an efficient instrument of domination, eliminating people's autonomy and integrity (Blauner, 1969). Indeed, as pointed out by Eide (in this volume) biological theories of race were developed at the time of European imperialist expansion. According to these theories, culture is determined by 'race' and a nation becomes equated with a racial type (Knox, 1850). Blaschke (in this volume) indicates that Germany, which had no history of empire initially, did not develop its own theory of race but imported it from France and Britain. The biological or 'scientific' foundation of a race theory has been dismissed completely but it is still widely pedalled in popular mythology and by common sense – such as anti-gypsy attitudes in Romania (see Matei in this volume) – and by some political organizations like neo-Nazi groups in Germany (Blaschke, in this volume). The exposure of false theories of race is evidently not sufficient to dispel racism and prejudice (Macgiver, 1952).

In the same way as racist stereotypes arise from the economic and social relationships of the populations concerned, racism initially follows from discrimination and not the reverse (Lapeyronnie, 1993). But the tenets of prejudices towards the 'other' involve complex processes of social interaction. The group prejudice against others might be a ricochet or an instrument of the in-group consolidation. Identity narratives are constructed which are both exclusive and inclusive to consolidate a particular community (Martin, 1995). This process, when it is concomitant with racism, can (but does not necessarily) involve colonialism. Miles (1993) examines how, in nineteenth-century Europe, racism and nationalism went hand in hand to serve the edification of nations and nation-states. He analyses racism as a process of ideological construction within a specific historical and structural context where relations of productions have a determining effect. It was the ideology of Nazi Germany to promote the 'Aryan' German race through the construction of another inferiorized race and its elimination. This process was to be witnessed again in the 90s as ethno-nationalism in former Yugoslavia, where it even led to the expulsion and/or extermination of the outgroup, named *ethnic cleansing* (Eide, 1994). These are extreme forms of a general phenomenon but it is necessary to examine carefully historical developments in a specific country to elucidate the racism and prejudices it displays. It is not sufficient, for instance, to call upon colonialism as an explanation of anti-Arab racism in France; one must also look at the specific form of colonization established in Algeria and at the decolonization process, i.e. the form of the Algerian war, and at the general perceptions of Islam and Muslim countries in Europe today. Racism is not to be considered as a general feature of all human societies, as Stuart Hall (1980) states: what actually exists are historically specific racisms.

SOCIAL STATUS

Hostility and prejudice against the out-group takes different forms and proceeds from different mechanisms. For instance, the Jews of the Middle Ages occupied a position of pariahs, as they carried out the activities which were necessary but which Christians were not allowed (morally and legally) to fulfil. This is often the position of immigrants in contemporary Europe (Rex, 1986). In modern times, the preservation of status is at stake, whereby the lower strata of the indigenous population stigmatize ethnic minorities in order to maintain their own 'superiority', in effect turning their own stigma to the ethnic minorities, conjuring away their own social exclusion (Gruel, 1985). In the USA Myrdal (1944) explains how the poor whites of the southern states developed discrimination and racism as a response to the threat which blacks were perceived to pose to their own status. The pariah and stigmatized 'other' are an easy target for scapegoating and hence a useful tool in the hands of political leaders who wish to divert the blame for a critical situation from themselves on to the out-group; 'One million unemployed, one million immigrants' is a facile slogan used by extreme right-wing political parties which offer quick and expeditious remedies. But it is also readily taken up by the native population, as it saves them finding a culprit among their own group and challenging the reassuring order to which they are accustomed. The stranger's objectivity, which enables him to see the harbingers of crisis with anticipation, also makes him suspect of doubtful loyalty (Schutz, 1944). Strangers are denied individuality and become a general abstract category. Simmel's (1964) stranger has a reduced affective relationship with the majority community, and is seen as mobile, devoid of roots in the community space, 'far' and 'objective'. The rejection of the stranger has sometimes been called the rejection of the 'tyranny of objectivity' (Lapeyronnie, 1993). This is best exemplified by the prejudice against Jews in Romania (Matei, in this volume). Strangers may be perceived as a threat either because they are deemed to undermine modernity or because they introduce it (Wieviorka, 1994). In Europe today, racism has been described as a defensive reaction to threatened identities and a crisis of society (Wieviorka, 1992). As for the victims of racism, they are denied their identity or equality, or both. If they want to preserve a collective identity, it is inferiorized and they cannot partake of an equality for which the elimination of difference is a *sine qua non* (Lapeyronnie, 1993). Competition is also a source of prejudice and hostility towards certain groups when they are competing for the same stakes and economic niches as groups from the majority society, and racism is likely to be enhanced when minority groups are successful. But throughout the debate over racism the notion of relations of power tends to predominate; this situation has sometimes been defined as institutional racism, which means that it forms an integral part of the institutions which govern our societies and perpetrate the discrimination of certain groups.

Several authors in this book develop the themes of racism, prejudice and discrimination. **Eide** analyses the history of ideologies used to justify discrimination, starting from the birth of racial theories in the second half of the eighteenth century, the heyday of the slave trade and colonialism. He shows how in Europe this contributed to nation-building and led in a direct line to the 'Aryan' superiority hailed by Nazism and to the extremes of ethno-nationalism in former Yugoslavia. Eide describes the current emergence of a European neo-racism/neo-nationalism with a culture base directed at non-Europeans and Muslims. He also traces the refutation of those theories in international human rights law which vouches the equality and dignity of all human beings and the elimination of discrimination. He warns us, however, of the delicate balance which exists between the prevention of discrimination and the protection of minorities. Eide remains fundamentally optimistic and proposes a framework for peaceful and constructive solutions to be guided by international human rights instruments.

For **Alt**, the contemporary upsurge of racism and xenophobia in Europe is a symptom and a consequence of the general crisis of the Western European model. He posits three components to this crisis: 1. the fragmentation of social life which leads both those who are disavantaged by and those who benefit from present socio-economic structures to turn to racism; 2. the increasing inadequacy of established political and social institutions which are incapable of facing both the elites and the electorates, hence the scapegoating of foreigners; 3. a crisis of Western values, tradition and civilization in its shift from a value-based to a consumer society, with national chauvinism providing a compensation for those who do not partake of material wealth and have lost the tenets of their identity, either as a result of an under-gratification or over-gratification of their desires. Alt concludes that the extent of racism corresponds to the scale of discontent with the norms of one's own society and offers three principles which political and other leaders of society need to adopt towards a solution: a new honesty in admitting to the size of the problem, the clarification of the root causes of the crisis, and the provision of channels for a contribution from the public to creative solutions.

Blaschke shows that Germany's specific history is not a sufficient explanation for the new racism flaring up at present. He argues that the latter finds its roots in polyethnic situations in which cultural demarcations and ethnicization are decisive. He identifies the principal arenas of racism in Germany: 1. in what he calls 'high politics', the lack of a concerted immigration and integration policy leading to an 'expulsion discourse'; 2. in the party system, the rise of populist parties; 3. the networking and increasing profile of neo-Nazi groups in the 80s; 4. the closer connection between youth culture and violence, mostly directed at foreigners since reunification; 5. a social predisposition; and 6. inadequate institutional structures which in effect lead to institutional racism. Blaschke portrays neo-racism in Germany as an expression of all-European activities in opposition to the transformation of a nation-state structure perceived as unitary into polyethnic patterns. He argues that as long as governments and their agencies fail to recognize the new polyethnic structures, hierarchization and delimitation along ethnic boundaries will remain an important element of social action.

Two chapters in this book deal with racism and discrimination in Eastern Europe. **Jarabova** focuses on the issue of gypsies in the Czech lands to argue for an evaluation of their current situation which should take into account the history of the discriminatory measures they suffered, official and non-official policies, attempts at assimilation and integration at the hands of mainstream institutions, communities and individuals. She finds that, as a consequence, gypsies have a low level of education, poor qualifications for jobs and a high degree of criminality compared to the rest of the population in the Czech lands. She sees in education the possibility of bringing about change and describes a project designed to introduce programmes aimed at improving the general situation. It sets out to provide better training of teachers through specialized courses in psychology, sociology and pedagogy and pilot projects in the classroom. Its objectives are to achieve a better knowledge of gypsies, to evaluate national and international experience to do with racial tolerance and intolerance and to spread enlightnment on the issue of human and civil rights. A first evaluation of this programme shows limited results and areas of possible improvement.

Matei examine prejudices against the main minority groups – Jews, Gypsies and Hungarians – in a country which is defined as 'a national unitary state' by its constitution. He unpacks the diverse social processes underpinning prejudice and racism in Romania. Noting that antisemitism in Romania (as in Poland) is singularized by the absence of Jews and anti-semites, but also by a strong tradition, he demonstrates how it is now used for clear political purposes of national bonding. In his words the term 'Jews' refers today to politicians and intellectuals as agents of an international cabal' which aims to subordinate the country to its interests; once again, the myth of the international conspiracy provides a scapegoat. Gypsies, on the other hand, are simply treated as biologically inferior by the population and as second-class citizens by the state. They are also used as scapegoats, but are said to represent an 'internal danger' and are considered as a 'police matter' rather than an ethnic question. Past progroms and the severity of present discrimination have hampered the awakening of a gypsy ethnic awareness, which is only beginning. The Hungarian minority, on the other hand, is vociferous, well organized and mobilizes its resources. Prejudice against Hungarians seems to be motivated by competition and the fear that their claims may lead to secession.

It is not sufficient to describe and analyse the social relations which account for racism and discrimination among the majority society. It is necessary to explore the possibility of other modes of interaction and how to bring them about. This can be attempted at an international level and at the level of normative sociology or can be found amongst the collective actions of civil society.

Phillips traces for us the recent strides taken in the work on new standards for minorities in international fora. He finds that in the OSCE and the Council of Europe, the emphasis has been on national minorities and agreements have included aspects of group rights and measures for empowerment; the references are primarily to 'persons belonging to minorities' but not exclusively so. These are political agreements linked to security that may become legally binding through a convention. Phillips argues that some Western governments are facing a dilemma which creates difficulties for the implementation of these agreed norms: how to limit violent conflicts between ethnic groups in Central and Eastern Europe, while retaining the sovereignty of Western governments to continue with existing practices on minorities that they would criticize elsewhere. The UN Declaration on minorities, in contrast to the above, refers to national or ethnic, linguistic and religious minorities, but it is a purely political declaration. According to Phillips, there is a recognition that standards alone, even if adopted, are not enough – that specific implementation measures are needed in countries, whether at state or local level, and that the new standards agreed have major implications: they place the treatment of minorities above the sovereignty of the state in a number of circumstances.

Rex expounds the two main tenets of what he calls the ideal of a democratic multi-cultural society: the notion of equality of opportunity for individuals and that of the tolerance of cultural diversity. According to him it implies two cultural domains in co-existence: (a) a political culture of the public domain, centring around the idea of equality, and (b) separate cultures in the private or communal domain based upon a tolerated diversity of language, religion and family practices. This definition, however, raises important problems for the sociologist, which leads Rex to ask several questions: how far is such separation of culture into two domains possible? What should be the place of the 'ethnic culture' of dominant groups? How far can religion be regarded as a matter of the private domain? Are there limits to what can be tolerated in immigrant and other ethnic minority cultures? He then considers these questions especially in the light of Western European experience in dealing with minority cultures.

Lloyd draws on the theory of social movements in her discussion of trends in the trajectory of anti-racist movements through a comparison of anti-racist mobilization in Britain and in France. In Britain she examines the period of the mid- to late 1970s as grassroots mobilization from local community groups was developed through Rock Against Racism and gave place to the Anti-Nazi league with its large and spectacular carnival-type activities. In France she concentrates on a slightly later period: the early to mid-1980s, where a similar process is taking place, i.e. the displacement of grassroots mobilization which culminated in the 1983 March for Equality and the formation of national organizations, in particular SOS Racisme.

Finally, ethnic minorities are active in their own right and may follow diverse paths in their interaction with the majority society. Assimilation, separation or ethnic group formation are the three main routes, although the first two are least likely and least desirable in the present situation. The strategy of ethnic group formation involves processes of boundary construction and resource mobilization and often leads to collective action through ethnic mobilization. The constitution of communities brings together tradition and modernity generally for an engagement with the majority society and for greater participation in the latter; they propose an alternative to a model of society divided by racist cleavages and ethnic reification.

The three chapters of this book dealing with ethnic groups and ethnicity concentrate on a section of these communities which is often left out, namely women.

Anthias first examines the problem of static and reified categories, particularly in the context of multiculturalism and its focus on ethnicity, but she supplements her deconstruction of categories by an attempt to theorize connections between them. For instance, she argues that racisms do not rely only on race categorization but also on ethnic category. She sees individuals as positioned at the crossroads of different categories of disadvantage: there is an ethnically diverse experience of racism and a gender-diverse experience, too. She links the categories of race and class and then those of race, ethnicity and gender, showing the limitations of the migrant labour paradigm, theories of patriarchy and the Marxist political economy model. Anthias stresses that ethnic minority women are subjected to two sets of gender relations: those of the minority and of the dominant majority and to racialization processes. She concludes that any attempt to correct disadvantage must take into account the intersecting categories of ethnic minority, class and gender.

Campani, after establishing the numerical importance of women in migratory flows, proceeds to analyse both the processes of settlement in some European countries of older migration (namely France and Great Britain), where different generations of migrant and minority women are present, and the new migratory flows.

As far as the new migratory flows are concerned, she studies in greater detail the case of Southern Europe: Italy, Spain and Portugal. She points out that these three countries present similar and different cases as far as women's migration is concerned: if the demand for domestic helpers and maids is common to the three countries, there are differences in the processes of family reunification, and in the ethnic origins of the migrants, for example. Campani considers the cases of women from the Cape Verde Islands in Portugal and Italy, and of Moroccan women in Italy and Spain.

She then turns to the life of associations among migrant and minority women, which varies greatly according to the host country, even if there are attempts to create international migrant and minority women's networks. Italy is presented as a case study to analyse the passage from informal networks to associations and the different forms of organization that immigrant women are developing.

Xavier de Brito and Vasquez write on Latin American exiles and note that most of the research on exile presents it as a life experience, without any distinction between genders, or where the female experience is necessarily subordinated to the universal male viewpoint. In this chapter they demonstrate that women have to be taken into account for a complete insight into the issue and that they have their own viewpoint. However, women do not constitute a homogeneous group and are split by a number of differences. Xavier de Brito and Vasquez draw on empirical observations and case studies to show what is universal and what is specific in women's experience of exile in the process of transculturation, and then analyse the diversity of directions taken by women.

BIBLIOGRAPHY

Blauner, Robert (1969), 'Internal colonialism and ghetto revolt', *Social Problems*, 16, Spring: 393: 408
Blauner, Robert (1972), *Racial oppression in America*, New York: Harper and Row
Bonacich, E. (1972), 'A theory of ethnic antagonism: the split labour market' American *Sociological Review*, 37: 547–59
Bonacich, E. (1976), 'Advanced capitalism and black and white relations in the United States: A split labour market interpretation', *American Sociological Review*, 41: 34–51
Castles, S. and Kosack, C. (1973), *Immigrant workers and class structure in Western Europe*, London: Oxford University Press
Cohen, Percy (1976), 'Race as a sociological issue' in Gordon Bowker and John Carrier (eds) *Race and Ethnic Relations*, London: Hutchinson, pp. 9–27
Eide, Asbjørn (1994), 'Minority and groups rights under the contemporary international order' in Panayotis Grigoriou (ed.) *Questions de minorités en Europe*, pp. 49–89
Gruel, Louis (1985), 'Conjurer l'exclusion: rhétorique et identité revendiquée dans des habitats socialement disqualifiés', *Revue française de sociologie*, 26(3), pp. 431–453
Hall, Stuart (1980), 'Race, articulation and societies structured in dominance', in *UNESCO, Sociological theories: Race and colonialism*, Paris: UNESCO
Knox, R. (1850), *The races of men: a fragment*, London: Henry Renshaw
Lapeyronnie, Didier (1993), *L'individu et les minorités*, Paris: PUF
Maciver, R.M. and Charles H. Page (1952), *Society*, London: Macmillan
Martin Denis-Constant, (1995), 'The choices of identity', *Social Identities*, Vol. 1, No.1, pp. 5–21
Memmi, Albert (1972), *Portrait du colonisé*, Montréal: L'Etincelle
Miles, Robert (1993), *Racism after 'race relations'*, London & New York: Routledge
Myrdal, Gunnar (1944), *An American Dilemma*, New York: Harper Bros.
Myrdal, Gunnar (1964), *Challenge to Affluence*, London: Macmillan
Rex, John (1986), *Race and ethnicity*, Milton Keynes: Open University Press
Rex, John and Sally Tomlinson (1979), *Colonial immigrants in a British City. A class analysis*, London: Routledge and Kegan Paul
Schutz, Alfred (1944), 'The stranger: an essay in social psychology' *American Journal of Sociology*, Vol. 49, No. 6, pp. 499–507

Simmel, Georg (1964), *The sociology of Georg Simmel* translated, edited and with an introduction by Kurt H. Wolff, New York: The Free Press

Simon-Barouh, Ida (1982), 'Minorités en France: populations originaires des pays de l'Asie du Sud-Est' *Pluriel* No. 32, pp. 59–71

Wieviorka, Michel (1992), *La France raciste*, Paris: Seuil

Wieviorka, Michel (1994), 'Ethnicity as action' in John Rex and Beatrice Drury (eds) *Ethnic mobilization in a multi-cultural Europe*, Aldershot: Avebury, pp. 23–29

Wirth, L., (1945), 'The problems of minority groups' in R. Linton (ed.), *The Science of man in the world crisis*, New York

1 Racial and Ethnic Discrimination in Europe: Past, Present and Future

Asbjørn Eide

INTRODUCTION: DISCRIMINATION AS IDEOLOGY

This paper does not examine the *causes* of racism and discrimination. These form a complex set of economic, social, cultural, scientific, technological and political factors which have been shifting over time and whose manifold combinations have caused great variations in the practice of discrimination in different parts of the world. I shall focus, rather, on some of the ideologies or belief structures which have been used and are being used in an attempt to *justify* discrimination and exclusiveness. The main focus will be on racism in the strict, traditional sense of the word, which for some time in European intellectual history was sought and justified by a pseudo-scientific tradition starting around 1750 and experiencing its downfall with the collapse of the 'Third Reich' in 1945.

Contemporary, post-1945 exclusion and discrimination is rarely sought to be justified by racism in its traditional way. To the extent that intellectual justification is sought at all (many racists care little about intellectual exercises), it is linked to allegations of more or less insurmountable cultural differences, often based on religious or ethnic classifications where the role of race, in terms of biological differences of descent, plays a less prominent role – the concepts we use in the discourse on discrimination. The words have changed in their semantic content over time, and not everyone understands the same things from the key words used in this chapter. I shall therefore first examine the evolution and demise of the mythology of race in pseudo-scientific discourse and follow this account with an examination of its replacement by xenophobia and related intolerance in our own time.

1　SOME CONCEPTUAL CLARIFICATIONS

This paper deals with racism, racial discrimination, xenophobia and related intolerance. None of those terms are free from ambiguity; they are filled with emotions and sometimes passion. They form a significant part of the arsenal of contemporary political discourse. The ambiguity of their use often causes political and even scientific discourse to become confused and thereby makes it difficult to find constructive solutions.

The closest we can come to an international consensus on the meaning of these words is by reference to declarations and conventions adopted by United Nations organs, which must be seen as approximations of the views of the world community. With all the weaknesses of the United Nations, there exists no other body with a similar claim to speak on behalf of the world community.

Racial discrimination is the widest concept. It is defined thus in the International Convention on the Elimination of all Forms of Racial Discrimination, art. 1:

> In this convention, the term 'racial discrimination' shall mean any distinction, exclusion, restriction or preference based on race, colour, descent or national or ethnic origin which has the purpose or effect of nullifying or impairing the recognition, enjoyment or exercise, on an equal footing, of human rights and fundamental freedoms in the political, economic, social, cultural or any other field of public life.

It will be noted that 'racial discrimination' covers more than race in the traditional sense: it also includes distinctions made on the basis of descent, national or ethnic origin. These are phenomena which are very real and serious at the present time. The Human Rights Commission in resolution 1993/20 pointed out that there is a fundamental difference between, on the one hand, racism and racial discrimination as an institutionalized governmental policy, such as apartheid, or resulting from official doctrines of racial superiority or exclusivity, and on the other hand other manifestations of racism, racial discrimination, xenophobia and related intolerance in segments of many societies and perpetrated by individuals or groups.

Racism as a concept has been the subject of several declarations by UNESCO. The Declaration on Race and Racial Prejudice adopted by the General Conference of UNESCO in 1978 reads in Article 2 para. 2:

> Racism includes racist ideologies, prejudiced attitudes, discriminatory behaviour, and institutionalized practices, resulting in racial

inequality, as well as the fallacious notion that discriminatory relations between groups are morally and scientifically justifiable. . . .

The core element in earlier versions of UNESCO declarations was to understand racism as attitudes and behaviour based on theories or doctrines involving the claim that some racial groups are inherently superior and others inferior. In the early declarations, only the words 'race' and 'racial' were used in connection with discrimination; by 1978 it was broadened to include 'racial and ethnic groups', thus probably adapting to the language of the International Convention on the Elimination of all Forms of Racial Discrimination, which had been adopted in 1965.

We should also take note of the notions of heterophobia and xenophobia. There are, to my knowledge, no legally relevant definitions of these social and cultural phenomena. They refer to pervasive, fluctuating and largely irrational feelings of hostility (and correspondingly hostile behaviour) towards groups belonging to different cultures, different ethnic and cultural backgrounds, and different religions. The strength of heterophobia and xenophobia varies with economic and political conditions. At times such feelings, and in particular the corresponding behaviour, are subordinated to and suppressed by other factors, such as ideologies directed against different political systems; at other times such sentiments reappear in strength and create serious political turbulence.

2   RACIST MYTHOLOGY IN HISTORY

Probably the most significant achievement in our time is the practically unanimous finding by contemporary scientists that theories of race postulating a superiority-inferiority relationship are without any biological foundation. Modern science has been able to show that the word 'race' is practically devoid of biological meaning. This is significant because racism has been built on pseudo-scientific assumptions, which have now been shown to be false.

UNESCO has on various occasions sought to define racism. In UNESCO's 'Fourth statement of race' it was defined as 'anti-social beliefs and acts which are based on the fallacy that discriminatory inter-group relations are justifiable on a biological ground'. It can be useful to review briefly the evolution of those theories in the light of modern knowledge.

At a meeting of scientists convened by UNESCO, it was noted that 'all attempts to classify the human species so as to give objective content to the concept of race has been based on visible physical characteristics. In fact, the concept of race can only be based on transmissible characteristics, that is to say, not on visible physical features but on the genetic factors that govern them.' (Science and Racism: 32.)

While *heterophobia, xenophobia* and *ethnocentrism* are world-wide phenomena, probably as old as the existence of ethnic groups, *racism* in the strict sense of the word is a European invention, dating less than 300 years back. It coincided with the European explorations of other continents of the world and Europeans' encounters with peoples who differed from themselves both in appearance and in culture. Gradually, Europeans developed theories about biological links between appearance and culture. The foundation of racism was thereby established. Racism in its strict sense asserts that biological differences determine capacities and culture.

Prior to the end of the seventeenth century, the word 'race' (Italian 'razza', Spanish 'raza', French 'race', when applied to human beings, referred primarily to their descent from a given family or lineage, such as a 'noble family' (Geschichtliche Grundbegriffe, vol. 5: 136).

In the late seventeenth century, the usage appears to have changed. The earliest efforts at classification, however, resulted from rather innocent scientific speculation. Explorers, geographers, philosophers and pioneers in biological science sought to systematize their observations of the existence of peoples of different colour and physiognomy. There was initially no assumption of superiority/inferiority among these classes.

François Bernier, a French geographer writing in 1685, appears to have been the first to use the notion of human races in an effort to introduce a new classification system of peoples in the world.[1] He did not attribute intellectual or moral differences to these groups. Gottfried Wilhelm Leibniz, writing about the same time, similarly divided humankind into five 'species' or 'races'.[2] His language was still unclear, since he insisted that all human beings belonged to one race. Like Bernier, he made no differentiation between the different races in terms of innate abilities.

It must be remembered that in Europe, religious dogmas preceded racist theories. The Biblical description of the Creation had most Christians up to in the eighteenth century believe that all human beings were descended from Adam and Eve, and were therefore all of one race. This, however, was combined with a strong religious fervour according to which non-Christians were 'infidels' or 'heathen'. This belief was used to justify the conquest and persecution of Jews, Muslims and followers of other religions. Spain, like other European countries, had its share of intolerance. Two examples could be mentioned: the first is the expulsion of Jews from Spain, based on the edict of March 31, 1492. The second and quite revealing expression of this religious fervour, or the political and economic exploitation of it, can be found in the 'Requerimiento', a document made at the Spanish court in 1513. It was requested by Dominican friars, to be used by *conquistadores*. The document based its legal validity on the Bulls by Pope Alexander VI in 1493, delegating papal authority over most of the Americas to the Spanish monarchs. These were assumed to have God-given sovereignty over not only the land but also its inhabitants. The *requerimiento* was to be used by the *conquistadores* to be read to the Indians. If the Indians accepted it, they would then become serfs of the Spaniards; if not, the document presented in stark terms what would then be done:

> With the help of God, we shall forcibly enter into your country and shall make war upon you in all ways and manners that we can, and shall subject you to the yoke and obedience of the Church and of their Highnesses [the Spanish King and Queen], we shall take you and your wives and your children and shall make slaves of them as their Highnesses may command; and we shall take away your goods, and we shall do all the harm and damage that we can as to vassals who do not obey and refuse to receive the Lord, and resist and contradict him. (Todorov: 147)

Only at the end of the eighteenth century did the idea take hold that different races existed, with different origins. This was later strengthened by the theory of evolution by Charles Darwin and his successors, which undermined the Biblical claim of the Creation but opened the way for more explicit racism. The first steps on this road had already been taken, quite unwittingly, by the early natural scientists.

Carl von Linné (Carolus Linnaeus) the Swedish botanist and explorer who became famous for his effort to systematize all living things in his work *Systema Naturae* (first published in 1735, followed by several editions, the last in 1758), placed the human being (*homo sapiens*) at the top of the 'animal regnum' and subdivided humankind into four 'species' based on their outward appearance, in line with Bernier and Leibniz before him. In his first edition (1735) he made no differentiation with regard to the innate qualities of the members of the different species, and held that the variations found within the genus *homo sapiens* are caused by differences in climate and culture. In the tenth edition (1758) it seems that he, like some of his contemporaries, started to introduce notions of a link between outward appearance and innate qualities, including temperament (Geschichtliche Grundbegriffe, vol. 5: 145).

It is this transition from a simple classification of outward appearance to assumed (and unproven) differences in innate capabilities and characteristics which was to lead later to the dramatic degeneration of science in regard to race. Apparently, this fallacy arises during the second half of the eighteenth century.

Neither Linnaeus nor his contemporaries had any way of investigating the genetic factors which governed transmissible characteristics. But, as pointed out two centuries later by the scientists assembled by UNESCO in Athens in 1981, modern biological techniques have made it possible to study these factors. They reveal a far greater genetic diversity than had been imagined:

> It has been found that the differences between the genetic structures of two individuals belonging to the same population group can be far greater than the differences between the average genetic structures of two population groups. This finding makes it impossible to arrive at any objective and stable definition of the different races and consequently deprives the word 'race' of much of its biological meaning. (Science and Racism: 32–33)

Race theories in Europe at the end of the eighteenth century and through the nineteenth century rarely differentiated between 'ethnic group' and 'race', nor was a distinction made between biological and cultural features. To this, the scientists assembled in Athens in 1981 said:

> Man has developed culture, which has enabled the human race to adapt itself to different ecological environments and to transform them according to its needs. The pre-eminence of culture makes the human species unique and invalidates any explanations of human behaviour based solely on the study of animal behaviour. There are no grounds for explaining variations in group behaviour in terms of genetic differences. (Ibid: 33.)

Race theorists during the nineteenth century either were not aware or did not pay attention to these aspects. The observed differences in peoples' cultures in different parts of the world were evaluated by European standards. Europeans considered themselves superior and held other cultures to be inferior, though in different degrees. A double fallacy was involved: the Eurocentric assessment of cultural qualities, and the inability to separate between biologically (genetically) transmissible characteristics and those culturally acquired. In the view of the scientists convened in 1981, however:

> The complexity of the interaction between biological and cultural factors makes any attempt to establish the relative importance of innate and acquired characteristics completely meaningless.

Race theories in the nineteenth century became increasingly assertive. Charles Darwin's theory of evolution was quickly exploited by Social Darwinists to consolidate the prevailing prejudices about superiority and inferiority.

Race 'theories' lost touch with serious science and relied instead on vague, theoretical postulates. 'Science' came to serve political purposes. A landmark in this degeneration was the notorious work of Joseph Arthur, Comte de Gobineau, who developed a grand theory of the history of humankind in the 1850s.[3] He was the first to give prominence to the concept of the superiority of the so-called 'Aryan' race. He was not, however, a nationalist – on the contrary, his vision was the existence at the apex of the human races of what he considered a noble, aristocratic lineage transcending national boundaries, which he considered to be doomed to extinction or degeneration due to the strength (which he deplored) of democratic ideas of equality.

His views were to influence others, however, who interpreted the message in a much more nationalistic way and harnessed it to the growing anti-semitism present in parts of Europe. Gobineau was not himself an outright anti-semite, but his theories of race were vague enough to allow them to be used in various directions. One of those who picked them up was the German composer Richard Wagner, who displayed a strong anti-semitic attitude and was possessed by an imaginary conception of decadence and rejuvenation. He had, in turn, a strong impact on Houston Stewart Chamberlain, an English-born author and a strong admirer of German nationalism, who settled in Germany and became the son-in-law of Richard Wagner.

The major work by Houston Stewart Chamberlain is entitled *Die Grundlagen des 19. Jahrhunderts*.[4] Its first edition appeared in 1899 and was followed by 28 editions, the latest in 1942, which became immensely popular in Germany. It had a strong impact on Austrian and German mythology in the first part of the twentieth century and deeply influenced Adolf Hitler, as manifested in his notorious book *Mein Kampf*, and Adolf Rosenberg, another Nazi German propagandist, in his book *Mythus des 20. Jahrhunderts* (Myth of the Twentieth Century). The main purpose for Chamberlain was to 'save' the Teutonic culture from what he saw as the threat of materialism. He depicted the Jews as the major agents of materialism and the Aryan-German culture as the embodiment of the highest spiritual culture.

Race theories in the nineteenth and early twentieth century were serving social, political and emotional ends in parts of the European and North American populations as well as in other parts of the world where Europeans had settled. The theories served to legitimate actions which have caused untold suffering to millions of human beings in a multitude of ways. Racism has been used for purposes of exclusion, marginalization, and subjugation. Exclusion, at its extreme, has sometimes taken the form of genocide. Marginalization has been effected by white settlers penetrating into territories populated by different peoples who in many cases have been pushed into the interior and inhospitable parts of the country concerned, or forced to live on reserves which very often provide them with little or no opportunity for a meaningful way of life. In a more recent expression of racism, such peoples have become victims of extensive ethnic cleansing. Subjugation in its extreme form took the form of slavery, a dark chapter in the history of the Americas.

It is now generally recognized that colonial expansion was strongly influenced by widespread assumptions that Europeans had a superior civilization and culture. In his study of racial discrimination, Hernán Santa Cruz described these assumptions as follows:

Europeans, it was explained, colonized portions of Africa or Asia in order to preserve the indigenous peoples from barbarism, to convert them to Christianity, or to bring to them the 'benefits' of civilization. Regrets were frequently expressed that the 'natives' were so incapable of self-government, so far from being ready for independence, so thoroughly unable to manage the machinery of modern technology. (Santa Cruz: para. 40)

This was often said to be 'the white man's burden'. These opinions, widespread in Europe during the nineteenth century, based on pseudoscience and confused thinking, were used to legitimize the colonial conquests in moral terms.

It has been pointed out above that race theories about superiority and inferiority started to emerge during the second half of the eighteenth century. This is also the time when the slave trade began to become profitable business. Santa Cruz writes (ibid, para. 20):

The nominally Christian slave trader found belief in the inferiority, and even non-human nature, of the black man to provide a convenient rationalization for his business. As Philip Mason points out, this affirmation of the inferiority of black people was an attempt to balance the rather unbalanced equation of the Western Christian ethic that preached human brotherhood and equality of all people, not only before God but also in any democracy, while seeking to enslave some human beings.

Before the outbreak of the American Civil War, a leader from one of the Southern states, Jefferson Davies, told the Senate: 'One of the reconciliating features of the existence of Negro slavery is the fact that it raises white men to the same general level, that it dignifies and exhorts every white man by the presence of a lower race.'

In Europe, racism was used mainly in the process of nation-building and its main target was the Jewish population, but that was only the top of the hierarchy of 'races' against whom Nazism was directed: others who were to suffer included the Romanies (Gypsies). From Gobineau onwards, the mythology of the superiority of the 'Aryan' people took hold on the imagination. Nationalist authors like Houston Stewart Chamberlain projected a struggle for world domination between the Jewish and German peoples. As we shall see below, the persecution of Jews in Spain and many other places had initially been based on *religious* intolerance. By the nineteenth century, however, it was increasingly seen as an issue of race. This was woven into the Nazi 'theories' of race which resulted in the catastrophe now called the Holocaust.

Racist mythology seemed to have collapsed by the end of World War II, partly as a result of the revulsion against the Nazi use of racism in its boundless cruelty, and partly because modern science by 1945 could prove the fallacies of racist theories. Where past racism had structured social relations, however, discrimination did not disappear. The UN has undertaken a complex mission to obtain its complete eradication.

3 RACE, RELIGION AND ETHNICITY

As noted above, those who engaged in classification or policies of separation did not always distinguish between the senses of belonging to a specific religion, race, minority or ethnic group. Discrimination directed against one and the same group has with the change of time been explained variously as religious intolerance, racial prejudice, social conflict, cultural antagonism or xenophobia.

3.1   Religion and Race: The Case of Anti-Semitism in Europe

Antagonism against Jewish people has existed through the centuries, although the *rationalization* has changed considerably over time. For centuries it was primarily an issue of religious intolerance practised by Christian communities, but affected by cultural conflict and a desire for national self-preservation – and also, in the nineteenth and early twentieth century, a fear of modernization and hostility to capitalism. Different groups with a wide variety of concerns directed their antagonism against Jewish people, drawing on various stereotypes propagated in anti-Jewish campaigns.

Until the 1870s, however, it was not cast in terms of race. The very concept of anti-semitism was not used. This can be illustrated by the fact that the expulsion of the Jews from Spain in 1492 was sought to be justified in religious not racist terms Jews who were prepared to convert to Christianity were allowed to stay.

Influenced by the race theories which came fully into the open around 1850, however, a major change took place during the last decades of the nineteenth century. The race theories of Comte Gobineau, who for the first time made use of the notion of the Aryan race, were reinforced by Social Darwinism and, as previously noted, were further cultivated, among other places, in the Bayreuth circle around Richard Wagner. They were finally translated through ideological writing into action by authors like Houston Chamberlain, who contributed to a consolidation of several strands of anti-Jewish sentiments which by 1870 were defined as anti-semitism, building on vague assumptions of a biological heritage.

Semantic and intellectual confusion was extensive, to a large extent deliberately so. The notion of anti-semitism builds on the word 'Semitic', which can refer to language and culture (those who speak Semitic languages or adhere to Semitic cultures) or to 'the descendants of Shem' (derived from the description in the Biblical Genesis, Chapter X). Those two elements do not coincide, but for the racists this was not important.

It has been shown above how assertions about different genetic inheritance, aristocratic assumptions about the predestination of their social position, and cultural manifestations such as language were woven together with the fear of the agents or carriers of modernization who allegedly destroyed national culture and the nation itself.

Small anti-Semitic political parties emerged in Germany during the end of the nineteenth century. In France, anti-Semitic sentiments culminated in the Dreyfus affair. By the end of World War I, it appeared that these emotions had to a large extent faded away, but they were unfortunately rekindled in the turbulent inter-war years, mainly by ethno-nationalist hegemonical groups in Central and Eastern Europe. The extreme case was that of Germany, where the impact of the defeat during that war, together with the subsequent economic dislocation, was to cause a most cruel reappearance of what was called 'scientific anti-semitism' by the Nazis.

The resulting Holocaust prior to and during World War II is sufficiently well known to need no recounting here. The experience of unbridled brutality, however, was an essential factor in the formation of a global consensus after the war to adopt and to implement an International Bill of Human Rights and to make the elimination of racial discrimination a key element in that process.

This very sketchy description of the evolution which took place in the muddled ideology of racism has been recounted here as a reminder of the conceptual obfuscations which often form part of discriminatory attitudes and behaviour, making anti-discrimination efforts particularly difficult to enforce.

3.2 Ethnicity and Race

The word 'race' has in most cases been used by the dominant group (usually white) implying a superiority/inferiority relationship. 'Ethnicity' does not necessarily entail any such ranking, but there may be conflicts between ethnic groups for numerous reasons: control over land, political influence, predominance of culture, religious struggle, affiliations to peoples in other countries, to mention only some. This is further aggravated by transmigrations of groups of people. Problems can arise both when those who move are forced to do so, and when the migration is voluntary on the side of those who move but forced upon those who already live in the region concerned.

The UN has been faced with a double task: to prevent discrimination against members of ethnic groups, and to protect the right of members of these groups to preserve their separate identity when they so wish. This duality is not always easy to manage, particularly during times of ethnic conflict. A substantial part of the violations of human rights communicated to the United Nations are related to ethnic and cultural conflicts, sometimes interspersed with religious elements. The most extreme case is that of Bosnia today, where the Muslims are targets of extreme acts of barbarity, including mass rapes, killings, arson and threats, making them flee their places of residence in thousands.

The origin of ethnic conflicts are many and complex. There can be intolerant ethnic 'entrepreneurs' on both sides, militants who simply do not want to live in a multi-ethnic society. In some cases, the conflicts arise from real or imagined discrimination directed against members of minority groups, or from efforts of assimilation whereby members of the minority are denied the possibility to maintain their characteristics as a group, through language, religion, culture, and local autonomy where applicable.

In extreme cases, ethnic conflicts escalate into genocide, where the dominant society seeks physically to destroy a national or ethnic group. This is clearly illegal under international law, not only under the convention on the Prevention and Punishment of the Crime of Genocide, but as part of international *jus cogens*. International supervision in this field is still very weak, however.

Denial of human rights protection for members of minorities is unfortunately not uncommon. The UN Sub-Commission on Human Rights has paid particular attention to the problem of discrimination in the administration of justice, including the study by the late Mr Justice Choudhury on 'Discriminatory treatment of members of racial, ethnic, religious or linguistic groups at the various levels in the administration of criminal justice' (UN Doc. E/CN.4/Sub.2/1982/7). In the conclusions, it is stated:

> Discriminatory treatment against members of racial, ethnic, religious or linguistic groups at the various levels in the administration of justice is, in a number of jurisdictions, a fact of current life. It would seem that as politically and economically subordinate groups seek to achieve self-determination and rise in the social structure, they are continually confronted by the legal structure. Many minority group members feel that the criminal legal system is heavily weighted against them and that the police represent a foreign, alien power. (Op.cit., para. 160.)

This aspect should be given more attention. When members of minorities feel that they are not provided with equal protection by the law enforcement officials of their country, this is likely to intensify ethnic conflicts and lead to an escalation of violations on both sides. It is essential, therefore, that equal and reliable protection is provided by the agents of law. If not, the situation easily slips into massive violence and counter-violence.

There is a delicate balance to be maintained between the prevention of discrimination and the protection of minorities. The Convention on the Elimination on Racial Discrimination defines racial discrimination broadly enough to include 'distinction, exclusion, restriction or preference based on . . . national or ethnic origin which has the purpose or effect of nullifying or impairing the recognition, enjoyment or exercise, on an equal footing, of human rights and fundamental freedoms for all . . .'.

The Convention allows for affirmative action for groups which in one way or another have been disadvantaged and which may need such protection until equality in fact has been achieved.

But the issue of ethnicity goes further. It is a question of maintaining a separate identity for the minority as a group. Establishment of the appropriate balance between non-discrimination and equality on one hand, and respect and protection of the separate identity on the other, would probably be facilitated if there were in existence international standards concerning the rights of minorities.

4 DISPERSED GROUPS, PARTICULARLY ROMAS (GYPSIES)

The problem of dispersed national minorities requires particular attention. The lack of a compact settlement pattern means that the identity of these minorities is in greater danger of disintegration. They lack political structures and appropriate economic programmes; they are in danger of losing their language and knowledge of their own history. Programmes designed to protect and promote cultural awareness are weak or missing. Few groups are as exposed as the Roma people to these dangers. Solutions to their problems require a co-ordinated approach extending across state boundaries. Possibly there should be a special human rights supervision mechanism and an international network established by representatives of such groups with financial assistance put at their disposal.

Some positive steps have recently been taken in several countries. In Austria, a Roma council has been established; in the Czech Republic, the Roma community has been recognized as a national minority with corresponding legal rights; in Romania, a network of municipalities has been established to co-ordinate the resettlement of repatriated

Roma; in Spain, the issues have been approached with success, except in some provinces in Andalusia. The Council of Europe is now taking several initiatives in this field. It may be that the experiences gained from addressing the Roma question can also be used to deal with other dispersed minorities. These minorities do not have any country which is 'their own' and which seeks to help them. They are generally not covered by bilateral treaties. They require special attention, because violations of their rights are even more common and prevalent. They are often the most vulnerable groups, lacking back-up from any particular state that might place abuses against them on the international agenda.

5 MIGRANT WORKERS

Problems that relate to aliens and migrant workers are sometimes cast in terms of race. Here, as in many other contexts, the notion of 'race' is used in a vague and imprecise way. Aliens (including migrant workers) often, though not always, belong to different cultures and are sometimes of a different colour. The greater the apparent differences from the majority population in the country of residence, the more likely they are to be exposed to xenophobic sentiments and behaviour from some segments of that population. Xenophobia is greater during periods of economic recession and competition for jobs and other scarce resources. It is sometimes also exploited by politicians using xenophobic emotions to extend their power base.

One set of problems arose in the wake of decolonization. During the colonial period, settlements of aliens had been encouraged by the colonial administration, for plantation and other forms of labour. After independence, tension and conflicts over land and resources have resulted in some cases. While this form of tension is comparable to other ethnic conflicts, the fact that some members of these groups did not have citizenship at independence led some of the governments concerned to expel those 'aliens' who might already have lived there for several generations.

In Europe there have been several indicators of a re-emergence of racism. Under the European Parliament, a Committee of Inquiry reported in December 1985 that there were some small groups still professing such ideologies:

> Forty years after the victory over the Nazi and fascist regimes, groups and individuals in the Community and in other countries of Western Europe still proclaim their adherence to those regimes' ideologies,

or at least some of their features, and especially those which are racist and anti-democratic. (Committee of Inquiry: para. 345.)

These groups are in general extremely small. Their multiplicity, due to ideological dissension, constant personal squabbles and occasional outlawing, can hardly disguise the smallness of the numbers and the meagreness of their resources. It may be said that the more radical their ideology and behaviour, the more peripheral these groups become. (Ibid: para. 346.)

Owing to their small size and their lack of support among a broader public, these groups were not found to constitute a major problem. There were other phenomena, potentially much more dangerous, which have been primarily directed against migrant workers, refugees and the new ethnic minorities in Europe:

There is cause for more concern over the rise of more or less diffuse feelings of xenophobia and the increase in tensions between different communities. It has a distressing effect on the immigrant communities which are daily subject to displays of distrust and hostility, to continuous discrimination, which legislative measures have failed to prevent, when seeking accommodation or employment or trying to provide services, and, in many cases, to racial violence, including murder. The situation is aggravated by the fact that, rightly or wrongly, these minorities have little confidence in the institutions on which they should be able to call to uphold their rights and to offer them protection.

The development of this situation is associated with a new global malaise, the elements of which are difficult to identify and assess and in any case may vary from context to context. They comprise the time-honoured distrust of strangers, fear of the future, combined with a self-defensive reflex which together often lead to a withdrawal symptom, prejudices arising from the way national and international news is presented, and occasionally a spiral of violence in which aggression and defence are almost inextricably intertwined. All these elements can be found in crisis-ridden urban centres, where physical, economic and social conditions gravely militate against dialogue and tolerance. (Para 354–55)

Too little attention is given to this unease and its future consequences:

Many Europeans have difficulty in getting used to the idea that their countries have irreversibly become mixed societies of people of diverse European and non-European origin. (SIM Special: 1.)

In one sense, the world is becoming more open. Transactions across state borders are multiplying. Capital is flowing freely to most corners of the world. Scientific and technological exchange is on the increase. It is but natural that in this process, the flow of human beings across state boundaries is also increasing. As a consequence, people normally used to living in a homogeneous society are now facing neighbours with different colour and different language as well as different cultures.

For those who feel insecure, this influx adds to their insecurity. The response is a frightened effort to stem the tide of access of other peoples to their shores. Some of the Europeans whose forefathers emigrated to the continents of North and South America, Australia, New Zealand, Africa and most other corners of the world are hostile to the presence of persons of other colours and cultures moving the *opposite* way – from Africa, Asia, and the Caribbean to Europe.

Western governments increasingly face the dilemma of pursuing an open-door policy in other parts of the world (access of trade, technology and investment) while meeting increasing resistance at home against new arrivals. This dilemma will not easily disappear, and will constitute a significant human rights problem in the years to come. Improved standards for the protection of human rights of migrant workers and aliens already lawfully resident in these countries is important, but the problem of access will become more rather than less accentuated in the years to come.

6 CHANGES IN THE STRUCTURE OF INTERNATIONAL SOCIETY AND ITS IMPACT ON CHANGING ETHNIC/RACE RELATIONS

The phenomena of racism and discrimination based on nationality, ethnicity and religion have been deeply influenced by changes in the structures of international society. The impact of migrations and imperial formations in the past was substantial and obvious, whether we refer to Chinese, Mogul, Hellenistic, Roman or the more recent European formation of colonies and empires. The grand European conquests, colonization and establishment of settler societies from the sixteenth to the nineteenth centuries, however, provided the strongest impetus for racial classifications and discrimination on a world scale. In the present century efforts are being made to undo this. International relations, and in particular international law, have changed significantly. The basic principles are now the equality of states and the equality of all human beings. This is a feature only of the post-World War II period.

When the League of Nations was established, Western states were not yet ready to accept the principle of elimination of racial discrimination. Efforts by Japan to introduce this principle into the Covenant of the League were then opposed by several Western countries, including Britain, which in turn was urged to oppose it by Australia and New Zealand. The latter feared that the principle of equality and non-discrimination on the grounds of race would affect their treatment of the aboriginal and Maori populations (McKean: 14–20).

In drafting the Charter of the United Nations, on the other hand, equality and non-discrimination on the grounds of race was seen by all to be essential. For the countries of the North, however, the main concern was to bring an end to anti-Semitism, which had been the most cruel manifestation of rampant racism prior to and during World War II.

With the entry into the United Nations of a large number of African states from 1960 onwards, the emphasis shifted to racism based on colour – white discrimination applied to non-white people. *Apartheid* became the major symbol. There is a growing awareness, however, that discrimination takes many other forms, based on nationality, ethnicity, culture and religion. When apartheid has finally disappeared, the international community will have to come to grips with those manifold situations where discrimination is not based on theories of superiority and inferiority, but on fear and rejection of those who are different – whether it be in Europe, Africa, Asia or in the Americas.

The new racism emphasizes allegedly insurmountable differences between cultures. 'These forms of neo-racism no longer presuppose biologist dogmatism and plain inequality in the relations between the races . . . but stem from a makeshift ideology that has two essential props: defence of cultural identity, and praise of the difference both between individuals and between communities, as reflected in 'the right to be different'. Racist theories, to justify a perceived need to keep communities separate, now stress the anthropological characteristics of the target groups – not in order to praise the benefits of multiculturalism, but in order to justify keeping members of other cultures apart – preferably, to exclude them altogether. In many Western European countries neo-racist ideology stresses the unique nature of the languages, religions, mental and social structure and value systems of immigrants of African, Arab and Asian origin. In some parts of Central and Eastern Europe, particularly former Yugoslavia and the former Soviet Union, we see an unprecedented explosion of ethnic hatred and large-scale, brutal and violent ethnic cleansing.

Sadly, the quest by minorities for respect for their identity has in many places been perverted, by them or the majority, into a quest for physical separation. Pressures in the West to force migrant workers and their descendants to leave is paralleled by a much more violent process in places like Bosnia, Abkhazia and others of a process to establish 'pure' ethnically dominated territories by mass killings, rape, arson and threats.

Nationalist exclusiveness is on the rise. In the West, it does not so much mean the traditional, chauvinist nationalism directed (for example) by French against Germans, or by Basques against Castilians. It is a Euro-nationalism directed against those who are not European. Unfortunately, there appears to be a quasi-religious element in it, since Muslims are targeted, even when they are European – as is the case of the Bosnian Muslims, or second- and third-generation descendants of migrant workers, as in several West European countries.

In the East, nationalism is of the old, nineteenth-century type of ethno-nationalism. Under this ideology, nations are to be defined in ethnic terms, referring to a common past history, tradition, and (preferably) also a common language; secondly, nations should have their own states, so the society composing a state should as far as possible be congruent with the nation as defined in ethnic terms; thirdly, the loyalty of members of nations to that nation should override all other loyalties.

This ideology, which contributed significantly to the outbreak of World War I and World War II, is reappearing with great and devastating vehemence in the Balkans and in parts of former Soviet Union, and is having an impact also on other ethnic conflicts in the world of today.

7   THE FRAMEWORK FOR PEACEFUL AND CONSTRUCTIVE SOLUTIONS

While territorial integrity is essential to peace and order, sovereignty is today, as a consequence of human rights, understood in a much more open way than before. Freedom of movement allows members of minorities to have easy access to members of the same ethnic or linguistic group who are citizens in neighbouring countries. States are expected to co-operate in solving problems of an economic and social nature, including bilateral and regional co-operation to facilitate practical aspects of the existence of ethnic groups straddling borders of different states. Contemporary sovereignty carries obligations of good government, in particular compliance with universal human rights. Part of this obligation is to ensure that no member of any group within the national territory should have reason to be considered a second-class resident in that society.

Every state thus has a dual task under international law: to participate at the international level in the adoption of the international law necessary to build the world order as described above, including the adoption of international measures to advance the compliance with that law; and on the other hand to implement, at the national level, those obligations contained in international law which are intended to ensure good governance and protection of human rights.

Under international human rights law, states have three levels of obligations: one, to respect universally recognized human rights in dealing with the inhabitants of the country; two, to protect those same human rights against violations by private or non-state entities; three, to assist their inhabitants in enjoying their human rights by the necessary positive measures.

CONCLUSION: ELIMINATION OF DISCRIMINATION THROUGH A PROCESS OF EMANCIPATION

The realization of human rights for all, including the elimination of all forms of discrimination, represents a process of emancipation for all human beings, which still is being only slowly and imperfectly achieved. Of particular importance for the present study is the elimination of discrimination based on race, colour, national or ethnic origin.

In the past, discrimination consisted in the denial of genuine citizenship; discriminated groups were effectively blocked from participation. The worst treated were the slaves and their descendants; even after the end of slavery (the first step in emancipation) it took a long time before the African-American population in the United States obtained genuine rights of participation. The US civil rights movement, which scored its greatest successes in the 1960s, pursued the task of achieving the second stage of the struggle: genuine emancipation and equal enjoyment of rights. In terms of equality, in fact, the task is not yet fully completed.

Until the previous century Romanies (Gypsies) were, in some parts of Europe, treated practically as slaves. Their emancipation has only been partial and incomplete; they were often forced to opt for ways to survive which were frowned on by the dominant groups in society, and in many places they still suffer the stigmas and discrimination which arose out of their previous inferior status.

For centuries, Jews were severely restricted in their participation in many European states; segregation in ghettos was forced upon them. The only way they could become 'emancipated' was made dependent on baptism, i.e. conversion to the dominant religion (Christianity). During the Enlightenment, they were gradually accepted, but in some places on the condition that they gave up their Jewish name and other aspects of their Jewish identity (i.e. a policy of assimilation); the subsequent emancipation has not prevented serious, recurrent outbursts of anti-Semitism.

The process of decolonization brought about the emancipation of populations in colonial territories, opening up possibilities for the free determination of their political status and for their economic, social and cultural development. The process goes on, however, both in terms of extending their genuine participation through democratic structures and through the elimination of inequalities that might exist for some of the ethnic, religious or linguistic groups in the newly independent states.

The framework for the solution of minority situations consists in a combination of several elements:

– Respect for territorial integrity
– Ensuring equality and non-discrimination in the common domain
– Arrangements for pluralism in togetherness
– Where appropriate, pluralism by territorial sub-division.

The obstacles in real life to such solutions are formidable. They can, partly or wholly, be overcome through the use of national mechanisms for recourse procedures and conflict resolution.

Guidance can now be taken from the *Convention on the Rights of the Child*, Article 29 which spells out the threefold requirement to education. States which are party to the Convention agree that the education of the child shall be directed to:

(a) the development of respect for the child's parents, his or her own cultural identity, for the national values of the country in which the child is living, the country from which he or she may originate and for civilizations different from his or her own. Important is also:
(b) The preparation of the child for responsible life in a free society, in the spirit of understanding, peace, tolerance, equality of sexes, and friendship among all peoples, ethnic, national and religious groups and persons of indigenous origins.

BIBLIOGRAPHY

Bernier, François (1685), *Nouvelle division de la terre, par les différentes espèces ou races d'hommes qui l'habitent. Journal des Savants* 12, Paris

Chamberlain, Houston Stewart (1968), *The foundations of the 19th Century,* 2 vols. Originally published in German 1899, English edition by Fertig

Choudhury, Justice Abouyeed (1982), *Discriminatory treatment of members of racial, ethnic, religious or linguistic groups at the various levels in the administration of criminal justice.* United Nations doc. E/CN.4/Sub.2/7

Committee of Inquiry into the Rise of Fascism and Racism in Europe, (1985), established October 25, 1984 by the European Parliament, Dimitrios Evrigenis (Greece). Report presented to the European Parliament in December

Encyclopedia of Philosophy (editor-in-chief: Paul Edwards), (1967), Macmillan, New York and London (reprint 1972), 8 vols.

Geschichtliche Grundbegriffe (1984), *Historisches Lexicon zur Politisch-sozialen Sprache in Deutschland.* Herausgegeben von Otto Brunner, Werner Conze und Reinhard Koselleck, Klett-Cotta (Heidelberg)

Leibniz, Gottfried Wilhelm (1728), *Otium Hanoveranum,* published posthumously in Leipzig

Linné, Carl von (Carolus Linnaeus) (1758), *Systema Naturae sive regna tria naturae systematice* (first published in Leiden 1735, followed by several editions, the last in Stockholm in 1758)

McKean, Warwick (1983), *Equality and Non-Discrimination under International Law,* Clarendon Press, Oxford

Santa Cruz, Hernán (1977), *Racial Discrimination.* Revised and updated version, 1976. New York: United Nations

Science and Racism (1981), Report from a meeting of scientists held in Athens, UNESCO, Paris

SIM Special No. 7, 1988: New Expressions of Racism. Growing Areas of Conflict in Europe. International Alert in cooperation with SIM (Netherlands Institute of Human Rights, Utrecht)

Taguieff, D.A. (1990), *L'évolution contemporaine de l'idéologie raciste: de l'inégalité biologique à l'absolutisation de la différence culturelle;* Rapport de la Commission nationale consultative des droits de l'homme, Paris 1990

Thompson, Leonard (1985), *The Political Mythology of Apartheid,* Yale University Press, New Haven

Todorov, Tzetvan (1984), *The Conquest of America,* translated by Richard Hower. New York

UNESCO (1969), *Four Statements on the Race Question,* UNESCO, Paris

NOTES

1. An examination of the usage by Bernier is found in Geschichtliche Grundbegriffe, vol. 5 p. 137. The reference is to François Bernier: *Nouvelle division de la terre, par les différentes espèces ou races d'hommes qui l'habitent (Journal des Savants* 12, 1685, p. 148).

2. His writings on these issues are found, i.a., in Gottfried Wilhelm Leibniz: *Otium Hanoveranum*, p. 158 following. This work was published posthumously in Leipzig, edited by Joachim Friedrich Feller, in 1728. His ideas were first expressed a few years after Bernier's article, apparently in a correspondence with Johann Gabirel Sparwenveld in February 1697; see further 'Geschictliche Grundbegriffe' vol. 5 p. 143 with references.
3. On Gobineau and race, see i.a. *Encyclopedia of Philosophy* vol. 3: 342–343, and Gesetsliche Grundbegriffe vol. 5: 161–163. The main publication of relevance here is Joseph Arthur de Gobineau: *Essai sur l'inégalité des races humaines*, 4 vols., Paris 1852–55.
4. There is a translation into English, based on the 1910 German edition, *Chamberlain, Houston Stewart: The foundation of the 19th Century*, 2 vols. (Fertig, 1968).
5. For a comprehensive discussion of these issues, see Taguieff, D.A.: *L'évolution contemporaine de l'idéologie raciste: de l'inégalité biologique à l'absolutisation de la différence culturelle*; Rapport de la Commission nationale consultative des droits des l'homme, Paris 1990, passim.

2 Racism Within the General Crisis of Western Civilization
Jorg Alt

INTRODUCTION

Let's face it: We have known for a long time that destructivity inherent in our 'performance-orientated society' (= 'Leistungsgesellschaft') has been postponed temporarily (ecological catastrophe!) and geographically (wealth based on increasing poverty in the East and South). In the stream of asylum-seekers comes back to us what we first created in co-responsibility . . . We should be grateful to them because they challenge us . . . to a necessary review of our life-style and concept of society.

We must think urgently of a causal 'therapy' as regards the radicalization within society. In no way must we commit the mistake of fighting violent youth as the new enemy of society or seeing asylum-seekers as a threat to our way of life. Both groups – violent youth and asylum-seekers – are symptoms of a social conflict in this world which has acquired critical dimensions (Maaz, 1993:31).

This quotation is not taken from a socialist or green/alternative politician, but from the East German psychologist, Hans-Joachim Maaz. One may wonder with what expertise a psychologist comments on issues relating to sociology, politics, economy and ecology, while the article's outspoken intention is to be a psychological analysis of violence in Germany.

However, this quotation reveals two important premises which everybody should consider who wants to enter the discourse on matters relating to racism and xenophobia in Europe:

1. The insufficiency of partial explanations given by the different disciplines, and the need for a more synthetic or even 'global' approach for the discussion.
2. Every participant in this discourse eventually faces a fundamental

choice when it comes down to locate one's argument, namely whether racism and xenophobia needs to be seen as
a) a crisis *within* the present socio-economical and cultural model, or
b) *also* a crisis *of* the present socio-economical and cultural model *itself.*

These two premises call for some comments. More and more people are acknowledging the fact that the present upsurge in racism and xenophobia is a very complex phenomenon. The more experts try to answer questions relating to these matters in a thorough and honest way, the more they are aware of questions and phenomena which cannot be answered within their own field of expertise. Many of those experts, realizing the limitations of their own discipline, are therefore entering into dialogue with people working on the same question in other fields and who experience the same problems and shortcomings. This is where people like Maaz and the author of this chapter find the courage to think and talk about issues in which they are not trained experts.

There are two main positions concerning the problem of racism and xenophobia in today's society: the first position, of which Miles is a well known contender, argues that racism is 'a "normal" feature of capitalist social formations'. In other words, racism is a problem *within* capitalist society. It needs to be taken seriously, but not to be overdramatized: 'Because capitalism itself is structured by contradictions it simultaneously creates the potential for anti-racism'. Following this view, today's racist and anti-racist manifestations are part and parcel of the world we live in. There is hope that the anti-racist forces will continue to 'become increasingly powerful in Europe' as has been the case 'in the past two decades' (Miles, 1993:20; Kowalski, 1993).

I would argue that the views expressed above cannot account adequately for what is happening today. Like Maaz, I posit that present developments are revealing also a crisis *of* the Western socio-economical and cultural model *itself.* Consequently this chapter will develop the following proposition:

The contemporary upsurge of racism and xenophobia in Europe is to be explained as the result of a general crisis of Western society which makes it difficult to solve all sorts of conflicts. This crisis reinforces expressions of fear and prejudice against all those who are perceived to be 'foreign'.

First of all, however, some remarks concerning the central terms used in this paper seem to be appropriate: the precise meaning of the concepts 'racism' and 'xenophobia' is contested and the subject of ongoing debate. For the purpose of this chapter, the following working descriptions are suggested.

As far as *racism* is concerned, the definition provided in Article 2, para. 2 of the Declaration on Race and Racial Prejudice at the UNESCO General Conference in 1978 seems to be adequate. It defines racism as a *theory* including 'racist ideologies, prejudiced attitudes, discriminatory behaviour, and institutionalized practices, resulting in racial inequality, as well as the fallacious notion that discriminatory relations between groups are morally and scientifically justifiable.' Racism thus refers to a more or less clearly defined set of values, principles, convictions and goals, and racists – especially neo-nazis and fascists – normally use the language inspired by this ideology.

Contrary to racism, *xenophobia* is more difficult to define. First of all, xenophobia is a *universal phenomenon*. It is certainly difficult to determine whether genetic developments and influences in the context of evolution underly human resentment of 'foreigners' and 'the foreign'. Some ethnologists argue that there might be diffuse and initially unspecified feelings of resentment which eventually attain content and direction in the pursuit of social, ethnic and cultural interests and ambitions. Xenophobic – or heterophobic – feelings may also be directed against members of one's own sociocultural group – for example, towards those who hold different political views, who adhere to alternative lifestyles and subcultures or who are generally marginalized or considered to be 'abnormal'.

In my opinion, racism and xenophobia can be seen as symptoms of three long-term developments within European history and society which now, at the end of the twentieth century, pose serious threats:

1 The fragmentation of social life
2 The increasing inadequacy of political and social institutions
3 The crisis of western values, tradition and civilization.

I THE FRAGMENTATION OF SOCIAL LIFE[1]

The central thesis of this section is that socio-economic conditions create a sense of alienation which is subsequently manifested as hostility against the 'foreigner'.

One main feature characterizing the socio-economic structure in today's Europe is an excessive 'individualization'. Individualism as such was always an integral and important element of European culture. So far, however, excesses were balanced by social and collective norms, values and structures. This is no longer always the case because of important aspects of the present socio-economical model, such as confusing complexity and diversity, speedy economical and technological modernization, competition, deregulation, 'lean-production' policies and standards of efficiency. These features require of the individual enormous efforts (sometimes even submission), high availability and qualification, flexibility and readiness to move around as the employment situation calls for.

On the positive side, individualization offers to every person a high degree of choice, self-determination and self-realization.

However, there are negative side-effects of individualization. Due to competition, mobility, deregulation and other essential features of the present order, traditional social and value-supporting milieux come increasingly under pressure. Relations with family and relatives are under strain, solidarity among the 'working class' or other professional groups or the cohesion of so-far supportive structures of civil society are undermined. Examples of the latter are the small rural community, church congregations, and other membership in various organizations which exercised a certain degree of social stabilization and control. This breakdown of traditional structures with its unquestioned 'matter of course' as far as guidance and orientation by norms and values is concerned is widely replaced merely by a utilitarian cost-benefit calculation with individual well-being as yardstick.

These conditions create two groups at both ends of the social spectrum, among both of which racist and xenophobic attitudes exist to a considerable degree.

At one end, there are those actually disadvantaged by the present societal dynamics: those who are unemployed or whose jobs are threatened, those with few opportunities for education or professional training, or those finishing a training programme without having a job afterwards. Living in such situations creates first a diffuse and unspecified potential of frustration and aggression which may then direct itself towards all sorts of scapegoats: prominent here are foreigners and Jews, but also marginalized members of one's own sociocultural group such as the handicapped, the homeless, political-ideological opponents, adherents of different lifestyles or subcultures, the police and others.

Some researchers demonstrate that the feelings created by contemporary socio-economic developments carry within them the potential for right-wing, racist and xenophobic ideas. Examples have been put forward by the German professor, W. Heitmeyer (1993), who discusses feelings of insecurity, powerlessness, isolation and inferiority.

Insecurity is caused in a world of bewildering complexity, when people are forced into situations which call for decisions. Very often today, people lack the guidance offered by perspectives, goals and values and are therefore looking for orientation and direction. Right-wing parties are providing just that by propagating 'natural' orders, hierarchies and 'traditional' values. They also offer simple policies to solve real problems.

Powerlessness is a central experience in a competing society which operates according to the motto 'Survival of the fittest'. Right-wing parties rephrase this slogan into 'The fittest shall survive', present it with a doctrine of race superiority and offer scapegoats held to be responsible for present-day miseries. This coincides with the desire for self-assertion felt by victims of the present socio-economical order. Hence the application of violence in the context of a right-wing world view offers the desired compensation.

Isolation and loneliness are widespread in a society of fragmenting traditional milieus. Here people are susceptible to all those group-defining features and values which are perceived as 'natural', such as colour of skin, race and national origin. Those features are, in contrast with social status, criteria which nobody can be deprived of and are therefore 'suitable' to define membership in a new kind of 'family', 'community' and 'home'.

At the other end of the social spectrum we find racist acts and attitudes among those benefiting from the present socio-economic structure. Their racist and xenophobic attitudes are strongly influenced by social-Darwinist concepts. Successful career and social status are seen by such people as personal achievements. This provides them with a sense of superiority towards all those who 'did not make it', and an attitude of aggressive defence against all those threatening their possessions. They, too, direct their aggression both towards foreigners and marginalized nationals.[2] Of course, those people would not actively condone racist and xenophobic violence. On the other hand, they are doing everything 'legitimately' possible to defend their individual and national wealth against those who appear to threaten it, both locally and globally ('the chauvinism of affluence').

An important factor contributing to the emergence of this group of people is seen in the correlation of the socio-economic mentality and its imprint on the education system. Education is no longer a place for the transmission of values such as social responsibility, tolerance, solidarity, participation, co-operation and sensitivity. Rather, from early on children are subjected to exercises of competition, comparison and efficiency rather than creativity, which thus eventually tend to become internalized features of their character.

The fragmentation of social life is a helpful frame of reference for other important observations. For instance:

- As already mentioned, it renders plausible the 'xenophobic' resentment not only of foreigners, but also *of members of one's own sociocultural group.*
- *It explains the violent radicalization of society at both ends of the political spectrum.* Those suffering under the present economical order tend to react in three distinct ways: some of those disillusioned and frustrated can be found at the left end of the political spectrum. They reject the present socio-economic order entirely and withdraw into 'alternative' forms of life. They are known by such names as 'Alternatives', 'Aussteiger', Punks or Autonomous Left. On the right wing of the political spectrum are those who want to 'put' the shortcomings of contemporary society 'right' by implementing clear and simple solutions to present problems (Fascists and Neo-Nazis). Finally, a third group are those who want to break away from the daily grind at least occasionally (Skins, Hooligans). They, too, justify their activities mainly with slogans taken from a right-wing repertoire.[3] All those groups have a varying number of sympathizers and supporters from whom future members may be recruited.[4]
- It also accounts for the *decreasing importance of family and school as primary locus for orientation and relationship.* Families are put under strain by requirements of the 'round-the-clock' society which constantly requires mobility and flexibility. Hence, even though the net amount of free time is growing, ability to spend this free time together declines. Furthermore, parents are increasingly absorbed and preoccupied by their own professional problems and therefore have less time for the worries and needs of their children.[5]

As to the importance of school, given the above mentioned characteristics and goals of education teachers are no longer in a position to be recommendable partners to young people in addressing and discussing personal problems.

The place previously held by family and school is increasingly taken by peer-groups. Those groups offer quite a number of features compensating for those deficiencies experienced by young people in families and schools, including protection, solidarity and a place to commu-

nicate problems. However, in their inherent insecurity and lack of personal and social orientation, such groups are open to all kinds of seducers and ideologists.[6]
– Finally, the fragmentation of social life lends credence to the view that quite a considerable amount of racist violence can be seen as a *desperate cry for help* (Kodderitzsch, 1992; Heinemann, 1993; Maaz, 1993; Pahnke, 1993). Young people experience real problems and perceive no likely improvement for a personal future. Simultaneously, they find no adequate understanding, support or dialogue on the part of their elders. As a result, they consciously or unconsciously resort to the breach of strong social taboos. Thus they hope to draw attention to their own critical situation and to force authorities into dialogue and action.

II   THE INCREASING INADEQUACY OF ESTABLISHED POLITICAL AND SOCIAL INSTITUTIONS

Knowing about the pitfalls of simplifications, we may assert three major premises as still dominating the present socio-economical order:

1 The concept of 'progress' and 'development' is linked to quantitative economical growth[7]
2 Job opportunities, income and consumption are linked to the growth of production
3. Political and social institutions are used, *inter alia*, to protect objectives 1 and 2. For example, in foreign politics, geo-strategical political decisions were devised under economical and financial interests. In the domestic area, a tax system was developed to mitigate emerging social tensions by a system of social welfare. Finally, a system of customs and duties served to protect national industry from cheap imports or competition from outside.

All these structures were largely developed and implemented towards the end of the last century when the frontiers of a nation state were – more or less – coinciding with the political, social, and economical interests of a given nation and people. Tensions emerged as soon as the balance between these three starting premises became upset.

As time proceeded, economic growth gained its own dynamics and momentum. It made economic interests grow beyond the boundaries of the nation state and, by doing so, created a sphere of influence of its own. In this context, events of recent years such as the energy crisis, the growing globalization of trade and production, cheaper labour in many so-called Third World countries, rising competition for limited markets, the so-called Third Technical Revolution, the breakdown of the communist societies and upheavals of the post-Cold War period have a continuously growing impact on the areas indicated in premises 2 and 3. Production could be increased without employing more people. Moreover, it was even possible to make the workforce redundant ('jobless growth'). Mechanization required more skills than many traditional employees could offer, rationalization and 'lean-production' policies had machines take over the places so far held by human labourers.[8]

The continuing globalization of trade, industry and finance increased tensions in the field of social and economic policies which are still formulated and implemented to a large extent within the boundaries of the nation states. Due to emerging disparities within these developments, existing financial resources available to national governments are no longer sufficient to 'soften' or mitigate the problems thus emerging.

Thus today's crisis is not only a crisis in the employment sector. Since major existing social and political institutions were devised and equipped to resolve conflicts emerging *within* the present socio-economic model, they are unable to address and resolve problems and events originating in the crisis and dynamic of the model *itself*. In other words: even though there were fragmenting tendencies in Western society long before the past decade, the present crisis of the Western socio-economical model prevents its institutions from regulating or softening emerging tensions.

It is certainly arguable whether 'inadequacy' is the best concept with which to characterize the situation of contemporary political and social institutions. It should be unquestionable, however, that these institutions are more and more in their actions depended on and influenced by decisions and developments within the financial-economical sphere.

This being the case, there are two further positions worth considering: the first argues that present institutions are inherently inadequate to cope with the present crisis. The second assumes that the political and social elites have either failed or are unwilling to adjust existing institutional structures to contemporary needs. First of all, it does not seem to be the case that both national and international institutions are inherently inadequate to cope with present problems. They could be adjusted in two ways: firstly, by using the potential still undeveloped within present structures and mandates, and secondly, by means of reform, namely extending and redefining their role, or by adding or regrouping the functions of existing institutions.

The more convincing explanation for the present institutional crisis lies in the link between job opportunities, consumption and the growth of production. After all, any serious attempt by present political and social elites to adjust present institutions to contemporary problems is to risk a battle on two fronts: the first opponents are other, powerful elites of the present society, especially those in the areas of trade, economy and finance. The reader may recall how often the threat of imminent redundancies by the employer's lobby forces national governments to abandon reforms in the tax or welfare sector. The second front would be the electorate: decisions which need to be taken are expensive. After all, strategies up for discussion involve global action towards a more healthy environment and climate as well as measures with which to narrow the gap between the rich and poor nations. The latter call for action in the field of credits and debts, trading conditions, protectionism and developmental aid. All this can only be financed if the developed countries change their style of production and consumption and accept a decrease in their living standards, at least temporarily. Naturally, all this is extremely unpopular with the electorate.

Most revealing in this context is the preference of present elites to *promote scapegoats* rather than to address the root causes of existing problems. The proportion of scapegoats can be defined as an attempt to personify abstract and complex problems which otherwise need to be analysed and tackled in social, political and economical terms (Mosse, 1993:268; Pinn/Nebelung, 1992:10–39; Heitmeyer, 1993). For instance, the major problems of contemporary society lie in the areas of housing, employment and social welfare. However, everybody familiar with the context of these problems knows the following:

- Refugees are not the cause of housing shortage. The problem rests with planning mistakes in urban development and housing policies during past decades as well as the contemporary upsurge in single households.
- The deepening global recession has more to do with unemployment than 'foreigners' who can be found largely in jobs which are unacceptable to native citizens.
- If there were equal opportunities for refugees and natives alike, quite a number of refugees could care for themselves. Often they are forced to rely on the social welfare system due to restrictive legislation.

Similar reflections could be undertaken by discussing issues relating to policies in the field of developmental aid, ecology and (im)migration. Given their privileged access to information and data, it can safely be assumed that present political and social elites are aware of these facts. However, distracting attention from the complex root causes underlying these problems is easier than addressing them. It also guarantees short-term benefits in elections, for example, and shifts the burden to the shoulders of future generations.

All in all, therefore, present political practice indicates once more the tendency of any system under pressure – be it in nature, ideology, society or politics – to conserve and defend its present structure rather than attempting reforms.

In this context also the influence of the mass media needs to be mentioned. Their (all too often) uncritical coverage of the 'asylum problem' largely contributed to the emergence of a distorted notion of the size of the problem in the minds of the public. A grotesque example is surely Germany's public discourse surrounding Chancellor Kohl's perception of a 'state of emergency' ('Staatsnotstand') at a time when every 150 Germans were 'swamped' by one asylum-seeker. What wonder that people over-reacted in a violent way because they eventually believed what they were told and shown on the television screen?

III   A CRISIS OF WESTERN VALUES, TRADITION AND CIVILIZATION

The third, major complex of underlying obstacles and reluctance towards the reception of foreigners lies within European culture itself. Here ambiguity has always existed as far as the acceptance and perception of 'foreigners' is concerned. Distinctions between 'citizens' and 'aliens', 'civilians' and 'barbarians', 'Europeans' and 'savages' have been long bandied about.

Also, present-day society reflects this ambiguity because of the philosophies and ideologies shaping the outlook of contemporary society. For example, influences coming from Humanism and the Enlightenment (Erasmus and Kant) and the 'romantic reaction' (Herder and the Idealists) are major determinants in the current polarization of European society into those rejecting, and those welcoming 'foreigners'.

The historic tension between those two groups became complicated by two more recent developments. First of all, in a pluralist society ethics will have a different status from that prior to the Renaissance and the Reformation, when 'European' society had strong unifying features. In a homogeneous society and culture with identifiable authorities responsible for settling disputed questions, the ethical concept of the 'common good' or 'personal good' is less disputed and more binding for everybody. The same applies, of course, for the ways and means necessary to obtain these ends. In a plural society with a wider range of different world-views, the 'common' and 'personal' good will vary in accordance with the premises on which the respective world-view of the person involved is based. Hence a Christian will define and justify those concepts differently from a humanist, and both will have a lot in common when compared with the attitudes of national-ists and racists.

Secondly, the tension is nowadays complicated by the position by which possession of material goods defines status in today's society. Material property needs to be balanced by values of solidarity, and private interests defined by taking into account common interests. Nowadays, however, material property and possession are widely used as an 'objective' yardstick with which to determine social status be-yond all ideological divides. Wealth increasingly is an end in itself, influencing personal and national ambitions. This being the case, how-ever, materialism also puts a new momentum behind all sorts of per-sonal and national egoism, weakening further the existing forms of solidarity.

Accordingly, mistrust, resentment and dissatisfaction are increasingly major elements determining the social climate and interaction. Perma-nent competition puts any human relationships under pressure and the widespread reduction of social status to the size of material possession is the source of particular tension if existing desires cannot be satis-fied any more, or if available resources become scarce.

As has happened in periods similar to the present, national chauvin-ism and racism are yet again a welcome substitute for those disadvan-taged by the present distribution of goods and resources:

– National chauvinism offers a possibility to see oneself participating in the abstract and general 'wealth of the nation' in spite of factu-ally being excluded from it.
– Racism offers experiences of self-assertion in directing frustration and aggression towards other groups, thus making people feel that they are participating in the mythological glory of some 'superior race'.

The exploitation of racism and national chauvinism performs a similar function to that which distorted forms of religion had in earlier times: a form of distraction from the failures of the sociopolitical system to resolve grave social problems. The question remains, however, how long such a highly problematic strategy can succeed in keeping a fragmenting society together, or will it rather result in its members turning against each other? As long as there is no positive social consensus on the acceptance of 'foreigners' and as long as materialism and egoism remain major determinants of social interaction, civil unrest will be unavoidable if present socio-economic developments continue. As the report 'Welfare in a Civil Society' concludes quite realistically: 'Europeans should know from their own histories that growing racist sentiments are the most obvious signs of impending social catastrophes.'[10]

This outline of European history and culture is confirmed by the following observations and theories:

The above-mentioned ambiguity within European culture towards 'the Other' accounts for the existence of racist patterns in everyday thinking and talking

The adoption of racist ideas, criteria of perception and evaluation in most cases does not happen consciously. Rather, as has been shown by discourse analysis, one absorbs those concepts unintentionally. It just 'happens' by the way in which education, newspapers and everyday language develop and shape mental and intellectual concepts of discourse participants. The following phrases may serve as illustration: 'I have nothing against foreigners, but . . .'; 'Of course, there are also intelligent blacks!'; 'Germans are not racist'; 'French culture and lifestyle need to be defended . . .', 'I believe, that we are a wonderfully fair country (. . .), [but] British citizenship should be a most valuable prize for anyone and it should not be granted lightly to all and sundry'.[11] Those examples contain preclusions, unjustified generalizations, patronizing attitudes or evaluations which are taken on the background of an existing prejudice. Such phrases contain hidden signals which, in certain situations, can (and will) be interpreted as encouragement to racist acts.

Latent racist patterns of thinking and talking are continually strengthened within the nation-state ideology

A frequent recurring assertion goes that 'foreigners' are a threat to the national identity. People promoting that view, however, seem to be unaware that national identities are historical constructs and subject to change. Racist and nationalist prejudices developed at an accelerated pace during the second half of the last century when the nation-state became the predominant political structure of Europe. At that time, the active propagation of emerging 'national identities' which should be shared by all members of the given society included:

- the promotion of identity creating symbols (flags, anthems)
- literature supporting a specific view of the relationship between different European nations or between the European and non-European cultures[12]
- the rewriting of history in the attempt to justify present territorial possession as well as interests of the majority ethnic group and/or ruling elites
- language chauvinism.

Admittedly, European integration nowadays contributes to a general improvement in the mutual perception of EU Member States. However, there are also indications of an emerging 'Euro-Nationalism' claiming a 'European superiority' towards other mentalities and cultures.

The crisis of Western civilization also helps to understand a frequently asserted correlation between materialism and the growing potential of frustration and aggression in society

As has been argued, materialism dominates to a growing extent other status-determining standards such as social relationships, education, cultural and religious-spiritual achievements. Thus a shift from a value-based society to a consumer society is widely perceived. An important feature of consumer society is the correlation between supply and demand. However, all too often demands are artificially created in order that someone can satisfy them. This creation of demands occurs via advertisements, role-models, 'stars' and trend-setters, and competition with the neighbour next door. Because of this highly sophisticated manipulation, negative side-effects can occur:

(a) There may be situations where outside stimuli arouse desires which cannot be satisfied because of the lack of money ('under-gratification' of desires)

(b) There are people whose desires are completely satisfied as far as money can buy gratification at all. Life threatens to become boring and 'excitement' is looked for ('over-gratification' of desires).

In both cases, frustration and aggression build up and look for outlets. After all, it is revealing that desire for 'fun' and 'pleasurable excitement' are frequently recurring motives of racist and xenophobic perpetrators (Heinz, 1992:80; Willems, 1993:91; Spiegel, 24.1.1993:18).

Another interesting theory in this context argues that the extent of racism and xenophobia can be interpreted as scale of discontent with norms and principles of one's own society and culture (Räthzel, 1992 and Maaz, 1993).

The proponent of this theory once asked a sample of people to name those features considered to be 'typical' of 'foreigners'. Those given are listed in the left column. However, if those features are supplemented by their opposite, it shows an interesting collection of important features of Western society and culture:

FOREIGNER	EUROPEAN
headscarf = religious	no headscarf = not religious
group-life	individuals and singles
many children	no children
friendly to children	hostile towards children
worker	entrepreneurs
not educated	educated
not cultivated	cultivated
dependent	independent
passive	active
warm	distant
emotional	rational
ready to help	egocentric
backwards-orientated	progressive
having time	having no time

These findings, supplemented by results of related disciplines, led to the conclusion that racism can also be understood as 'rebellious self-submission'. In other words, many people submit to an existing socio-economical structure and culture only with clenched teeth and fists. People living a different life might then be experienced as a mirror of one's own desires and needs. In such a situation a person may be unable both to admit his/her own, suppressed desires and/or to change the conditions who force him/her into those resented attitudes. As a result, temptation lurks to release the tension caused whilst fighting 'the Other within oneself' by kicking the foreigner met outside.

CONCLUSION

The question remains as to what should be done in order to soften or even to counter the developments described above.

First of all, attention is drawn to the fact that the author of this chapter prefers to speak of a 'crisis' of present social, economical, political institutions and cultural values rather than of 'decline', 'decay' or even 'collapse'. The term crisis, coming from the Greek word 'krinein' – to judge – should indicate the author's basic optimistic belief that the present situation can be influenced for the better or worse. A crisis signifies a situation where old certainties, norms, codes of conduct and values are being questioned and new certainties, norms, etc. are not yet clearly visible, definable or accepted by widespread social consensus. This view is supported by the kind of language used by many analysts when describing the contemporary situation in its historical context: this situation is largely characterized in negative terms such as 'post-modern, post-secularized, post-industrialized, post-Cold War era', etc. Positive terms, such as 'New World Order', are still wanting in conceptual clarity or content.

Finding solutions for the current crisis is further complicated by the fact that many people confuse the absence of alternatives to present structures and values with the positive assessment that present structures and values are the best attainable *in principle*. More pragmatic people prefer to believe that the present situation is the *status quo* from which to start the search for reforms and improvements. Among the latter, there are at present two distinct approaches employed in attempts to find ways out of the present crisis. The first looks backwards and tries to revitalize old norms and values. Within this category not only racism, fascism and nationalism rank highly: all kinds of religious and ideological fundamentalism have to be mentioned alongside the 'acceptable' conservative revival among established conservative political and social groups all over Europe. Proponents of this approach, however, all too often try to superimpose firm sets of norms and values upon people of diverging convictions. In so doing, they not only negate the good and positive achievements of pluralism and secularization; they increase the possibility that a dangerous situation will develop in which particularistic and egoistic interests are strengthened and polarization and division within society are fostered and increased.

The second approach involves people who try to respond dialogically to contemporary needs by developing ways of co-operation beyond pluralistic divides. Most obvious are alliances of groups and individuals engaged in issues relating to ecology, human rights and global justice. Here, polarization is not deepened. By identifying common interests, a new social consensus can be established and a balance of particular interests aimed for. Combined efforts in working towards the implementation of common interests and goals are instrumental in bridging differences in beliefs and convictions. This approach seems to be far more promising as far as permanent solutions are concerned.

The author is pessimistic, however, as to whether this process of emerging social consensus will succeed as long as present elites continue to ignore or even combat it.[13] Facing the dimensions of local, national and global problems, the author is also doubtful whether there is sufficient time available to leave this process at the mercy of market forces or the outcome of a contest between free-floating opinions.

To the author, the present situation requires various forms of leadership. There are two imperatives justifying that demand:

- The imperative based on the insight as to what will happen if present developments are permitted to follow their own dynamic and quick and effective action is not being taken;
- The imperative arising from the ethical *and* legal obligations of the Code of Human Rights.

By way of a conclusion, three principles are suggested which should guide future activities of political and other leaders of society.

First of all, a new honesty is called for which (a) admits to the size of the problem instead of ignoring, negating or diminishing it and (b) admits helplessness or the absence of promising strategies and solutions if there are none.

Secondly, the root causes and dimensions of the present crisis and the interrelation and complexity of its symptoms have to be brought to the attention of all people. After all, the revolutionary changes needed today will require sacrifices by, and the co-operation of, everybody.

Thirdly, it can be assumed that an increasing public awareness of the present crisis will stimulate creativity and thought on possible solutions. Political leadership has to provide for channels and fora where this potential can develop and articulate itself.

All this should be done in the spirit of mutual respect and tolerance as well as in accordance with democratic principles and transparency.

BIBLIOGRAPHY

Alt, J. (1994), *Racism and Xenophobia in Europe*. European Council on Refugees and Exiles, London

Alt, J. (1993), *Pourquoi la xénophobie en Allemagne?* Etudes, Paris, Septembre

Annaun, W. (1995), 'Die Braune-Armee Fraktion'. Dossier in *Die Zeit, 13 January*

Bauböck, R./Feldmann, K. (1993), *Welfare in a Civil Society – Report for the Conference of European Ministers Responsible for Social Affairs* – United Nations European Region, Bratislava, June 28–July 2, 1993. c/o. European Centre, Vienna.

Boyer, R. (1986), *La théorie de la régulation: Une analyse critique*. Paris

Drieschner, F. (1993), 'Gestiefelte Schwäche'. Article in: *Die Zeit*, 6.8.93

Eide, A., Racial and ethnic discrimination in Europe: Past, present and future. Unpublished manuscript.

Ford, G. (1991), *Report drawn up on behalf of the Committee of Inquiry into Racism and Xenophobia*. (*Ford Report*). Office for Official Publications of the European Communities, Luxembourg

Friedrich, W. (ed.) (1992a), *Ausländerfeindlichkeit und rechtsextreme Orientierung der ostdeutschen Jugend*. Friedrich Ebert Stiftung, Leipzig, February

Friedrich, W. (ed.) (1992b), Studie Ostdeutsche Jugend '92. Zentralstelle Sozialanalyse e.V., Leipzig June 1992. (*Quotations in the article are taken from the press-handout, not from the study itself*)

Heinemann, K.H. (1993), 'Ihr wollt nicht wissen, wer wir sind – also wundert Euch nicht, wie wir sind'. In Verlagsinitiative gegen Gewalt und Fremdenhass (ed.): *Schweigen ist Schuldein* Lesebuch. Piper, München

Heins, Volker (1992), 'Krise des Fordismus und parapolitische Phänomene'. In Jäger, M. and S.: *Aus der Mitte der Gesellschaft* (I)

Heitmeyer, W. (1992), *Die Bielefelder Rechtsextremismus-Studie: Erste Langzeituntersuchung zur politischen Sozialisation männlicher Jugendlicher*. Juventa, Weinheim

Heitmeyer, W. (1993), 'Gesellschaftliche Desintegrationsprozesse als Ursachen von fremdenfeindlicher Gewalt und politischer Paralysierung'. In: *Aus Politik und Zeitgeschichte*, Supplement to the German paper 'Das Parlament', 8 January

Held, J./Horn, H./Leiprecht, R./Maravakis, A. (1992), '*Du musst so handeln, dass Du Gewinn machst . . .*' – *Empirische Untersuchungen und theoretische Überlegungen zu politisch rechten Orientierungen jugendlicher Arbeitnehmer*. Duisburger Institut für Sprach-und Sozialforschung (DISS), Duisburg

Jäger, M. and S. (1992a), *Aus der Mitte der Gesellschaft (I): Zu den Ursachen von Rechtsextremismus und Rassismus in Europa*. Duisburger Institut für Sprach– und Sozialforschung (DISS), Duisburg

Jäger, M. and S. (1992b), *Aus der Mitte der Gesellschaft (II): Rechtsextremismus und Rassismus in Russland und in der ehemaligen DDR*. Duisburger Institut für Sprach-und Sozialforschung (DISS), Duisburg

Jäger, S. (Ed.) (1992c), *BrandSätze-Rassismus im Alltag*. Duisburger Institut für Sprach-und Sozialforschung (DISS), Duisburg

Jäger, S./Link, J. (eds) (1993), *Die Vierte Gewalt-Rassismus und die Medien*.

Duisburger Institut für Sprach– und Sozialforschung (DISS), Duisburg

Ködderitzsch, P. (1992), 'Rechtsextremismus in der DDR'. In Jäger, M. and S.: *Aus der Mitte der Gesellschaft (II) Rechtsextremismus und Rassismus in Russland und in der ehemaligen DDR*. Duisburger Institut für Sprach-und Sozialforschung (DISS), Duisburg

Kowalski, W. (1993), 'Rechtsextremismus und Anti-Rechtsextremismus in der modernen Industriegesellschaft'. In *Aus Politik und Zeitgeschichte*, Supplement to the German paper 'Das Parlament', 8 January

Lipietz, A. (1990), 'Apres-fordisme et démocratie'. In *Les Temps modernes*, No 524/1990, pp. 97–121

Lipietz, A. (1987), *Mirages and Miracles. The crisis of global Fordism*. London

Maaz, H.J. (1993), 'Gewalt in Deutschland- Eine psychologische Analyse'. In *Aus Politik und Zeitgeschichte*, Supplement to the German paper 'Das Parlament', 8 January

Miles, R. (1993), Racisms in Contemporary Europe. Talk given at the 9th Nordiske Migrantionsforskerseminar, Esbjerg, 16.–19.9

Mosse, G. (1993), *Die Geschichte des Rassismus in Europa*. Fischer, Frankfurt

Oakley, R. (1993), *Racial Violence and Harassment in Europe*. Report comissioned by the Council of Europe, Strasbourg

Pahnke, R. (1993), 'Zur Faszination von Gewalt und dem Versuch, sie zu überwinden'. In Posselt/Schumacher (eds) *Projekthandbuch: Gewalt und Rassismus*. Verlag an der Ruhr, Mühlheim

Pinn, I./Nebelung M. (1992), *Vom 'klassischen' zum aktuellen Rassismus in Deutschland*. Duisburger Institut für Sprach- und Sozialforschung (DISS), Duisburg

Posselt, R.E./ Schumacher, K. (eds) (1993), *Projekthandbuch: Gewalt und Rassismus*. Verlag an der Ruhr, Mühlheim

Räthzel, N. (1992), 'Formen von Rassismus in der Bundesrepublik'. In: Jäger, M. and S.: *Aus der Mitte der Gesellschaft (I) Zu den Ursachen von Rechtsextremismus und Rassismus in Europa*. Duisburger Institut für Sprach-und Sozialforschung (DISS), Duisburg

Renan, E. (1992), *Qu'est-ce qu'une nation?* Presses pocket, Paris

Schuler, U. (1993), 'Krise der Gesamtgesellschaft'. Article in the paper *Frankfurter Rundschau* 13 July

Schumann, K. (1993), 'Nur jeder zehnte Gewalttäter ist arbeitslos'. Speech documented in the paper *Frankfurter Rundschau*, 1 July

Spiegel, German news-magazine, ed. No. 24/93. Article 'Party bis zum Einsargen', pp. 18ff

Studie- en Informatiecentrum Mensenrechten (SIM/ed.) (1987), *New expressions of Racism – growing areas of conflict in Europe*. SIM Special No 7

van Dijk, T. (1991a), *Rassismus heute: Der Diskurs der Elite und seine Funktion für die Reproduktion des Rassismus*. Duisburger Institut für Sprach-und Sozialforschung (DISS), Duisburg

van Dijk, T. (1991b), 'Analyzing Racism through Discourse Analysis – Some methodological reflections'. In *Race and Ethnicity in Research Methods*, pp. 92–134, Newbury Park, CA: Sage

van Dijk, T. (1991c), Elite Discourse and the Reproduction of Racism. Manuscript by the author, July 1991

van Dijk, T. (1992), Elites, Racism and the Press. Paper for the Congress of the

International Association of Mass Communication Research, Guaruja, Brazil

van Dijk, T. (1993), Political Discourse and Racism. Unpublished manuscript by the author, February

Verlagsinitiative gegen Gewalt und Fremdenhass (ed.) (1993), *Schweigen ist Schuldein Lesebuch.* Piper, München

Willems, H./Würtz, S./Eckert, R. (1993), *Fremdenfeindliche Gewalt: Eine Analyse von Täterstrukturen und Eskalationsprozessen.* Forschungsbericht vorgelegt dem Bundesministerium für Frauen und Jugend und der Deutschen Forschungsgemeinschaft im Juni

NOTES

1. This chapter is based on the research by W. Heitmeyer (1992 and 1993), the Duisburger Institut für Sprach- und Sozialforschung (DISS) and Willems (*et al*, 1993) as well as the articles by Schuler (1993) and Drieschner (1993).
2. For example: the homeless, beggars, unemployed, families with many children.
3. Many Skins and Hooligans are 'normally' known as very industrious and polite citizens, whereas in the evenings or at the weekends they are out to compensate for all the frustration which had been accumulated in the meantime. Cf. articles by Ködderitzsch (1992) and Schumann (1993) as well as Willems (1993).
4. Some figures concerning membership, sympathizers () and opponents [] of radical and extremist groups in East-Germany provided by Friedrich (1992b), p. 9:
   1% Republicans (11%) [60%]
   1% Skins (7%) [76%]
   1% Faschos and Hooligans (5% each) [71%]
   2% Punks (12%)
   1% Autonomous left (8%)
5. Cf. Friedrich (1992a), pp. 18f and Pahnke (1993) pp. 73ff. Needless to say, that there is no 'atmospheric' improvement if parents are unemployed and therefore socially stigmatized.
6. Cf. Willems 1993: On the social function of membership in Skin-groups esp. pp. 78ff.
7. More recently confirmed at for example, the G7 summit in Naples, June 1994.
8. Here, it seems at best questionable whether new jobs in the emerging high-tech and service sector can balance these losses.
9. Among those are most noteworthy to mention: the changing 'industrial profile' of entire geographical regions, the crisis of whole professional sectors, the 'Two Thirds' society, multi-ethnic society and immigration, international debts, pollution and environmental damage.
10. Bauböck/Feldmann (1993), p. 207. At present, this insight is in danger of being neglected. News of racist and xenophobic attacks disappears from

the papers, mainly for two reasons. Firstly, public interest gets used to these events and they therefore are no longer 'worth the message'. Secondly, repressive measures initiated by Home Offices, Secret Services and the Police seem to succeed. In my view, however, they succeed mainly in pushing their adherents into clandestine activities with the risk of nurturing terrorist tendencies. (Latest contribution in the German context: Annaun, 1995.) Referring back to the quotation at the beginning, the author firmly believes that repressive measures against racist and xenophobic perpetrators are equally unsuited, as restrictive policies in the asylum and immigration sector are adequate means with which to address the root-causes of forced migration.

11. The last example is taken from a speech made in the British House of Commons, May 15, 1990 (Van Dijk, 1991c).
12. The latter was of particular importance during the period of colonialization. Cf. examination by van Dijk, (1991c), pp. 16ff and Pinn/Nebelung 1992.
13. Indications of such attitudes are, for example, the continuing claims that ethnic homogeneity or the 'preservation of national interests' are still realistic goals in an increasingly interdependent world. Another dangerous development is seen in the more or less accepted fact that Western democracies more and more mutate into 'lobbycracies'.

3 New Racism in Germany[1]
Jochen Blaschke

Right-wing radicalism has become a major issue in German politics. Since the incorporation of the territory of the German Democratic Republic into that of the Federal Republic of Germany, questions of racial violence and prejudice towards foreigners have received greatly increased coverage in the press and the electronic media.[2] Since 1989 more than fifteen hundred related books, brochures, essays and scientific articles have been published, so that we now have a more or less comprehensive overview and sufficient empirical data in the area of this phenomenon.

German discussion of right-wing radicalism and racism can be understood only in the light of its history. It has been influenced, firstly, by the early reverse suffered by Germany's colonial aspirations in the Third World. The German Reich had to renounce all its colonies after World War I. German racism was not functional in the years between the wars in terms of colonial supremacy. Secondly, the subject became taboo after 1945 as a result of the Nazi crimes against Jews, Gypsies and other minorities. And thirdly, the radical right-wing parties of the post-war period tried, in their political programmes at least, to suppress racism and hostility towards foreigners.

The dissolution of the German colonial empire after World War I removed at an early stage any material foundation there might have been for discriminatory notions that ruling systems correspond to racial hierarchies. As a result, the violence and the colonial racism of the German occupants in Africa, the Pacific and other parts of the world remained a subject of theoretical reflection which had little to do with life as it was lived in Germany. From the German perspective the international argument about roots of racist thinking in the imperial division of labour up to decolonization in the second half of the twentieth century could be seen as a problem of the British, French, Belgian, Dutch and other colonial powers. Nevertheless, it is possible to point to occasional racist images and stereotypes from the context of the international division of labour.

In Germany, racism was never a popular ideology – except in the thirties and forties of the twentieth century. In the nineteenth century it was racism as anti-Semitism that dominated intellectual debates influenced by Protestant theologians and historians. Racism developed into a subject of scientific debate: ethnographers, sociologists, anthropologists and human biologists were in great demand in the twenties and thirties. Racist ideas were formulated not in the political arena but at universities (Weingart *et al.*, 1988). Racism was transferred from Britain and France, where it played an influential role as a device for interpreting colonial structures, to Germany, where, like other nineteenth-century ideologies, racism was just a romantic but a scientific experience.

In practical terms, it was the 'volkish'[3] movement in particular which posited the superiority of German traditions of civilization and culture. The 'volkish' supporters linked nationalism with 'volkish' theories. Superiority was related to traditional status positions. The king, the duke and other nobles were mysticized into a Germanic Valhalla.[4] Hierarchies were bound to Germanic mythologies. Racism played only a minor role in 'volkish' publications and discussions. However, 'volkish' thought was open to racist discourses as anti-Semitism. Talking about the ostracism of Jews was a main area of interest for 'volkish' intellectuals in church or university circles.

Alongside the 'volkish' movement there were the statist nationalists who made a distinction not between ethnically alien nationals and natives or ethnic Germans, but between nationals and foreigners. This type of nationalism had its roots in the labour movement and in Catholic conservatism. The frequent recourse to national interests and nationalist ideologies in the German labour movement can be explained in part by the fact that social democracy, like the Catholic Church in the Kulturkampf, was perceived as nationally unreliable.[5] Yet even in the initial phases the Prussian conservatives attempted to arrive at a social compromise with labour leaders under nationalist slogans. Thus Prussian-orientated nationalism made particularly rapid headway among Social Democratic parliamentarians.

The constitutional law specialist Carl Schmitt, who became the state philosopher of the Third Reich after 1936, had a Catholic background. His statist nationalism was indeed rooted in Europe's conservative Catholic philosophy.[6] His main assumption was that the national interest could be defined as the expression of an ontologically assumed tendency to think in terms of friend and foe. Anti-Semitism appears in many of Schmitt's writings, but it is not a central element.

It was not until the Nazi period that 'volkish' traditions, racist science and statist nationalism merged into an aggressive political concept which regarded struggle against the political enemy as being the only way of overcoming social anachronisms. Since there were no longer any enemy images as there had been in the colonial era, however, the Nazis had to come up with new enemies. The result was a mixture of anti-Semitism and a specifically German form of racism: the mobilization of the masses to counteract imaginary conspiracies was accompanied by sermons on the relationship between the size of a person's cranium and various stages of human civilization. The holocaust, perfectly organized in technical terms, was an expression of totalitarian anti-rationalism. It has cast a shadow on German politics and culture ever since. Inconceivable as it is, it was the first outcome of a positively interpreted purposeful, technological, finalistic concept of rationality.

After World War II, the old German ruling elite succeeded in reestablishing itself. The principles of parliamentary democracy, introduced at the insistence of the Allied occupation forces, acted as a political bonding agent for the new society. However, a far-reaching analysis and debate on Nazi irrationalism and outrages was largely blanketed over. At the most, the theory of fascism formed part of the democratic reeducation process or else an aspect of the theory of totalitarianism which was directed more than anything else against Communism (Jänicke, 1971).

The lack of any discussion of racism, of the 'volkish' movement and of nationalist statism meant that the subject remained taboo. Moral categories were used to maintain this taboo. The prohibition of certain terms and anxiety about any analytical approach to the subject acted as deterring factors. Words such as 'ethnos', 'ethnicity', 'race', 'racism', 'volkish', etc. were removed from the German political vocabulary.

However, tabooing was only one side of the problem. The other side was that post-war development showed that although they were politically marginalized, survival was possible for marginal political groups which cultivated national socialist traditions and drew their inspiration from mass experiences under German fascism and their participation in the war. These were for the most part associations of expellees and veterans' associations which cultivated extreme nationalist thinking, although only as an unofficial and inner group ideology (Dudek, 1989). But alongside these there continued to exist small, smoothly functioning networks of former members of the SS and police and representatives of the 'volkish' national mind set (Dudek and Jaschke, 1984). The 'volkish' segment stabilized their ideologies in the context of the 'Europäischen Volksgruppenbewegung' ('European national minorities' movement'), referring back to their human rights traditions of the twenties, when the German Volkstum theoreticians dominated the European minorities' movement (Blaschke, 1984).

Also among the survivors were the national revolutionary circles with a distinctly anti-national socialist self-perception that identified themselves with the early phase of National Socialism, when traditions of the labour movement and socialism were of central importance for the members of the NSDAP. Despite taboos, a marginalized organizational tradition was thus maintained. The taboo could not erase the collective recollection of mass and wartime experiences.

ARENAS OF RACISM

Racism is customarily taken to mean the disparagement or hierarchization of social groups on the basis of ethnic symbol formations. Such discrimination and deprecation on the basis of group membership takes place at various levels.

- The first level is everyday life: one important aspect of the new racism in Germany is social predisposition. Between three and five per cent of the population are manifestly afraid of foreigners and are prepared to take aggressive action under certain circumstances. About 30 to 45 per cent tend towards xenophobic reactions to differing degrees. In certain conflict situations, groups of sympathizers, fellow-travellers and onlookers are formed from these circles. In addition there are racist sentiments in the collective consciousness that in certain situations can easily lead to racist prejudices and aversions being recalled. The centuries-old state formation process is also a part of this complex of institutionalized racism. There are many laws, guidelines, administrative routines and rules of etiquette that do not conform to the situation in multi-ethnic countries. In Germany this applies in particular to the definition of 'Bürger' as citizen.
- The second arena of racism is the body politic: government and state. The pressure of national interests and the inclusion of citizens are the dominant political ideas. In 'high politics' Germany continues to be described as a non-immigration country. The political class refuses to pursue a systematic immigration policy or to implement a coherent policy of integration. Restriction of migration has been the dominant political ideology. The state is seen nationalistically as a vehicle in which a people links together and fences itself off from others. 'The boat is full' is a slogan shared by all the political parties. The welfare system is a contributing factor: it has not been able to adjust to a massive entry of asylum applicants.

- Populism in elections and party politics is the third political arena of racism. The party system is currently in a deep crisis, expressed in particular in the upsurge of populist parties since the mid-eighties and in the populist strategies of established party elites. Populist parties recruit members mainly by channelling the people's fear of losing their livelihood into diffuse criticism of the existing party system. In this political strategy the fomenting of hostility to foreigners is an important instrument of political mobilization.
- Fascist mobilization is the fourth arena. Since the mid-eighties, neo-Nazi groups have been speaking out more explicitly. They have built up a tight network in the meantime and used it to gain influence over the populist parties and youth cultures. The new federal Länder have been a testing-ground in this endeavour.
- Aggression against structural power (Galtung, 1973) is the fifth arena. With reunification, the connection between youth cultures and violence has become evident. As a rule, the violence is directed against all outsiders. Foreigners have been preferred targets, however. This violence is generally attributable to group processes.

Thus racism has different arenas. The theatre of racist policy keeps finding other stages. In the Federal Republic of Germany the racist theatre had a successful run for several years following reunification. Now it is playing in changing arenas, but there is no simultaneity. It has become marginal and has thus lost some of its significance. It is still dangerous, however, as a latent threat to parliamentary politics and civil society. Its claws have not been clipped and its base, namely the aloofness to foreigners that is prevalent in everyday life, has been retained.

GERMANY AS A COUNTRY OF IMMIGRATION

The racism of the nineties has thrived on the political impotence of the federal, state and local governments in the face of surprisingly high numbers of immigrants at a time of rising unemployment and a simultaneous state financial crisis. Immigration and ethnicization still needed to be defined as fields of policy-making. It was not until the nineties that this political sphere became a theme for established professional politics.

In recent years there have been considerable changes in the types of immigrants coming to Germany. They can be assigned to such axial categories as hierarchical groups, regions of origin, and racial and ethnic demarcations linked with those regions on the one hand and, on the other, status classification – modified by the immigration processes – with respect to guaranteed access, via the statutes on human and civil rights, to the political processes and the resources of the welfare state (cf. Ashkenasi, 1988).

After the Second World War, the labour market in Germany was filled by displaced persons and those expelled or forced to emigrate as a result of the war. These groups of immigrants were quickly integrated into the labour markets and – with the aid of financial compensation programmes – into the social structures without there being any open discrimination along ethnic lines. This group of immigrants makes up almost a quarter of the German population.

The economic upswing in the fifties and sixties led to a system of labour recruitment from the immediate European periphery being introduced. Immigrant workers linked up with the last of the internal migrants from the countryside and for the most part they were employed for the purpose of maintaining traditional industries (in particular the textile mills and heavy industry). This system was discarded following the economic crisis which set in during the late sixties and early seventies.

Characteristic features of the migration processes in the seventies were family completions and chain migrations. These immigration waves, which incorporated the second and third generations of immigrant labourers added to the pool of low-paid workers available. At this point education and vocational training measures became cost factors in the system of labour migration. The immigration of family members in particular increased the demands made on the services of the welfare state. There are around five million people in the country today who immigrated in this way.

During the eighties there was a marked increase in the immigration of diaspora Germans from Eastern European countries. These new migratory movements can be attributed, firstly, to the generous naturalization and integration measures for these population groups. Secondly, the conservative governments under Chancellor Helmut Kohl made a political issue of the ethnic Germans and thus intensified the 'pull' factors. Thirdly, the radical changes in Eastern Europe have intensified this type of chain migration. In the past three years more than one million diaspora Germans have entered the country.

From the seventies onwards the labour markets were steered for the most part by means of the discrimination of immigrants. Immigration bans and reforms of immigration legislation replaced recruitment policies.

Immigrants, therefore, began to look for new ways of entering the industrial countries. Family reunions represented an extension of immigration patterns. Immigrants began increasingly to cross the borders of the Community as refugees and applicants for asylum or else as tourists and illegal entrants. This steadily diminished the civic status of migrants. Asylum in all its various forms, marriage, short-term residence permits and illegality had a differentiating effect on the legal status of immigrants. On the other hand, these new immigrants added considerably to the labour force in the countries of immigration and thereby improved the basis for the structural transformation of the German industrial society. The different regulations on residence had a considerable influence on access to the labour markets. The number of these migrants is comparatively small at present but it is on the increase.

The distribution of labour to the factories in the Eastern German Democratic Republic formed an integral part of the bureaucratic planning system. The only way of adding to the overall labour force was to tap the international labour market. The overall economic figures for the GDR in 1988 revealed for the first time a drop in the total labour force (a reduction in the number of GDR workers by 3,000) which according to demographic predictions was not due to occur until 1990/91. That provided an additional motive for employing more foreigners. It transpired that the overall data was imprecise and that the decisions taken on the basis of diffuse information and complex interests were erroneous.

This situation led to the GDR importing immigrant labour from the middle of the 1980s onwards. Workers were recruited solely from what were called the 'fraternal socialist' countries. There is no exact chronological data for this labour immigration. The workers were under contract to specific companies. In the spring of 1990 there were 190,000 foreigners living in the GDR. Of these 106,500 were in employment, 28,900 were undergoing vocational training and 10,200 were enrolled at universities and colleges.

In the first six months of 1990 the deployment of Soviet troops increasingly came to be perceived as a problem of foreigners. In our inquiry we treated 'the Russians' as an ethnic group. This group is not included in the statistical data.

Foreigners in the GDR worked almost exclusively in production – in light industry, vehicle construction, and in the production of chemical fibres and tyres. Data on the factories and branches concerned is still not available. Nevertheless, a few examples can be given: 30,000 immigrant labourers worked in light industry, 650 were employed at the car-producing plant in Eisenach and 550 at the port in Rostock. As was the case in the Federal Republic, foreigners in the GDR were employed in jobs that were low on skills and pay.

In early 1990, foreign employees in the GDR came from the following countries: Vietnam (60,400), Mozambique (15,100), Cuba (8,000), Poland (6,400), and Angola (1,300). These figures refer to workers employed in the GDR on the basis of bilateral agreements. The overall total of foreign employees cannot be broken down into countries of origin. Polish immigrant workers who entered the country in 1990 on an individual basis are not included in these statistics.

Gainfully employed foreigners were accommodated exclusively in hostels which were barely accessible to Germans. The hostels were supervised by wardens; on no grounds were workers allowed to be joined by their families. Bilateral agreements regulated the payment of wages, child and separation allowances as well as home leave. The contracts also covered such issues as the forwarding of parcels and clothing allowances.

The unification of the Federal Republic of Germany and the German Democratic Republic meant that foreigners resident in the eastern part of Germany became subject to the Federal Republic's legislation on foreigners. It is not anticipated that there will be a general deterioration in their social standing as a result, although individual factories did terminate a large number of contracts with foreign workers in the first half of 1990. In other words, the job contracts with immigrant labourers were put on an individual footing. In the meantime, a large number of the immigrants have left the country. At present, applicants for asylum and foreigners who do not have the status of immigrant labourers make up the ethnic populations in the eastern parts of the country.

MULTI-ETHNIC STRUCTURES IN GERMANY

Immigrant populations can be statistically registered in Germany only by citizenship, so that an exact demographic classification is not possible. At present there are 6.5 million aliens in the Federal Republic of Germany, about 1.3 million of them children and adolescents. Twenty-eight per cent of the foreigners come from Turkey, and of these more than 70 per cent have resided in the Federal Republic of Germany for more than ten years. Half a million Turks have permanent resident status.

On 31 December 1994 there were about two million refugees in

Germany. Of these about 230,000 had been granted asylum or were relatives of asylum applicants. Another 200,000 persons had the status of contingent or short-term refugees. The residence status of these immigrants was to a large extent secure. Some 640,000 persons were tolerated as *de facto* refugees and thus had more or less the status of immigrants.[7]

Roughly 150,000 more immigrants are in Germany at present under other immigration procedures as service contract workers, seasonal workers, guest workers and cross-border commuters. In addition to these there are the GDR's former guest workers, who are tolerated. The estimates of the number of illegal immigrants vary between 200,000 and 1.5 million.

It is not only the migrations that have made Germany a country with a multitude of ethnic populations. The country is rather in a crisis situation in which cultural symbols are increasingly being used to promote group formation. The reasons for this lie in the change in modes of production and in the globalization of the production of cultural symbols. In the industrialized societies, people are increasingly being individualized and try to document their special status through style formation, through the production of distinctive clothing and the development of distinctive eating and consumption habits. This also applies to the native population with its growing subcultures. Political behaviour and social relationships are determined increasingly by culturally moulded social backgrounds rather than traditional class organizations such as trade unions and associations, political parties and sports clubs. Even old people, blue and white collar workers, the jobless and the homeless are to some extent generating their own middle-class or cultures of poverty. These now separate only certain occupational groups and no longer 'blue-collar' from 'white-collar' workers. There are shops, restaurants, meeting-places and supply points for all fashions and styles. Young people in particular evolve such subcultures, since before their identity change they relied on demarcations imposed from outside. This is not a new phenomenon. Youth cultures have always been manifestations of modernism. Owing to the ethnicization of society at large, however, the tendency has become more pronounced in the last few years.

The ethnicization of society also includes its regionalization and localization. Here the rather universalist medium of television deserves mention; it presents a picture of large-scale cultivation of so-called customs. Brass bands and traditional costumes are presented professionally and marketed as local 'folk music'. The television viewer gets a taste of local costume and music groups from all parts of the country.

They are presented as representatives of valley-dwellers, villages, small towns and regions. Their symbols, however, are centrally pre-cast: whether it is the costume dance group from Heligoland with Viennese waltzes and south German country dances or the Zillertaler Musikanten with polkas and Prussian marching music. The tourist industry with its advertising and visitor entertainment reinforces this commercial regionalization and localization. The politicians, with reified conservatism, also try to purvey their messages under the mantle of folklore associations and folklore broadcasts, seen by them as the preservers of handed-down, parochial cultures.

Immigrant groups are particularly affected by ethnicization. The effect of belt-tightening programmes in the sphere of the integration of diaspora Germans has been that these are assimilated less rapidly. The older guest worker minorities have formed ethnic communities with their own organizations and views of the world. This applies to many refugee groups from the Third World as well.

The refugees who have arrived in recent years, at the rate of 450,000 persons per year – before the change of asylum laws – at the last count comprised five groups. One especially large group embraces the gypsies from Yugoslavia, Rumania and Bulgaria. This is a particularly problematic migrant group, since it has not been able to become integrated in the German labour market. This group is subjected to particularly strong demarcation mechanisms on the part of the administration and the population. The second group consists of civil war refugees from former Yugoslavia; they are increasingly being admitted under the contingent procedure or through private initiatives. The latter support the expansion of Croatian, Bosnian, Albanian and Serbian aid networks. The third group of refugees consists of Turks and Kurds, not all of whom have come to Germany as a result of the Turkish civil war. Instead there has been a form of family reunification via the gate of entry of asylum. The other two groups consist mainly of refugees from Eastern Europe (prominent among them the Russian Jews) and from the Third World.

What we have is an extensive dispute and competition for resources among a large number of culturally differentiated groups. Immigrants, who as a rule are still denied 'inlander' status in Germany, increasingly resort to ethnic symbols in this competitive situation.

THE FIRST ARENA: EVERYDAY LIFE AND ALOOFNESS TO STRANGERS

In the context of a presentation of neo-racism in Germany, it seems necessary to draw attention to two phenomena. Firstly, xenophobia correlates clearly with a low level of education. The electorate and the members of right-wing populist parties can easily be a corresponding segment of the population. Secondly, scales of preference of population groups in the two parts of Germany largely correspond. They clearly show a racist structure aligned to the phenomena of outer appearance and the distance from the country of origin of the preferred persons: the darker the skin colour, the greater the aloofness.

It is certain that we have a hard core of five to six per cent xenophobic persons with diffuse but aggressive inclinations and 35 to 45 per cent of generally xenophobic people in the Federal Republic of Germany. This corresponds roughly to the six to seven per cent who vote for neo-populist political parties. It is not possible to say as yet whether the two statistical quantities overlap or not.

THE SECOND ARENA: IMMIGRATION RESTRICTIONISM AND ASYLUM POLICY

Immigration and integration policy has always been an *ad hoc* policy in Germany. Immigrants were summoned to the country or accepted in response to the economic requirements of various economic sectors. The most recent of these were the restaurant sector with its demand for work permits for asylum applicants, the building industry with its demand for the conclusion of service contracts with Poland, and agriculture with its demand for seasonal workers. Gates of entry for migrants were thus opened in a diversified and intricate manner, although officially the policy of a recruitment stop still applied. The discussion concerning the right to asylum was mainly a debate on the question of whether the fundamental right to asylum was a suitable gate of immigration. The majority of the asylum applicants remained *de facto* in the country, although they had never been recognized as refugees. The administration of the process took so long that asylum applicants became a special kind of immigration category.[8]

This *ad hoc* policy led to an intricate assembly of associated costs that have repeatedly provided concrete grounds for resistance to further emigration. Most recently it was resistance to the consequences of service contract work that led to protests on the part of the trade unions and the construction industry. Before that it was complaints from the municipal authorities about being overburdened with the costs of the asylum process as they had to bear the bulk of the costs of immigration. Seeing in this a threat to their financial scope, they agitated for an anti-immigration policy.

At the same time, leading politicians distinguished themselves with openly racist remarks and comments. The debate on alien and asylum legislation that has been going on since 1985 stylizes the exclusion of immigrants as a central national mission. The perception was thus spread among the German population that immigrants threatened the prosperity and stability of the Federal Republic of Germany.

Frequently, however, immigration to Germany was distinguished by the lack of any policy. The immigration of gypsies from eastern Europe was not followed by any political debate on their possible integration. Instead, a strong feeling of distrust towards these ethnic groups was discernible from the beginning. The problem was made taboo; euphemisms such as 'Rumanians' or 'Sinti and Roma' were used to designate the gypsies, and all political responsibility was denied when they turned up. It was not a sense of post-Auschwitz responsibility that determined the policy towards arriving gypsies but the Auschwitz taboo. The policy towards their arrival was at best repatriation assistance. But then the arrival of gypsies was the occasion for the first racist riots.

The policy towards former Yugoslav immigrants revealed a similar lack of interest. The mass immigration made the establishment of quotas in the range of less than 10,000 persons unrealistic even when it was being discussed. A reception policy for civil war refugees has still not been formulated. In the context of former Yugoslavia policy, however, the failure of a common Europe-wide reception policy should be mentioned.

An adequate problem of adaptation is lacking for the Turkish and Kurdish refugees as well, who basically are arriving family members outside the terms of the law on aliens. There is no assignment of this refugee policy to the 'integration tasks' for earlier foreign workers.

Instead of an immigration and integration policy, there were political discourses about possibilities of association with immigrants. These were reduced to expulsion discourses, namely debates about the repatriation of migrants and the abolition of the right to asylum. And a discourse developed about foreign penetration, which strangely took up the 'volkish' body of thought but was often expressed in a directly racist form. A discourse also developed about the costs of immigration in which liberal politicians figured out how many immigrants contributed how much to the gross national product and to the social insurance systems. Even the political groupings that were friendly towards immigrants did not realize that human rights obligations do not have to do justice to a cost-benefit analysis, perhaps out of tactical consideration for these 'good' findings. Conservative politicians, on the other hand, tend to stress the costs of immigration.

These discourses have become a central field of politics because the parliamentary parties increasingly fear the competition of populist parties. The fear of a rightward shift has radicalized the xenophobia in the parliamentary system.

THE THIRD ARENA: NEW POPULISM

The German party system has been characterized by unbroken stability during the last forty years. The three established parties, the CDU, the SPD and the FDP, have shared the monopoly over parliamentary politics. Since the eighties, however, this has been called into question. On the one hand there were the new social movements, the ecological positions that were brought into the parliaments by grassroots democratic parties. On the other hand were populist right-wing groups such as the Republikaner or the Deutsche Volksunion threatening the integrity of the party system. Both movements are characterized by their criticism of indirect democracy; they want the political system to have closer links with the electorate.

The political parties of the new movements are trying to achieve this by defining a distinct target, counting on the political interest in pollution control. They also criticize parliamentary procedure and the political establishment's distrust of direct democracy. Left-wing populism makes use of disaffection with the complexity and cumbrousness of parliamentary politics by calling for grassroots democracy.

The neo-populist parties of the right try to mobilise the masses with a rather diffuse programme that has scarcely any political contours and with the formulation of the general unease that exists with regard to politics. Xenophobia and racist speeches are a favoured resource, although violence, anti-Semitism and racism are officially banned in all these parties.

In 1992 the neo-populist parties and right-wing voters' groups had a membership potential of about 41,900, although membership of more than one group is not unusual (1991: 39,800). Their voter potential amounts to at least six per cent of the population. In some regions and constituencies, however, it could rise to 20 per cent. Major electoral successes have so far been denied them owing to the five per cent clause usually applied in the Federal Republic of Germany and periodic clashes between neo-populist parties.

The oldest party of this complexion is the NPD, the National Democratic Party of Germany, which, however, almost vanished in the seventies and eighties and is still deep in an organizational crisis. The NPD has about 5,000 members and defends volkish-collectivist ideas according to which the individual has to subordinate himself or herself to community goals. Its aim is the so-called 'Volksstaat' in which the ethnic community and the population merge into one.

The main party of the populist right is the party of the 'Republikaner' (REP). The Republikaner was founded by a former member of the SS and later director of Bavarian Television, Franz Schönhuber, and has chalked up an unbroken series of electoral successes since the mid-eighties. Since 1992 it has been under surveillance by the intelligence service; according to that service, it has distinctly anti-democratic tendencies and its officials regularly make racist utterances.

In political bodies the Republikaner regularly loses its internal coherence in factions and working parties following elections and is characterized by schisms. Its mass-oriented propaganda with its xenophobic and racist undertones is supplemented by abstinence from politics in political bodies. Thus the Republikaner seems to have no long-term political perspective. At present the Republikaner has about 23,000 members.

This was one of the reasons for the rise of the Deutsche Volksunion (DVU) to the status of an autonomous party. The initiative in founding this organization came from a publisher of radical right-wing writings (Gerhard Frey), who evidently never formulated a coherent philosophy himself. The policy of this party is characterized on the one hand by appeals to the existential fears of the electorate and on the other hand by enemy images. This friend-foe concept is directed especially against migrants, against 'vagabond gypsies', 'lazy Poles', 'criminal asylum-seekers' and 'Jews who blackmail the Germans'. The DVU has about 26,000 members. Owing to its close links with its founder's publishing business, it is financially secure. Electoral analyses show that it is most successful among workers and young people. In the September 1991 elections in Bremen the success of the DVU was expressly due to the asylum legislation. The DVU and the REPs can count on the votes of up to 20 per cent of the under-25s in elections in the Federal Republic of Germany.

The 'Deutsche Liga für Volk und Heimat' (Deutsche Liga), emerged from the internal schisms in the large right-wing populist parties. It is the product of splits and disputes in the DVU and among the REPs. It sees itself as the 'national collecting party', but it is presently in a deep crisis with its 800 members.

The internal arguments in the populist parties are not only due to the lack of political contours in these groups. They are also an expression of their special position in the party system in the Federal Republic of Germany. These parties claim to appeal to the national conservative camp in Germany. But in its behavioural predilections that camp continues to be deeply rooted in the Christian Democratic circles and their traditions of Catholic-conservative or German-national politics. Only a few old-line conservatives find their way to the new parties. The new parties are rather political vehicles for a few traditional Nazis and many political entrepreneurs who expect personal advantages from their political involvement.

The large parties also suffer from the new political entrepreneurship phenomenon. But they can still defend themselves to the extent that they have established elite recruiting systems and systems of inner party democracy. The right-wing populist parties, on the other hand, are dependent on the handful of 'movers', since the majority of the members have a very low educational level or are simply protest voters who have joined but have little loyalty to the organization. Their electoral success and the seats won do not correspond anywhere to their ability to fill those seats with persons capable of political activity. In contrast to the fascist parties of the period between the wars, the members of the right-wing populist organizations are not revolutionary followers of charismatic leaders but as a rule ordinary people who are dissatisfied with the present proportional representation of the parties.

Their few political entrepreneurs do, however, achieve isolated successes. They try to use marketing and advertising skills to turn these parties into modern political parties. But as long as their efforts are not supported by a 'modern' membership the long-term continuity of such a policy does not seem to be assured. In the German federal and länder parliaments the right-wing populists have so far been isolated. They therefore have little chance of using the parliamentary forum as a propaganda instrument. Instead, their political performance has so far been seen by the voters in a rather negative light. The strength of the right-wing populists lies in everyday political discussions in the pubs and the municipalities. Political coalitions with the right-wing populists have repeatedly been formed at the local government level.

THE FOURTH ARENA: NEO-FASCIST POLITICS

The history of neo-Fascism in Germany goes back to the end of the war, when 'old comrades' got together to resist persecution or to conquer new political and economic positions through common networks. Many of those groupings did not distinguish themselves by their own efforts but attempted to become integrated in new political parties and associations. Parties with distinctly National Socialist ways of thinking also emerged, however. The Socialist Party (SRP) was banned in 1952. This was an initial defeat for the independent policy of the old Nazis in the Federal Republic of Germany. Until the mid-sixties, neo-fascism seemed almost to have vanished.

The first right-wing populist party in the Federal Republic, the National Democratic Party of Germany (NPD), emerged in 1964. At that time it still had close links with cliques of old National Socialists. In essence, however, it grew up as a protest party during the first great recession of the post-war period. Even then it was with anti-foreigner slogans that this party attempted to mobilise voters. Its greatest electoral victory was in Baden-Württemberg in 1968, when it got 9.8 per cent of the votes. In the seventies, neo-fascism was once again a politically marginal phenomenon.

At the end of the seventies, however, a new phenomenon drew attention to itself on the extreme right: action groups emerged whose doings had their roots in war romanticism and liberation nationalism. The transition to terrorism was gradual. A few older extremists tried to recruit like-minded younger people and were to a certain extent successful. Contacts with international terrorist groups were established. The importance of individual grouplets and their leaders showed how little they were anchored in society; they included the lawyer Manfred Roeder and his 'German Action Groups', the 'Martial Arts Group Hoffman' and the 'Hepp Kexel Group'. What all these groups had in common was their sectarianism with regard to a national (National Socialist) renaissance. The German government responded with a series of individual bans, so that by the mid-eighties there were hardly any organized neo-Fascists to be seen. Their activities at that time, however, led to the emergence of a communication network for neo-Fascist policy that made it possible to rebuild such organizations later.

The year 1985 was marked on the one hand by a decrease in neo-Fascist violence and on the other by the beginning of a new wave of right-wing populist policy and violence. The problems connected with the right to asylum began to be an agitation theme at that time: immigration policy has remained so ever since. Since 1985, xenophobia has been the salient characteristic of extreme right-wing policy; it was to be joined in 1989 by the new greater German nationalism that was expected to come from reunification. For the most part, however, it remained limited to antiquated, rather rhetorical demands for a German Reich within the pre-war borders.

The Freiheitliche Deutsche Arbeiterpartei (FAP) was founded in 1978 by a former leader of the Hitler Youth Organization (HJ) who later joined the NPD. The FAP was a little-known group that came out with rather diffuse volkish-nationalist slogans. The militant Aktionsfront Nationaler Sozialisten/Nationale Aktivisten (ANS/NA) was another neo-fascist organization of the early eighties. Founded by the charismatic young politician Michael Kühnen, it took violent and militant action and was consequently banned in 1983. After the prohibition of the Kühnen group, the FAP was its cover organization. Almost all the known militants on the right assembled in it from the mid-eighties onwards. The party was systematically infiltrated and is now regarded as the most militant neo-Fascist party. Kühnen was not a regular member of the FAP, as this could have meant the end of its legal activities. Nonetheless, he was clearly the man in charge until his murder in Dresden early in 1991.

Now the FAP has attempted to distinguish legalistically between its party programme with its non-violent provisions and the demands of its officials for open violence to 'keep the German spirit and German blood pure'. For that reason the federal authorities were for some time reluctant to ban the party, although hundreds of members were investigated on charges of incitement of the masses and neo-Fascist symbols were openly displayed, and neo-Fascist slogans chanted, during FAP marches. The FAP always had a few hundred members, mostly young men with low and irregular incomes and low levels of education.

At the end of the eighties there were sharp disputes within the FAP that led to a split and the reduction of its membership to about 100 persons. The occasion was the argument about the place of the party programme in history. The Kühnen group had a tendency to identify with the former SA, the National Socialist militia. The other faction tended to see the SS as its model. The latter group made use in particular of Kühnen's homosexual leanings to attack his charismatic position.

Despite its militancy, the FAP declined into insignificance at the beginning of the nineties. It was only when neo-Fascist groups were banned in December 1992 that the FAP recovered some of its importance; the group had 220 members in 1992 in Lower Saxony alone and was led in that state by a skinhead.

The neo-Fascist spectrum is very complex. It includes about 1200 to 2000 individuals who romp about on the dance floor of militant and extreme-right alliances. There are small circles among these groups that have survived since the fifties and groups that were formed *ad hoc* only recently. They include voters' communities, military sports groups, associations for maintaining traditions, publishing collectives, groups for maintaining memorials, associations and political parties.

There have been few attempts to form a single organization of neo-Fascists. The ideologies and philosophies of their members and organizations are too diverse for that. The only one currently functioning is the so-called 'Hilfsorganisation für nationale Gefangene und deren Angehörige' (Organization to Help National Prisoners and Members of their Families, HNG). At the same time one of the few intellectuals in these circles is trying to launch a so-called 'Anti-Antifa Campaign' to combat the anti-Fascist movement and its militancy. At present emergency telephones are being set up under his auspices to mobilise hoodlums when left-wing demonstrations take place. Since the death of Michael Kühnen, no tendency towards a collective organization has been discernible. His 'Gesinnungsgemeinschaft der Neuen Front' is now simply the publisher of one of many neo-Nazi papers.

The Nationalistische Front (NF) was founded in November, 1985 and it sees itself as a follow-up organization to the Nazi SA. In the neo-Fascist spectrum it functions as a substitute organization in case the FAP should be banned. The NF was likewise founded on the initiative of Michael Kühnen. This group openly proclaimed itself to be the successor to Strasser's SA, using the national Bolshevist argument that National Socialism had been a socialist workers' party at first and was later betrayed by the NSDAP leadership. In spite of that ideology the NF was never able to recruit more than 150 members. These, however, were militant and not averse to violence. Until 1991, the strongholds of the group were Berlin, Bielefeld and Bremen. The NF managed to recruit the bulk of its membership in the newly formed federal states. The NF was banned after police raids turned up weapons and explosives.

The Deutsche Alternative (DA) was the umbrella organization of the Kühnen wing. It was founded in May 1989 in Bremen. On 7th July, 1990 it was established on the territory of what was still the

GDR under spectacular circumstances in Cottbus, with Kühnen being temporarily arrested. The founding followed the setting-up of regional organizations here and there.

In East Berlin, the DA operated under the name of 'Nationale Alternative' (NA) due to difficulties with the DA's registration. The DA is the most important neo-Nazi network party. Its major figures are at the same time officials of the relevant groupings of the Kühnen wing. The number of DA activists in Germany is estimated at some 250 to 300. Although Michael Kühnen was not the chairman of the party, he was its ideological and organizational head, as was also the case with the FAP.

The Cottbus and Dresden areas were particularly affected by the activities of the DA. There the DA was able to fall back on radicalized adolescents and found some backing in skinhead circles. Following the death of Kühnen, the DA became an East German group with more than 200 members in the Cottbus region alone. The DA chose an East German leadership clique headed by a Cottbus native who had been deported to the Federal Republic after serving prison sentences in the GDR. The DA was banned because of its evident militancy, which made it particularly attractive to adolescents. The ban also extended to the 'Nationale Offensive (NO)', a group that emerged in 1990 from the splits in the FAP, and the militant 'Deutsche Kameradschaftsbund Wilhelmshaven (DKB)'.

The neo-Fascist scene in the late eighties and early nineties was characterized by organizational splintering on the one hand and concentration on one charismatic figure, Michael Kühnen, on the other. After his death in April 1991 a neo-Nazi from Austria tried to take over his political role. After he was barred from entering the country in May 1991, Christian Worch of Hamburg became the driving force in the neo-Fascist organizations.

At the end of 1992 the 'Nationalistische Front, (NF)', the 'Deutsche Alternative, (DA)', the 'Nationale Offensive, (NO)' and the 'Deutsche Kameradschaftsbund Wilhelmshaven, (DKB)' were hit by a series of party prohibitions. These associations and parties were thus deprived of their capacity to acquire and hold rights and duties, their property was confiscated, their offices and the homes of their members were searched, and writings were confiscated. Since that time the Republikaner have been under surveillance by the German intelligence service. An action for deprivation of civil rights was brought against two neo-Nazis, Heinz Reisz and Thomas Dienel, under Article 18 of the German Constitution.

ATTEMPTS AT RECRUITING MEMBERS OF OTHER GROUPS OR YOUNGSTERS WITH RIGHT-WING EXTREMIST ORIENTATIONS

Radical right-wing parties and organizations apply a whole series of methods to recruit potential right-wing youngsters. A distinction can be made between recruitments from a 'more bourgeois environment' and those from a 'rather non-bourgeois environment, the so-called lower classes'. In the 'more bourgeois environment' youngsters are recruited by direct approach, activities such as excursions, camps and outings, as well as training courses and discussions, and among school and university students. Since the autumn of 1987 radical right-wing groups became very active at schools in German cities, where they distributed racist and anti-semitic pamphlets.

Youngsters from the 'non-bourgeois environment and the so-called lower classes', on the other hand, are approached by intervention in certain sub-cultural scenes, such as among football fans, hooligans and skins. Here they have been partly successful in the recent past.

It is not just non-bourgeois people who come together in subcultures, however. The process of ethnicization is proceeding in all strata of society. But it is the marginalized youth cultures in the poorer sectors that are the protagonists of racist violence. The multiplicity of violence and its organizations points again to neo-racism as a heterogeneous phenomenon.

Violence is seldom expressed through continuous organization, although the influence of neo-Fascist groups should certainly not be underestimated. The intelligence service estimates the number of 6,400 militant right-wing extremists in 1992. Of these, 3,800 reside in the eastern and 2,600 in the western part of Germany. The majority of these persons are probably skinheads. There were a total of 82 extreme right organizations in the Federal Republic of Germany, most of them neo-Fascist organizations, although neo-populist parties and their youth groups are included in the figure. A low degree of organization of the extreme right and xenophobic scene is evident.

The number of acts of violence motivated by hostility to foreigners is steadily increasing. In 1992 alone there were 2,548 cases in which a total of 17 people died, including seven foreigners (since the founding of the Federal Republic of Germany, 51 people have fallen victim to such acts of violence; twelve people died in 1986 in one bombing in Munich). Of the acts of violence committed in 1992, 63 had anti-Semitic causes. The targets were, besides foreigners, homeless people, homosexuals and disabled people. Thirty–three per cent of the incidents occurred in the newly formed federal states. Sixty–seven per cent of the perpetrators in 1992 were under 20 years of age and only 2.5 per cent were over 30.

EVENTS

The Rostock Conflict

The first major signal after Hoyerswerda came from Rostock. The Rostock district of Kleinhagen, consisting of new housing blocks made of concrete slabs, lies between Rostock and the seaside resort of Warnemünde and is a dismal working-class complex despite the recreational landscape surrounding it. In GDR times, successful skilled workers, public employees and office workers with a sense of their own prosperity were settled there. They had a self-contained flat and most of them had a family car. Their political orientation was towards their families and the private sphere. Their housing area accounted for a large part of their self-fulfilment. There were various social facilities within that housing area.

One of those facilities was re-dedicated to the accommodation of asylum applicants from eastern Europe. The bulk of the asylum applicants were gypsies, but there were also a few Vietnamese. The number of asylum applicants was out of proportion to the accommodation available: far more applicants were admitted than there were beds, so that tents were set up in the midst of the residential area. Acculturation problems arose, in the main problems of hygiene and differing views about access to resources. Complaints were made to the city administration, which failed to respond for several months. The accommodation of the asylum applicants became a familiar topic beyond the limits of the city of Rostock.

The conflict began in Rostock with protest campaigns and stone-throwing on the part of skinhead groups from outside the area, who were joined by neo-Fascists. The police reacted slowly and not very appropriately. The ranks of the rightist radicals swelled in the course of the whole operation. The police scarcely reacted and were not capable of protecting the home from attack. A part of the home was gutted by fire, to the approval of nearby residents. Politicians were not able to intercede in the overall situation either and after the operation they had to resign because of scandalous remarks.

The campaigns in Rostock were clearly the work of small, well organized youth groups facilitated by the under-reaction of the state as well as a large crowd of silent or cheering residents.

Other Incidents

A Berlin writer described the mobilization of right-wing conservative activities in a small town in Schleswig-Holstein. Right-wing conservative circles characterized by Nazi traditions, the tabooing of the subject of offences under German Fascism and withdrawal into the private sphere have survived there during the last 50 years. On the other hand, the local power elite was able to fall back on such old affinities at election time and when political decisions were taken (Morshäuser, 1993).

In the course of the general economic crisis the rural underclasses were especially subject to the threat of unemployment and other fears. There was a growing tendency to form gangs which admitted more and more neo-Nazis as ideologists. There was little resistance to this, but rather fear of individual terrorism, among the local population.

The youth of the radical right formed gangs and organized regular drinking sessions, and there were continual violent disputes. They affected not only gang outsiders but also the wives and families of the young radical right-wingers. In the course of the industrial restructuring of the region the rural idyll of this locality had early become a focus of social crisis.

In this situation, asylum applicants were accommodated all over the region in village inns and restaurants which had had to close not long before because of low revenues and mounting debts. These local changes in particular gave rise to ill-humoured discussions in all parts of the population. In the end the violence broke out in brutal attacks against a few guest workers in the town, closing the circle of xenophobia and neo-racism.

This example serves to show how the growing significance of the inflow of foreigners has led to direct violence by youthful gangs in materially and intellectually deprived right-wing circles. It also shows that the slogans that made the immigration policy of the Federal Republic of Germany towards migrants possible have fallen on fertile soil here.

Mölln and Solingen, by contrast, were expressions of individual *ad hoc* violence. Here too the perpetrators were adolescents. They developed only loose relationships with gangs, however. The target of the acts of terrorism were not new arrivals, but the Turkish population, which otherwise displays deep roots in the West German population.

YOUTH CULTURES AND VIOLENCE

All studies so far have shown that violent behaviour is in the main a problem of youth cultures. The evaluation of court records and attempts at journalistic or ethnographic research confirm this thesis. Violence on the part of youth takes place in heterogeneously structured arenas and is difficult to typify. It can nevertheless be said that mere individual violence is infrequent. It is more likely to be carried out by groups. Three types need to be differentiated.

The first type relates to individuals who come together on a casual basis as drinking partners. They drink together, insult people together and go out looking for an enemy together. Violence is expressed here on the basis of a general predilection to xenophobia, which results mainly from existential fears and a lack of self-esteem on the part of the perpetrator. The fact that adolescents in particular allow themselves to be carried away and commit acts of brutal violence can no doubt be attributed primarily to identity and puberty crises. Such individually structured violence is not the rule, however. In most cases individuals submit instead to existing group processes. This applied to the events in Rostock and those in Hoyerswerda and other towns where widespread violent conflicts occurred.

The second type is hooliganism (Dunning *et al.*, 1990). This type of violence can be traced to group formations that are orientated towards mass events such as concerts and football games. These are typical mass processes as described, for instance, by Elias Canetti. Group affinities are generated by the mobilization of the masses around a few targets and a separation between one's own group and other groups. The expected or current ritual of the concert or the game puts the groups in a trance. It only needs a few confrontations and provocations to lead to violent conflicts. This violence can be redirected *ad hoc* away from the enemy groups and degenerate into damage to property or vice versa. Such mass behaviour is often found in the right radical scene.

A third type is that of the closed groups (Douglas, 1996). This is generated through regular meetings where the procedure is highly ritualized. Skins in particular, but other youth groups as well belong to this type. The organized grid of these groups is very close-knit. Outsiders and insiders are precisely identified. They differentiate themselves not only through the identification of acquaintances but also quite distinctly through ethnic (cultural) symbols, which frequently follow international fashions but are often generated locally as well. Those involved make group membership the centre of their personality definition, and in the group context they subordinate themselves absolutely to the group dynamics.

Such group behaviour particularly affects young men who are threatened with unemployment or who, owing to progressing individualization processes, increasingly drop out of the job or family-orientated life planning patterns. Recently increasing numbers of women have been observed to join such groups, seeking a vanished world of trust and security. The quest for trust seems to be one of the strongest bonds in these groups. Ideologically the rituals are supplemented by fashionable bands and gossip about those who do not belong to the group. In extreme cases these are foreigners and racially defined persons. Since many of these groups are made up of men, male fantasies play a special role, and homosexuals and women are favourite targets of aggression.

Individual violence in *ad hoc* groups as demonstrated in Solingen and Mölln is easy to define sociologically. Mass violence too has entered the literature as a sociological law. The explanation of collective violence on the basis of the narrow grid of organizations is likewise a sociological law that can scarcely be doubted. There are few such laws, but these, together with case-orientated context analysis, seem to be adequate for the particular purpose of explaining the new violence from the extreme right.

It is not helpful, however, to name skins *per se* as the repositories of this violence. Often, neo-Fascist groups join the skinheads. In the meantime a functioning network has evolved here. Many skinheads describe themselves as being on the left, and some as enemies of violence. It can be left to future studies to establish whether that is really the case. The people most knowledgeable about the skinhead scene in Germany say that it is much larger than the police estimate. There are probably about 8000 skinheads in the Federal Republic of Germany, of whom perhaps 2000 have made themselves conspicuous through far-right violence. The skinhead scene is characterized at all times by strong internal group cohesion. But it is becoming increasingly differentiated in political leanings that relate to the variety of their international magazine literature and the music scene.

THE EAST-WEST DIFFERENCE FOLLOWING REUNIFICATION IN WEST GERMANY

Skinhead groups emerged in the GDR as early as the beginning of the eighties. They stood in pronounced resistance to the regime of the GDR. Their number is estimated at between 600 and 1000. They were confronted with the regime of the GDR in the sharpest form, and their attitude was massively anti-socialist. They followed the Western skinhead fashions and were a part of the neighbourhood culture in some major GDR cities. When the change came their violent tendencies developed into sheer brutality. Although eastern Germany, including Berlin, has only about 20 per cent of the West German population, about 33 per cent of the acts of violence take place in eastern Germany.

Even before the change, neo-Fascist activists such as Michael Kühnen tried to get a toe-hold in eastern Germany. They had few adherents among the skinheads at first, however. This changed in 1991 and 1992. The neo-Nazis themselves formed autonomous groups. Eminent among these is the Deutsche Alternative, which came to prominence in Cottbus and Dresden in 1992.

The neo-populist parties, the Nationaldemokratische Partei Deutschlands, the Deutsche Volksunion and the Republikaner, made little headway in eastern Germany. They lacked functionaries who had rightist personal convictions. No funds came from the membership: one reason the population kept its aloofness from such parties was that it mistrusted party structures generally. The large parties also suffer from this development.

THE REACTION OF THE GOVERNMENT MACHINERY

The government machinery has up to now proceeded against right extremism with bans and the establishment of new institutions. Thus in 1992, belatedly, various neo-Fascist groups were outlawed. The neo-populist party of the 'Republikaner' is under surveillance by the intelligence service. An application for repeal of civil rights has been lodged against two prominent neo-Fascists. The most important reactions of the state machinery, however, concern the establishment of new coordinating bodies and complaints about the lack of civil servants. Here once again we see a typical failure on the part of the state, resulting in particular from the fact that the problems are discussed not so much from the point of view of their solution or combating their causes as from that of justifying new posts and additional funding.

A departmental group on 'right-wing terrorism' was set up at the Conference of Ministers of the Interior in April 1992. The group co-ordinated the work of the individual ministerial departments that were responsible for police operations against right-wing radicals. At the end of 1992 the Ministers of the Interior decided that the Federal Criminal Police Office, the state police forces, the judicial departments and the intelligence service would assign the task to an 'Information Group for Observing and Combating Right Extremist, Terrorist and especially Anti-Foreigner Acts of Violence' (IGR). This national inter-ministerial co-ordination group was responsible for a large-scale operation against the distribution of material with neo-Fascist content at the beginning of 1993. 'Operation Clef (Notenschlüssel)' took place on 3 February 1993. During that police operation, ten skinhead bands and two music publishing companies were raided and their writings and texts were confiscated.

Even during the term of office of former Federal President Weizsäcker, criticism of racist and right-wing extremist actions in Germany, most of it coming from abroad, was perceived by the public as threatening national interests. This perception was reinforced by the media, non-governmental organizations, churches and many politicians. Anti-racism became a civic duty. Anti-racist demonstrations, organized from above and placed under the patronage of the Federal President, were grouped together and centrally planned. Chains of people holding candles and huge demonstrations showed the social potency of the anti-racist citizenry. Their symbolic power was overwhelming. Other imposing actions followed, including a broadly funded programme to combat youth violence.

NEW AND OLD RACISM

With regard to the theory that the status of the Federal Republic of Germany is special because of the experience of National Socialism in dealing with racism and nationalism, it can be said that Germany does indeed have a special status. It has to do in particular with the taboo that prevailed for a long time regarding this group of problems and the reconstruction of Fascism in the collective consciousness of various groups. Thus there are indeed relationships with the old racism in the sphere of the formulation of racist patterns. Scales of xenophobic aloofness show distinctly racist features.

It must nevertheless be said that the new racism in Germany has its causes more in multi-ethnic situations in which cultural demarcations are decisive. The frequently cited significance of neo-Fascism with its roots in National Socialist networks should not be overestimated.

It can be seen at all levels that neo-racism is a Europe-wide movement. This applies above all to the xenophobic proclivities in the collective consciousness of the population. It also applies to the networking of neo-populism and its political parties in Europe. It applies to the networks of right-wing conservative and far-right intellectuals, more so to the close-knit ritual bounded organizational grids of youth cultures, and finally to the activities of far-right hoodlums as combatants in Croatia and Bosnia and as start-up groups for right-wing nationalist movements in eastern Europe.

The new racism is also an expression of a global culture that has resulted not only in multi-ethnicity but also in the worldwide communication of resistance. The close links that German neo-Fascists have with American and Canadian groups is a clear indication of this, as is the international perception of immigration.

If we consider racism in Germany from a comparative perspective, we can see that German neo-racism is an expression of all-European activities. It stands in opposition to the changing of nation-state structures regarded as unitary into multi-ethnic patterns, and it expresses xenophobic fears stoked up by the political elite in the face of new waves of immigration.

In the final analysis it is up to the state whether it chooses to pursue a nationalist policy of social uniformity or transforms multi-ethnic structures into multiculturalism. As long as government agencies around the world resist recognizing the new multi-ethnic structures, hierarchization and delimitation across ethnic boundaries will remain an important element of social action. That is the core of neo-racism in Germany too.

BIBLIOGRAPHY

Ashkenasi, Abraham (ed.) (1988), *Das weltweite Flüchtlingsproblem,* Sozialwissen-schaftliche Versuche der Annäherung, Bremen
Bergmann, Werner/ Erb, Rainer (1991*), Antisemitismus in der Bundesrepublik Deutschland,* Ergebnisse der empirischen Forschung von 1946–1989, Opladen
Berliner Institut fr Vergleichende Sozialforschung (ed.), Blaschke, Jochen,

Frackmann, Helmut, Maáholder, Frigga, Schendel, Jürgen, Schwarz, Thomas, and Winter, Werner (1991) *Regionale und strukturelle Faktoren von Rechtsradikal-ismus und Ausländerfeindlichkeit in West-und Ostberlin*, (BIVS-Arbeitshefte), Berlin

Blaschke, Jochen (1984), *Volk, Nation, Interner Kolonialismus, Ethnizität*, Konzepte zur politischen Soziologie regionalistischer Bewegungen in Westeuropa, Berlin

Blaschke, Jochen (1991), 'Foreign workers in Germany: demographic patterns, trends, and consequences', in *Regional Development Dialogue*, 12/3, S. 127–144

Blaschke, Jochen (1991), 'Kurdische Communities in Deutschland und Westeuropa. Ein Überblick über ihre soziale und kulturelle situation', in Berliner Institut für Vergleichende Sozialforschung / (ed.), *Kurden im Exil. (Ein Handbuch kurdischer Kultur, Politik und Wissenschaft*, Band 1). Berlin, P.2.1

Blaschke, Jochen (1991), 'Die Diaspora der Kurden in der Bundesrepublik Deutschland', in *Österreichische Zeitschrift für Soziologie*, 16/3, S. 85–93

Blaschke, Jochen and Germershausen, Andreas (1992), *Sozialwissenschaftliche Studien über das Weltflüchtlingsproblem*, Band 1, Berlin

Blaschke, Jochen (1993), 'Gates of immigration into the Federal Republic of Germany', in *International Migration*, 31/2–3, S. 361–388

Blaschke, Jochen (1995), 'Multicultural strategies in the Federal Republic of Germany', in Hjarno, Jan (ed.), *Multiculturalism in the Nordic societies*, Proceedings of the 9th Nordic Seminar for Researchers on Migration and Ethnic Relations, Final report. Kopenhagen, S. 322–331

Broszat, Martin (1958), 'Die völkische Ideologie und der Nationalsozialismus', in *Deutsche Rundschau*, 1, S. 53ff

Broszinsky-Schwabe, E. (1994), 'Handlungsstrategien gegen Fremdenfeindlichkeit. Fachkonferenz in Hoyerswerda', in *Informationsdienst zur Ausländerarbeit*, 1, S. 10–11

Childs, David (1995), 'The far right in Germany since 1945', in Cheles, Luciano, Ferguson, Ronnie and Vaughan, Michalina (eds), *The far right in Western and Eastern Europe*, London/New York, S. 290–308

Conze, Werner and Groh, Dieter (1966), *Die Arbeiterbewegung in der nationalen Bewegung. Die deutsche Sozialdemokratie vor, während und nach der Reichsgründung*, Stuttgart

Dann, Otto (1994), *Nation und Nationalismus in Deutschland, 1770–1990*, München

Dohse, Knuth (1985), *Auslandische Arbeiter und bürgerlicher Staat. Genese und Funktion von staatlicher Ausländerpolitik und Auslanderrecht*, Vom Kaiserreich bis zur Bundesrepublik Deutschland. Königstein/Ts

Douglas, M. (1966), *Purity and danger*, London. (Ritual, Tabu und Krpersymbolik. Sozialanthropologische Studien in Industriegesellschaft und Stammeskultur. Frankfurt/M.)

Dudek, Peter and Jaschke, Hans-Gerd (1981), *Revolte von rechts*, Anatomie einer neuen Jugendpresse. Frankfurt/Main/New York

Dudek, Peter and Jaschke, Hans-Gerd (1984), *Entstehung und Entwicklung des Rechtsextremismus in der Bundesrepublik. Zur Tradition einer besonderen politischen Kultur (2, Bnde). Opladen

Dudek, Peter (1989), 'Thesen zum Rechtsextremismus unter Jugendlichen', in *Die Grünen*, Bundesvorstand, Argumente gegen REPs und Co. Bonn, S. 162–165

Dunning, Eric, Murphy, Patrick, Newburn, Tim and Waddington, Ivan (1987), 'Violent disorders in twentieth-century Britain', in Gaskell, George and Benewick, Robert (eds) *The Crowd in Contemporary Britain*, London, S. 19ff

Dunning, Eric, Murphy, Patrick and Williams, John (1990), *The roots of football Hooliganism. A historical and sociological study*, London

Dupeux, Louis (1985), *'Nationalbolschewismus' in Deutschland 1919–1933. Kommunistische Strategie und konservative Dynamik*, Mnchen

Farin, Klaus and Seidel-Pielen, Eberhard (1991), *Krieg in den Städten. Jugendgangs in Deutschland*, Berlin

Farin, Klaus and Seidel-Pielen, Eberhard (1992), *Rechtsruck. Rassismus im neuen Deutschland*, Berlin

Farin, Klaus and Seidel-Pielen, Eberhard (1993), *Ohne Gewalt läuft nichts! Jugend und Gewalt in Deutschland*, Köln

Farin, Klaus and Seidel-Pielen, Eberhard (1993), *Skinheads*, München

Galtung, Johan (1973), 'Eine strukturelle Theorie der Revolution', in Jänicke, Martin (ed.), *Herrschaft und Krise*, Opladen, S. 121–169

Heitmeyer, Wilhelm (ed.) (1994), *Das Gewalt-Dilemma. Gesellschaftliche Reaktionen auf fremdenfeindliche Gewalt und Rechtsextremismus*, Frankfurt/M

Herbert, Ulrich (1986), *Geschichte der Ausländerbeschäftigung in Deutschland 1880 bis 1980: Saisonarbeiter, Zwangsarbeiter, Gastarbeiter*, Berlin/Bonn

Herbert, Ulrich (1994), 'Saisonarbeiter – Zwangsarbeiter – Gastarbeiter. Zur historischen Dimension einer aktuellen Debatte', in Friedrich-Ebert-Stiftung (ed.), *Von der Ausländer-zur Einwanderungspolitik. Gesprächskreis Arbeit und Soziales*, Nr. 32. Bonn, S. 61–78

Hermand, Jost (1992), *Old dreams of a new Reich. Volkish utopias and national socialism*. Bloomington. (1988, *Der alte Traum vom neuen Reich. Völkische Utopien und Nationalsozialismus*, Frankfurt/M.)

Hirsch, Kurt and Metz, Wolfgang (1989), *Die Republikaner – die falschen Patrioten*, (Schriftenreihe der bayerischen SPD), München

Hirsch, Kurt (1989), *Rechts von der Union. Personen, Organisationen, Parteien seit 1945. Ein Lexikon*, München

Hirsch, Kurt (1990), *Rechts, REPs, Rechts. Aktuelles Handbuch zur rechtsextremen Szene*, Berlin

Hirsch, Kurt and Sarkowicz, H. (1989), Schönhuber. Der Politiker und seine Kreise, Frankfurt/M

Husbands, Christopher T. (1995), 'Militant neo-Nazism in Germany', in Cheles, Luciano, Ferguson, Ronnie and Vaughan, Michalina (eds.), *The far right in Western and Eastern Europe*, London/New York, S. 327–353

Jänicke, Martin (1971), *Totalitäre Herrschaft. Anatomie eines politischen Begriffes*, Berlin

Keßler, Hermann (1995), 'Das Höllentor der "Neuen Rechten"', in *Die Brcke*, 81(1), S. 23–24

Kleff, Broszinsky-Schwabe, Albert, Marburger and Karsten (1990), *BRD – DDR. Alte und neue Rassismen im Zuge der deutsch-deutschen Einigung*, Frankfurt

Kowalsky, Wolfgang and Schroeder, Wolfgang (1994), Rechtsextremismus. Begriff, Methode, Analyse in *Berliner Debatte*, 3. Zeitschrift für sozialwissenschaftlichen Diskurs, S. 87–94

Kowalsky, Wolfgang and Schroeder, Wolfgang (ed.) (1994), *Rechtsextremismus. Einführung und Forschungsbilanz*, Opladen

Langewiesche, Dieter (1992), 'Reich, Nation und Staat in der jüngeren deutschen Geschichte', in *Historische Zeitschrift* (HZ) 254, Seite 341–381

Langewiesche, Dieter (1994), *Nationalismus im 19. und 20. Jahrhundert: zwischen Partizipation und Aggression*, Bonn

Mohler, Armin (1994), *Die Konservative Revolution in Deutschland 1918–1932. Ein Handbuch. Hauptband*, Darmstadt

Morshäuser, Bodo (1993), *Warten auf den Führer*, Frankfurt/M.

Morshäuser, Bodo (1992), *Hauptsache Deutsch*, Frankfurt/Main

Mosse, George L. (1979), *Ein Volk, Ein Reich, Ein Führer. Die völkischen Ursprünge des Nationalsozialismus*, Königstein/Ts.

Murphy, Patrick, Williams, John and Dunning, Eric (1990), *Football on trial. Spectator violence and development in the football world*, London, New York

Noack, Paul (1996) *Carl Schmitt – eine Biographie*, Frankfurt/M.

Pfahl-Traughber, Armin (1993), *Rechtsextremismus. Eine kritische Bestandsaufnahme nach der Wiedervereinigung*, Bonn

Plessner, Helmuth (1974), *Die verspätete Nation. Über die politische Verfügbarkeit des Geistes*, Frankfurt/M.

Rüthers, Bernd (1990), *Carl Schmitt im Dritten Reich – Wissenschaft als Zeitgeist-Verstärkung?* München

Schmidt, Anne (1994), 'Chronologie des Rechtsextremismus in der Bundesrepublik Deutschland und anderen westeuropäischen Ländern ab 1945', in Kowalsky, Wolfgang and Schroeder, Wolfgang (eds.), *Rechtsextremismus, Einfhrung und Forschungsbilanz*, Opladen, S. 383–407

Seidel-Pielen, Eberhard (1993), 'Rechte und linke Gewalt', in *Blickpunkt*, 42/1, S. 26–27

Sontheimer, Kurt (1994), *Antidemokratisches Denken in der Weimarer Republik – die politischen Ideen des deutschen Nationalismus zwischen 1918 und 1933*, München

Weingart, Peter, Kroll, Jürgen and Bayertz, Kurt (1988), *Rasse, Blut und Gene. Geschichte der Eugenik und Rassenhygiene in Deutschland*, Frankfurt/M.

Winkler, Heinrich August (ed.) (1995), *Nationalismus – Nationalitäten – Supranation-alität*, Industrielle Welt Bd. 53, Stuttgart

Winkler, Heinrich August (1993), 'Nationalismus, Nationalstaat und nationale Frage in Deutschland seit 1945', in Winkler, Heinrich August and Kaelble, Hartmut (eds.) *Nationalismus – Nationalitäten – Supranationalität*, Stuttgart, S. 12–33

Winkler, Jürgen R. (1994), 'Die Wählerschaft der rechtsextremen Parteien in der Bundesrepublik Deutschland 1949 bis 1993', in Kowalsky, Wolfgang and Schroeder, Wolfgang (eds), *Rechtsextremismus. Einführung und Forschungsbilanz*, Opladen, S. 69–88

Wippermann, Wolfgang (1995), 'Sinti und Roma in Deutschland', in Berliner Institut für Vergleichende Sozialforschung (ed.) *Handbuch Ethnischer Minderheiten in Deutschland*, Berlin, 3.4.1.ff

NOTES

1. This paper is the product of discussions in various projects at the Berlin Institute for Comparative Social Research on the theory and experience of racism in Germany. The work began with a theory report in the eighties; in 1990 and 1991, empirical studies on racism were carried out in East and West Berlin. After that the Institute was entrusted with research on racism in various special fields. Parts of this manuscript were read at the Kenilworth Conference on European Racism in 1991. It was given its basic structure in the context of a conference at Loughborough University. I have to thank Alec Hargreaves here for his patience. The most recent version was presented at the conference from which the book arises.

2. The tenor of the debate in the early 1990s was that a differentiation had to be made between West Germany and East Germany, with East Germany being considered as particularly susceptible to hostility towards foreigners and to right-wing radicalism. This differentiation has now been shown to be at variance with reality. What we have instead is differing manifestations of racist activity.

3. Volkish is a translation of the German term 'völkisch'. The standard work on volkish theory is by Martin Braszat (1958); see also George Mosse (1997), where it says *Seit dem Beginn der Romantik im späten 18. Jahrhundert bezeichnet der Begriff 'Volk' für deutsche Denker eine Gruppe von Menschen, denen eine metaphysische 'Wesenheit' eigen ist* (Since the beginning of the Romance period in the late 18th century, the term 'Volk' has been applied by German thinkers to a group of people possessing a metaphyscial 'essence'; page 10). The volkish ideas are reviewed in an exciting book of more recent date by Jost Hermand (1988/1992).

4. In Germanic mythology, Valhalla is the place where heroes find their heavenly retreat after being killed in war. The German romantic Valhalla is a pseudo-Greek temple on the shores of the Danube with memorials to German celebrities.

5. The Social Democrats erected a socialist theoretical structure in the multi-ethnic Austrian context that left ample room for the national question: positive law, consideration of national minorities at the federal state level and the development of the welfare state, became the central themes of Austro-Marxism, in the evolution of which Social Democrats from the German Reich participated. German Social Democracy split on the national question in the face of World War I. The right-wing majority argued that democratic socialism required increasing participation in national questions as the emancipation of the working class progressed. The numerically small left wing remained internationalist. There were roots for both positions. The patriots surrounding Bernstein were in the tradition of Lassallian populism (Lassalle was the founder of Social democracy). The left based itself on Austro-Marxism and the rejection of nationalist positions by Karl Kautsky.

6. For Schmitt and his activities in the Fascist system, see Rüthers (1990); for his Catholicism see Noack (1993).

7. These figures are taken from statements of the Federal Chancellor's Office. They are estimates only. No precise statistics on the refugee population exist. Not even its composition by sex and occupation is known. Double

applications and family affiliations render numerical estimates more difficult to make.

8. There is very little empirically grounded material on the history of immigration policy. As part of a project sponsored by the Volkswagen Foundation, The Berlin Institute for Comparative Social Research is currently studying the immigration policy discourses that have taken place since the seventies.

4 The Romany Minority in the Czech Lands

Zdenka Jarabová

The post-totalitarian societies of Eastern and Central Europe seem to show not only an effort at reunification with the rest of the continent and the world but also unexpected tendencies of fragmentation. We face various new manifestations of nationalism and new attempts at ethnic identification and self-identification. In addition to the fact that Czechoslovakia as a federation has divided itself into two independent national states, ethnic minorities, especially that of Romanies, have become more visible than before. It is noticeable that quite a few of the problems encountered by Romanies today are either direct or indirect consequences of inherent racism within Czech and Slovak societies. People in general in the Czech Republic would, therefore, hardly understand or care that Romanies may have problems; the Czechs would rather believe that they have problems with the Romanies and that the Romanies themselves simply are 'a problem.'

All those phenomena may have existed under the cover of the totalitarian regime and only after the liberation of our societies did they start coming to the surface and taking their own, often unpredictable, paths of development.

Proportionately, that is, as a percentage of the total population, Czechoslovakia's Romany minority used to be among the largest in Europe, ranking between the third and fifth position (while Slovakia on its own is, in fact, the first). Because of the rather imperfect census in 1991, official figures cannot be very accurate; the estimated number at present is about three hundred thousand, which represents some three per cent of the total population of the Czech Republic.

HISTORICAL AND LEGAL FACTS

There are reports suggesting that Romanies (gypsies) may have moved into the area of the present Czech lands in the beginning of the thirteenth century. Originally they came to Europe from India via Asia Minor and the Balkans. Their origin can be deduced from their language, which is related to Sanskrit. Certain Romany dialects are among the surviving fragments of Sanskrit as a living language.

Throughout the Middle Ages, Romanies in the Czech lands and elsewhere in Europe were not permitted to settle in one place. They were not allowed to own land or to follow any trade, and their nomadic life was therefore largely a result of necessity. Change only occurred during the reign of the Habsburg monarchs Maria Theresa and her son Josef II in the latter part of the 18th century, when the first attempts to assimilate the Romanies were undertaken. The Empress assigned areas where they could settle and their children were ordered to attend school; they were also introduced to Christianity. The policy to convert them to a new way of life did not fully succeed and yet it could be said that the Romany population adjusted itself at least partly to a more or less settled existence for some two centuries and, therefore, differs culturally from Romanies in the rest of the continent. Interesting (and perhaps unique) demographic documentation of the process of settlement exists and reaches back to the eighteenth century. In the earlier stage, the act could be a result either of tolerance or of purposeful regulation on the part of the authorities; by the early twentieth century a demographic pattern appeared from which it was obvious that Romanies lived a settled life in some parts of Moravia (especially in the southeastern area and partly in the southern and central areas) while in the remaining territory of the Czech lands they kept roaming.[1]

Despite a certain degree of assimilation, however, Romanies never achieved the status of citizens of the majority population; in 1927 a Czechoslovak law even put Gypsies in one category with vagabonds and thieves.[2] Although the law, which had been discussed from the founding of the state in 1918, never verbally mentioned Romanies, by making it its objective to declare nomads, loafers and idlers illegal or undesirable, it was clearly aimed at persecuting them. In a discussion following the passing of the law, objections were raised, pointing out its unconstitutional nature; amendments and decrees were to revise its predominantly repressive character, but in April of 1928 the law was enforced. Romanies obtained from the authorities 'gypsy cards' (with fingerprints) and wanderers needed an official permit; thus Czechoslovakia became the first country trying to deal in legislative terms with the Romany issue, and the law was used as a source of inspiration for other countries in the years to follow.

The fate of Romanies in the Czech Lands reached its tragic point during World War II when the 'gypsy question' was resolved by the Nazis in sending members of this ethnic group to labour camps. There some fifty per cent of the Czech Romanies died of malnutrition, exhaustion, dysentery and typhoid; others perished in the extermination camp in Auschwitz. Of the original five to six thousand Czech Romanies, only a small part survived; the estimate of the number of survivors is 600.[3] Although quite a lot of documents and literature exists about the Holocaust history of the Romanies, general knowledge of the facts is tellingly poor, close to nil.

In the years after the war a great migration of Romanies to the Czech lands took place, first from Slovakia and then also from Romania, where the still nomadic Olah tribe lived. There were a number of reasons for the movement. There was, of course, space vacated by those who perished, and, in the border areas, by Germans who had been deported. Northern Bohemia and industrial towns in the Czech lands offered jobs and housing and looked quite attractive when compared with the conditions in Romany settlements in Slovakia. The increase in the Romany population, though, soon appeared to the majority as 'a gypsy problem.' In 1958 a new law came in force prohibiting the nomadic way of life for Romanies.[4] In practice it meant that their caravans were burned and their horses shot, and that Romanies were forced to accept the habits of the majority population, if only in a superficial way, by emulating the pursuit of materialistic values as goals to be achieved at whatever cost and by whatever means.

In 1965 the Government decided to introduce organized action aimed at the dispersion of Romanies throughout the country.[5] This legal act was followed in 1988 by a decree which attempted to address the immediate social problems and needs of the Romany population. Families with more than three children were granted free lunches from nursery school to the end of compulsory school attendance without any means testing. All the measures were based on the assumption that improved social conditions and a 'higher standard of living' would change 'the gypsy mentality.' What happened, however, was that the social advantages granted to Romanies as a group evoked hostility in the dominant population which looked upon decisions made by governmental authorities with growing distrust and disapproval anyway. It was also believed, and not without justification, that Romany families could live on subsidy provided by the Government for every new-born child and did not care much for any more ambitious social involvement.

The trouble, no doubt, was that nobody ever asked the members of the ethnic group for their own views; their existence, their way of life was always a matter of someone else's decision. There was no interest in the country in preserving their national and ethnic identity or making use of and even getting to know better their culture. The goal, indeed, was never integration but, at best, assimilation.

THE CURRENT SITUATION

When in 1978 the spokesmen for the Czechoslovak dissident group, the Charter 77, issued a statement on the position of Romanies in Czechoslovakia, it was the first serious criticism in many decades expressing disapproval with the official policy of the Communist regime regarding this ethnic minority.[6] The impact of the statement was quite limited, however, because of the limited publicity that documents issued by the Charter 77 had in those days; it was only on the wavelengths of Radio Free Europe that people could learn about them and not everyone who listened was necessarily convinced of the use, purpose or feasibility of the ideas expressed. On the issue of the Romanies in our country, therefore, most people remained uninformed and indifferent. Even after the revolutionary changes in Czechoslovakia in 1989, the document by the dissidents of Charter 77 remains the only demonstration of doubts as to the legitimacy and appropriateness of the acquired 'gypsy policy' of the state that deliberately, if not intentionally, disregarded ethnic or national differences and, in an insensitive and even brutal manner, pursued the objective of assimilation of the minority into the mainstream society, both without the consent and against the interest of the people concerned.

Only after the official acceptance of the Charter of Human Rights and Liberties in 1991 by the Parliament of the Czech and Slovak Federal Republic, which made any form of discrimination illegal were the Romanies in Czechoslovakia granted the status of a national minority. This appeared as a dramatic improvement but on its own it could not mend all the historically rooted inadequacies and manifestations of injustice; as most of the legislative measures relating to the Romanies have been of a repressive nature, there remains much to be done in the field before the democratic principles of the rule of law are in force. The most recent problem appeared after the split of Czechoslovakia and with the introduction in the Czech Republic of a new (and rather discriminatory) Law of Citizenship.

A positive feature of recent developments is, undoubtedly, the emergence of a few Romany organizations and political parties, the strongest of which is the Romany Civic Initiative, based on national principle. In the wake of November 1989 Romanies joined the population of the country in the enthusiasm and determination for changes in society. A few of their representatives were included in the list of candidates of the Civic Forum in 1990 but two years later, when their own parties could not reach agreement and no other political party would offer its platform for campaign, no Romany candidate made it to Parliament. So, nearly four years after the revolution, questions must be asked as to the efficiency and representativeness of the existing political organizations for Romanies.

Progress can be noticed in endeavours to raise the ethnic and national consciousness and, consequently, the identity of the Romanies in our country. The use of their language is encouraged and events promoting their cultural traditions are supported by various organizations and the Ministry of Culture. The problem again is in the mass of people who are being addressed by such activities; their eventual effect may also be lessened by lack of experience, unavailability of a greater number of professional organizers, and indifference and different interests of the Romanies themselves. It is worth mentioning that a few periodicals are being published by Romany organizations with parts of the contents in their own language (a bi-weekly paper *Romano Kurko*, for example and a monthly magazine, *Lacho Lav*).[7]

Unfortunately, a growth of unfavourable attitudes toward Romanies can be witnessed in our country. Negative features strongly overshadow positive ones when the majority population evaluates their coexistence with Romanies; only about fifteen per cent of respondents in a poll could see them positively as against 35 per cent who would have a predominantly negative assessment.[8] It appears socially acceptable to describe the whole minority as consisting of criminals, alcoholics and prostitutes. In criminal records even some leading Czech newspapers report the Romany nationality of offenders, disregarding whether they identified themselves as such in the census; if the offenders are ethnic Czechs, the point is never mentioned as noteworthy. Not surprisingly, then, the critical mass of news about Romanies concerns crime, especially when the crime rate among this minority is, indeed, significantly higher than in the rest of the population. The facts themselves, further enhanced by biased interpretation, build up an atmosphere favourable to racially motivated violence. Since 1990, right-wing extremists (skinheads, members of a 'Republican Party') have repeatedly initiated conflicts with Romanies and their communities; public marches were organized and aggressive racist slogans were chanted, including such vicious ones as 'gas the gypsies'. The discouraging fact is that almost no demonstrations of the Czech public protesting against such extremist violence and neo-fascist rhetoric has been noticed so far.

The most relevant area of discrimination is that of employment: while the present national rate of unemployment remains at the level of about two to three per cent, for Romanies it reaches into the double-digits. Due to problems with the definition and identification of who is a Romany, it is hard to establish accurate figures, but in some regions the estimated number of Romanies who are jobless is about seventy to eighty per cent. Although the principal reason for this degree of unemployment is lack of qualifications, many companies state that they 'don't employ Romanies' even if they meet the requirements and so the group's unemployment is higher than that of the unskilled part of the Czech population. Signs of racist and segregationist policy can also be seen in some restaurants and at discos, where owners may deny entry to Romanies and provoke no legal prosecution for such an unconstitutional act. The outlook for the future, then, is not very promising as far as a desired decrease of tension, conflict and even violence is concerned, unless something vital is changed in the situation and in the mentality of the general population.

The statement on the Romanies in Czechoslovakia issued by Charter 77 is related to all the major problems (still very topical at present) and includes housing, work opportunities and employment, social care, education, and, unfortunately, involvement in criminal activities. I believe there exists an obvious correlation between all the problems and yet there is no way of dealing with all of them in a complex way at once; what is most desirable is success, even if only a partial one, for psychological and tactical reasons also. The Czech population will have to deal also with deeply-rooted prejudices, with growing manifestations of racism and xenophobia, but what is most important, it will have to learn something about its Romany co-citizens, as general knowledge so far remains greatly insufficient. What prevails is a group, and stereotypical thinking that is well reflected in traditional Czech sayings referring to gypsies as liars and thieves. More factual information about Romanies and their way of life is an indispensable condition for a revision of attitudes on the part of the Czech majority which should also be a safeguard, then, against extremist views and behaviour in society.

THE QUESTION OF NATIONAL IDENTITY AND CITIZENSHIP

After 1948 Romanies were not recognized as a national minority and could be considered either Czech or Slovak. In fact, it was rather the administration that decided their nationality for them, judging by birth-place or abode. Officially they could choose between the two languages and their mother tongue was only spoken in the family, showing the influence of Czech or Slovak and indicating that knowledge of their native tongue was gradually declining even among its users. Legally the Romanies ceased to exist but their real existence was undeniable. Paradoxically, then, authorities collected various data about this 'non-existent' minority and this was exploited in the realization of the social policy regarding this particular group of the population. For the Communist regime the 'gypsy problem' was a matter to be dealt with through diverse bureaucratic decrees, some of which had a discriminatory or coercive character. For example, a decree recommended, but in fact ordered, Romanies to leave Slovakia and settle in the Czech lands; this resulted in a great number of lasting difficulties and in the dislocation of communities which caused the loss of traditional and valuable ways of life. (Cf. note 5).

The most recent problem appeared after the split of Czechoslovakia in 1993 and with the introduction in the Czech Republic of a new, rather dubious and even discriminatory law of citizenship. The law, which was passed in December 1992, was based on a previous one of 1969 which defined adult individuals born in the Slovak part of the country (i.e., those who were at least fifteen years old in 1969 and, therefore, born before 1954) and the children thereof as Slovak citizens; a similar rule applied for Czechs in the Czech Republic. At the time of the Federation the citizenship of one of the respective republics was a mere formality. In fact, it was less than that, because it was not even mentioned in any personal document and the vast majority of the population were not aware of the fact that they were citizens of anything but the Federal Republic.

When in 1992 the law of 1969 was taken as a basis for the new one, almost all Romanies living in the Czech Republic automatically became Slovak citizens, because the older generation was born in Slovakia before 1954, and those born in the Czech Lands after 1954 received the Slovak citizenship of their parents. For historical reasons then, as has already been pointed out, virtually all Czech Romanies came from Slovakia. According to the law, however, all of them now had to apply for Czech citizenship, including those who were born in the Czech Republic and had never even been to Slovakia. The application for Czech citizenship has to be supported by a proof of a two-year permanent residence in the Czech Republic, a clean penal record of five years, and a proof from Slovak authorities that the individual had resigned his or her Slovak citizenship. It is obvious that quite a few Romanies will fail to receive Czech citizenship because they will be unable to meet these requirements.

While the totalitarian authorities denied the official recognition of Romanies as a national minority but knew who they were, institutions of public administration after 1989 and the acceptance of the Charter of Human Rights and Liberties refuse to collect and issue data on minorities, as it is deemed illegal and unconstitutional. This seems to be a stumbling-block for projects in social and health care, and in education as well. There are justified doubts also about the results of the 1991 census, when Romanies could for the first time declare their nationality; the recorded 33,000 may only be one tenth of the actual number. Many members of this ethnic minority did not consider it necessary to admit that they were different; others may have felt it dangerous to have an identity card with Romany nationality stated. The low official number gave the authorities a good excuse for setting the issue aside, at least for the moment. All in all, what seems obvious is a need for a more realistic analysis of the current situation and, perhaps, an establishment of a clearing house for data and ideas, plus a co-ordinator of projects striving for the improvement of general conditions. Last but not least, all the effort should be made to involve in the activities the Romanies themselves in every possible capacity.

PLANS AND HOPES FOR CHANGE

There exists a growing conviction that education could play a key role in the process of breaking the vicious circle that so many of the Romany population fall into.[9] Traditionally, education has been highly valued in the Czech community and that is why Czechs have difficulties understanding the entirely different view of and attitude towards school instruction that they witness with Romany families and children. It is simply that formal education does not rank high on the value scale of the originally nomadic people whose traditional crafts and talents happened to be quite different from those cultivated by the dominant nations in Central Europe. Intellectuals are rather scarce among the Romanies, and they do not necessarily enjoy the greatest prestige or authority in their own community. In addition, they frequently join the mainstream society and, therefore, can hardly be appreciated and used as 'models' either by the majority or the minority. And yet the need for educated leaders is great, especially if coexistence of Czechs and Romanies is the goal. (Cf. note 14.)

Family ties seem to be very strong with Romanies, as they have always been. Statistics show that their families are large, but they also reveal that very few children make it to high school and an alarming percentage never completes basic school education. And yet, in comparison to neighbouring and other European countries, the policy of compulsory school attendance has been quite successful in Czechoslovakia, as schools are relatively accessible and the obligation of parents to send children to school has been systematically emphasized and presented as a condition for various social benefits. It has to be said that children from Romany families enter schools from a socially rather unsatisfactory environment and with a poor knowledge of the Czech language, which is a serious handicap not only in their understanding of other subjects but also in their communication with other children and with teachers. What ensues from such a situation is frustration, stressful reaction – including purposeful disregard for generally shared values – and attempts to draw attention and gain respect through negative and destructive conduct. The next step towards delinquency and crime is only logical.

On the basis of a verdict of intellectual and social inadequacy, Romany children are frequently sent to special schools for mentally retarded or handicapped pupils, even if their intelligence quotient is no lower than average. They are, of course, measured by social criteria and by the yardstick corresponding to the general cultural and hygienic requirements, which is far from fair. Among teachers there still prevails an attitude of distrust, conditioned by indifference and ignorance, from which the desire to get rid of the Romany children in the class as potential 'troublemakers' ensues. What is saddening is the fact that even some Romany parents, too, prefer to have their offspring in special schools as this takes away from them partial responsibility for the children's accomplishment and performance. In this way, then, the vicious circle is being constantly reiterated – young and often semi-literate parents have children who seem to be predestined to go to institutions for special education and become juvenile delinquents.

Ideas for programmes of alternative education for Romany children do exist.[10] The blueprint of the Romany Civic Initiative is of special appeal as it reflects the views of insiders. So far, however, the community of educators at large has not been involved in the discussion and it does not seem to be anxious to be involved. But without the interest and assistance of educational administrators and teachers there can be no progress in the field. It is high time, however, for the dominant population to realize that problems of and with gypsies are their problems as well.

THE OLOMOUC EDUCATIONAL PROJECT

Some projects designed to improve the conditions of education of Romany children are beginning to appear. The basic idea is to influence the mentality and thinking of both teachers and students who would become teachers in classes with Romanies in the basic school system; the general objective is to disseminate more information, to increase interest and, consequently, professional and human involvement.

One such programme at Palacký University, Olomouc, has now completed its second year. It was designed to help understand and overcome the dangers of stereotypical thinking and to challenge intolerance, racism, xenophobia and various prejudices. A better understanding of notions of ethnic pluralism, national diversity and multiculturalism was set as the primary objective of a series of lectures and courses in political philosophy, history, ethnology, psychology, sociology and pedagogy, in the hope that the discussion of racial and ethnic matters would considerably raise the awareness of the issue in all its aspects among the students and in the faculty.

From this viewpoint it appears encouraging that the second year proved more successful than the first one, when above all the introduction of new and unusual facts and phenomena, such as the Romany vision of the historical and current reality (especially if coming from an ethnic speaker), was still perceived with suspicion, if not irritation. As the first course of lectures proceeded during the year, the initial audience of eighty dwindled to less than half.

In the following year the programme seemed to be more effective after further well-known lecturers were brought in (the President of the Supreme Court, for example) and the scope of subjects was enlarged to include racism and cultural anthropology, the communal relevance of Romany language and other topics);[11] interest was also boosted by the availability of a few publications which resulted from the research done in the field and were issued as part of our Romany project.[12] Not only did the course retain its attractiveness for the audience throughout its duration but student participation in the discussion was more lively and to the point. It can also be considered a real breakthrough that nine students of pedagogy, psychology and sociology have decided to write their graduation theses on topics related to Romany subject matter,[13] thus becoming a part of the research programmes in the corresponding departments. The team in the Department of Psychology concentrates on the investigation and assessment of differences in the structure of cognitive abilities and skills of children from Romany communities and the majority population; the other objective is to state whether differences exist in the motivation of children from the two groups as a result of dissimilar value preferences.[14] The project in the Department of Applied Sociology undertakes research concentrating on relations within Romany families and evaluating how the majority population sees and views the Romany minority.[15]

From February to June 1994 a practical experiment was undertaken at one of the Olomouc schools. It aimed at providing children from Romany families with some pre-school training. In classroom work with the children, the teacher received continuous consultation from the experts in the project and was assisted by Romany mothers, whose participation was considered important for cultural, emotional and linguistic reasons. Soon it appeared that the problem did not lie so much with the children but rather with the parents and families. Attendance was irregular and the mothers seemed to value the meals provided at schools more than any of the activities; they were also easily discouraged from sending their children when even a nominal financial contribution was required. Even unemployed parents could not 'find time' to bring their children in in the morning and collect them in the afternoon. The general situation made it very difficult for the programme organizers to justify the whole project in the eyes of the school authorities, who were quite reluctant to support it in the first place. Obviously the experiment was not a success, but it was not a total failure either, as everybody involved learned a lot; even though all the acquired experience was not always pleasant it was, undoubtedly, useful and may lead next year to the opening of a modified programme for Romany children who would not be accepted into the first form of the basic schools and could do with a whole year of special training aimed at helping them deal with social and cultural differences. Such programmes could give them a more equal opportunity in the majority school system.[16]

The Palacký University Romany education programme, which was launched in 1993, can hardly be more than the beginning of a long endeavour, if not a lasting challenge; its partial success in the pursuit of the general goal, beyond the obvious and very specific results that have already been achieved, lies in the recognition of the relevance and the potential of educational activities in the creation of a just, truly democratic and pluralistic society. The most important achievement seems to lie in the very variety and number of those who have reached or are at least approaching such recognition; such people include a growing number of students, many of them future teachers and social workers, individuals from various paths of life, and last but not least, the Romanies themselves.[17]

BIBLIOGRAPHY

Charta 77: 1977–1989 (1990) *Od morální k demokratické revoluci*. Ed., Vilém Precan. Cs. stredisko nezávislé literatury, Scheinfeld-Schwarzenberg a Archa, Bratislava

Crowe, David and Kolski, John, (eds) (1991), *The Gypsies of Eastern Europe*. M.E. Sharpe, Inc., Armonk, N.Y. and London

Necas, Ctibor (1992), *Aušvicate Hi Khér Báro. Ceští veznové cikánského tábora v Osvetimi II – Brzezince*. Masarykova univerzita v Brne, Brno

Necas, Ctibor (1992), *Spolecenská problematika Romu v minulosti a prítomnosti*. Masarykova univerzita Brno, Brno

Struggling for Ethnic Identity: Czechoslovakia's Endangered Gypsies (1992). A Helsinki Watch Report, Human Rights Watch. New York, Washington, Los Angeles, London

NOTES

1. Necas, Ctibor: *Romové v Ceské republice vcera a dnes*. Olomouc 1993, pp. 21–23.
2. Ibid., pp. 31–32. The text of the law, 'Zákon ze 14.cervence 1927 o potulných cikánech', is quoted on pp. 74–79.
3. Ibid., p. 45.
4. Ibid., the text of law, 'Zákon ze dne 17.ríjna 1958 o trvalém usídlení kocujících osob', is quoted on p. 84.
5. Ibid., the text of governmental decree, 'Usnesení vlády CSSR ze dne 13. ríjna 1965 c. 502 o opatreních k rešení otázek cikánského obyvatelstva', quoted on pp. 84–85.
6. Ibid., the text of the statement, 'Dokument Charty 77 ze 13 prosince 1978 – O postavení Cikánu-Romu v Ceskoslovensku', is in part reprinted on pp. 86–89. It is worth mentioning that the two spokesmen were Václav Havel, later the President of Czechoslovakia and the Czech Republic, and Ladislav Hejdánek.
7. Some activities in the field of Romany education are carried out by the Institute of Romany Culture at the Purkyne University, Ústí nad Labem. The MENT (Man, Education and New Technologies) association, located at Karolíny Svetlé 4,110,00 Prague, organizes a wide variety of seminars concerned with educational programmes for and with Romanies. The Ministry of Culture of the Czech Republic has been sponsoring the publication of Romany papers and journals which appear partly in Romany language; in

1994 the monthly *Amaro Lav* was replaced by *Nevo Romano Gendalos*. Among the organizations of the Romanies themselves the Association of Moravian Romanies ('Spolecenství Romu na Morave', Rašínova 2,602,00 Brno), headed by the devoted personality of Karel Holomek, may be of special notice.

8. Cf. Vztah obcanu CR k Romum je špatný, *Lidové noviny*, 1 Dec. 1993; Josef Vohryzek: Anatomie rasismu, pp. 2–3, and Jindrich Šídlo, Tomáš Horejší: Nezacneme jako první, pp. 7–8, in *Respekt*, no. 11, 15–21 March, 1993; Rasismus na vzestupu, *Lidové noviny*, 29 March 1994.

9. Cf. Zdenka Jarabová: Pomoci Romum je v našem zájmu, *Hanácké noviny*, 15 October 1994, p. 13.

10. Cf. Soukromá ostravská škola pro romské deti, *Lidové noviny*, 1 September 1993; Oldrich Matoušek: Romskýoríšek: Domov kontra škola, *Nedelní lidové noviny*, 11 December 1993, p. VIII.

11. The second, amended, cycle of lectures presented in eleven weeks from October to December 1994: 1. Introducing the Issues and the Problems (Zdenka Jarabová), 2. Cultural Pluralism and Multiculturalism (Josef Jarab), 3. Human and Minority Rights in Czech Legislature (Otakar Motejl), 4. Racism Viewed as a Problem of Cultural Anthropology (Stanislav Hubík), 5. History of the Romanies in the Czech Lands up to 1938 (Ctibor Necas), 6. Romanies in the Czech Lands during the War and in the Post-war Period (Ctibor Necas), 7. Romany Material Culture and Ways of Life (Eva Davidová), 8. Romany Spiritual Culture and Social Ties (Eva Davidová), 9. The Relevance of the Roma Language for the Community (Milena Hubschmannová), 10. Czechoslovak Social Policy towards the Romanies after 1945 (Ludmila Typovská), 11. The Education and Upbringing of Romany Children (Jitka Cízková).

12. Publications issued by Pedagogická Fakulta Univerzity Palackého, Olomouc; the first two titles in 1993, the remaining ones in 1994: 1. Ctibor Necas: *Romové v Ceské republice vcera a dnes* (Romanies in the Czech Republic in the Past and Present); 2. Milena Hubschmannová: *Muzeme se domluvit – Šaj pes dovakeras* (We Can Make Each Other Understood); 3. Vlasta Kladivová: *Konecná stanice Auschwitz-Birkenau. Vznik a historie cikánského tábora 1943–1944* (The Terminal Auschwitz-Birkenau: The History of the gypsy Camp); 4. Ctibor Necas: *Nemuzeme zapomenout – Našti bisteras. Nucená táborová koncentrace ve vyprávavních pametníku* (We Cannot Forget: Recorded Memories of the Survivors of the Gypsy Concentration Camp); 5. Bartolomej Daniel: *Dejiny Romu – Vybrané kapitoly z dejin Romu v západní Evrope, v Ceských zemích a na Slovensku* (Chapters from the history of the Romanies in Western Europe, the Czech Lands and Slovakia); 6. Ruben Pellar et al.: *Tišten výstup z databáze romistické literatury* (A Printed Database of Sources Dealing with Romanies).

13. The chosen theses deal with the media coverage of the Romany issue, the problems of Romany children at school and in foster homes, housing and other social aspects of coexistence of the ethnic minority and the majority population, the role of the Romany family, the value scale within the Romany community, the history of mutual relations between the Czech population and the Romany minority in the society.

14. Cf. Cízková, Jitka: Hodnotová orientace romských detí (Value Scale of

Romany Children). To appear in *Acta Universitatis Palackianae Olomucensis*, Psychologica VI, 1995.

15. Cf. Typovská, Ludmila: Informace o projektech prípravy ucitelu a sociálních pracovníku pro práci s romskými detmi (Information on projects concerned with the training of teachers and social workers to work with Romany children). To appear in *Sborník sekce sociální patologie MCSS* in 1995.

16. Cf. Nultýrocník pro romské deti pred první trídou je úspešný, *Lidové noviny*, 28 October 1994.

17. The paper has been updated in January 1995, especially in its latter part and in the Notes section. At present, the Romany project at Palacký University is seeking support through national or international grants that would make the continuation of the work possible.

5 Discrimination and Prejudice: Minorities in Romania

Ioan Aluas and Liviu Matei

INTRODUCTION

The paper analyses stereotypes and prejudices of the Romanian majority about three ethnic minorities: Jews, Gypsies and Hungarians. The specific role those stereotypes play, their origin, and several examples of discrimination are explained in relation to demographic, economic, political and cultural factors, including types of prejudices other than ethnic. The nature of the interaction between international public opinion, the Romanian state and civil society is considered to be responsible for the specific forms which prejudice and discrimination take in contemporary Romania.

In a recent study Kleinpenning and Hagendoorn (1993) tried to develop a synthesis of the literature about ethnic attitudes. Providing experimental evidence, they conclude that attitudes towards ethnic groups form an array of a cumulative dimension. The (negative) ethnic attitude starts with the rejection of contact with ethnic groups in personal and public contexts and is followed by the demand for adjustment, the belief that ethnic groups are a threat to the culture of the in-group and the belief that ethnic groups have more social and economic rights than they deserve. Non-racism, aversive racism, ethnocentrism, symbolic racism and biological racism represent the particular steps in the ethnic attitude continuum.

Identifying similar elements in Romania is not a difficult task for an observer accustomed to its present situation: claims for ethnic pluralism coexist (not always peacefully) with demands for either uniformity (assimilation) or group 'segregation' (in terms of social or juridical distances). Words like 'deportation' or 'extermination' might even occur in some public speeches. Different ethnic but also professional or class groups hold a variety of beliefs in a quite complicated mosaic. On the other hand, explaining the origin of the situation and the specific role ethnic attitudes play is rather difficult. Social-psychological factors alone, as used in Kleinpenning and Hagendoorn's (1993) study, might not be sufficient. There are cultural, historical and economic factors one has to take into account as well.

Before analysing different aspects with respect to this mosaic, it might be useful to mention another general fact. What characterizes contemporary Romanian society is a deep state of entropy. The recent Communist past and the present transition are probably the best explanation (but not the only one) for that. This feature takes specific forms throughout the areas of both public and private life. To mention only one example: different and sometime opposite mentalities influence the nature of inter-group relations. Pre-modern, modern or post-modern beliefs and convictions make it hard to find a set of common types of argument. The social consensus is rather low also because of the 'incompatible' kinds of argument currently used. Specific groups resort to medieval-like superstitions, beliefs in a unique truth or radical liberalism, and this creates barriers to effective communication and cohesion.

The Romanian Constitution (1992) defines Romania as a 'national unitary state'. However, the proportion of different ethnic minorities is estimated at about 20 per cent. From a purely numerical point of view, there are two main ethnic minorities: Hungarians and gypsies (Romanies). But if one is to consider the magnitude of the prejudices then one has to pay attention to a third group: the Jews.

JEWS

The Jewish population represents about 0.1 per cent of the total population according to the last census (1992). This is quite a small figure and seems to provide little support for anti-Semitic attitudes. But the fact is that anti-Semitism continues to play an important role, particularly in political life. As long as nobody claims to be an anti-semite, the situation is similar to that of Poland: anti-Semitism 'without Jews and without anti-Semites'.

The Jewish population diminished considerably after World War II, a period of massive emigration. It is well known, for example, that financial benefits determined Ceausescu to allow thousands of Jews to leave for Israel. Less that 20,000 Jews now live in Romania. However, these 20,000 Jews are not necessarily the real target of 'anti-Semitism'; in most cases the targets are intellectuals or politicians expressing liberal views. The label 'Jews' serves to discredit them and it is used in

various contexts. Anti-Semitism represents a major issue mainly because of the interest the media has at stake. Two weekly magazines,
Europa and *Romania Mare*, are considered as the ones which express
the most extreme anti-Semitic discourses. Both are organs of parliamentary parties, currently supporting the governmental political line.

However, anti-Semitism has a tradition in Romania. The reluctance
to allow Jews to obtain Romanian nationality at the beginning of the
century and the pogroms during Antonescu's dictatorship (1940–1944)
might illustrate it. Romanian public opinion is still confused about this
subject, as there are few reliable historical reports available. It is possible that what explains the persistence of the stereotypes about Jews
relates to this 'tradition'. Stereotypes continue to exist as 'residues'.
But there is less or no evidence at all for their former content and
formal justification. This is probably why the use of the word 'Jew'
does not refer today to 'rapacious' bankers or capitalists but to intellectuals and politicians as agents of an international cabal which aims
at subordinating the country to the economic and political interests of
foreigners. The theme of an international conspiracy has been inten-
sively used before the first free elections in 1990 and it is still largely
present as an important 'concern' for several political groups. The idea
of an infusion of foreign capital in Romania was considered as nothing
other than the expression of this conspiracy's intentions. Anti-Communist
and anti-nationalist parties and their leaders were being presented as
'Jews' in order to make the electors vote against them.

Obviously, this strategy, proven to be successful, is closely related
to specific economic interests. The Communist regime created the political nomenclature, being transformed now into something like an
economic Mafia. The coming of international capital is being perceived
as threatening and this is what determined the resort to old stereotypes,
kept in a latent state during the Communist period. One of the main
slogans in the above mentioned elections was 'We don't sell our country'.

Anti-Semitism proves to be in fact the expression of a mixture of
deeply associated components like xenophobia, nationalism and Communist nostalgia. From a more global point of view, attitudes towards
foreigners play their specific role with respect to every other important minority group. It should constitute the subject of a separate analysis,
keeping in mind both negative and positive attitudes and expectations
towards Western countries. Anti-semitism in Romania is the attempt
to use old stereotypes about the Jews, exploiting (and sometimes creating) xenophobic feelings.

From another point of view it is interesting to analyse the attitude of the political powers towards anti-Semitism. The violation of several Jewish cemeteries or the attempt to print Hitler's *Mein Kampf* have been quite quickly condemned by the representatives of political power, including President Iliescu. The Attorney-General has been asked to intervene for the 'repression' of all similar attempts (with reference to the former Romanian Fascist movement). The magazines mentioned above (and some others) considered to express governmental obedience but also overt anti-Semitic attitudes have not been subject to such interventions.

Formal statements about the rejection of any form of anti-Semitism have recently been made by government officials in order to prove the democratic views of the political powers. However, anti-Semitic attitudes in Romanian society prove to be an instrument that certain political groups use rather than an actual characteristic which influences interpersonal relations in everyday life.

The stereotypes about Jews do not rely on beliefs in cultural or biological superiority v. inferiority but on the feeling of an economic and political threat. Is there any discrimination that follows this prejudice? It is difficult to evaluate to what extent both Jews or people labelled as 'Jews' are victims of actual discrimination. The use of those stereotypes obviously aims to impose different standards for their targets. This is not clear directly in the sense of some restricted rights (political or civil) but refers rather to the extent of the public confidence they deserve, which is to say, less directly, to the legitimacy of their presence in public life.

Attitudes towards Jews outside Romania have received less attention so far. One could consider the question whether there is, for example, a different attitude towards Jews and Arabs with respect to the process of privatization as far as both people from Israel and Arab countries expressed their willingness to start business in Romania. Unfortunately, no informative reports are available on this issue.

GYPSIES

Gypsies probably represent the most important ethnic minority in Romania, although there is debate concerning their actual numbers. The last census offers the figure of 409,723 Romanies, which is to say 1.8 per cent of the total population. Several gypsy organizations speak of 2.5 million (more than 10%) and even five million. A national survey conducted in 1992 by the Research Institute for the Quality of Life found that there were 1.010 million people (4.6%) living according to traditional Gypsy standards.

Such variation in the figures is relevant in itself. For several reasons, gypsies consider it better not to declare or even not to consider themselves as gypsies, and for both the State and civil society, accepting gypsies is rather uncomfortable. In the last years of the communist regime, for example, the tendency to deny the very existence of a massive gypsy minority had been very strong, and the use of the words 'Gypsies' or 'Romanies' was almost forbidden. Ceausescu used to mention the ethnic 'Paradise' Communism had installed in Romania in every one of his public speeches. His favourite phrase was to exhort 'Romanians, Hungarians, Germans, *etc.*' with no respect to their ethnic membership, to take part in the general welfare. Knowing that that *etc.* included mainly the gypsies, people used to talk about them as *Etceterists*!

Ignored for years, the situation of the gypsy group is now rather precarious. The above-mentioned survey speaks about a high percentage of illiteracy (above 50 per cent) and a high rate of unemployment (above 50 per cent, against a national average of 12–15 per cent). Another study conducted by a non-governmental organization (Save the Children Fund) mentions the fact that more than half of all abandoned children in Romania in 1991 (which is to say between 50,000 and 100,000), were gypsies. Our own research provides support for the statement that gypsies' life expectancy is 10–15 years less than the average.

If prejudices about Jews are not directly related to discriminatory behaviour and the topic is mainly a political one, this is not the case for gypsies. Gypsies live somehow at the borders of both the State and civil society. One analysis focusing on these aspects (Matei, 1993) found that according to general stereotypes gypsies are considered as second-class human beings (inferior from both biological and cultural points of view) by ordinary people, and as second-class citizens by the State.

There is no significant difference between Romanians, Hungarians or other non-gypsy groups in relation to this topic. A survey conducted in order to provide theoretical support for a Médecins sans Frontières assistance programme for several under-privileged gypsy communities proved as statistically significant the assertion that both the Romanian and the Hungarian population in three Transylvanian countries do not consider the gypsy 'problem' as an ethnic issue. To use the statement of a Hungarian politician, this is simply 'a problem police have to deal with'. It is so because the majority Romanian population as well as the minority ethnic groups consider gypsies not as just another ethnic group but as a racial group (an inferior one) which does not deserve the same rights. Using Kleinpenning and Hagendoorn's (1993) terms, this is nothing other than biological, old-fashioned racism.

The fact that more than twenty gypsy villages have been burnt in the last three years as reprisals for individual gypsy crimes against non-gypsies could also be used as empirical evidence for the above statements. Not only Romanians, but also Hungarians and even members of smaller ethnic groups such as Macedonians or Tartars, took an active part in those attacks.

If Jews are identified as agents of an international conspiracy, responsible for Romania's bad image abroad and its bad internal situation, gypsies represent another kind of 'scapegoat', they represent the 'internal' danger. Research on stereotypes about gypsies showed that people believe that they are criminal and rich because they control the black market. But a report of the Romanian Ministry of the Interior speaks of a percentage of delinquency among gypsies which does not exceed their percentage in the total population. The Research Institute for the Quality of Life survey proved that the gypsy population is in fact poor. Some other aspects of those stereotypes could be analysed in a similar manner.

It is important to mention that both positive and negative attitudes towards Jews are currently expressed, so as to draw a quite balanced picture. Attitudes towards gypsies tend to be negative most of the time. A survey of the Romanian press in 1990 (Bozo, 1993) found no positive reports about them either in government newspapers or in the opposition ones. A common practice still very strong today consists in identifying gypsies as such in every context that one specific individual or group is mentioned. This practice, which uses description for explanation ('delinquent because of gypsy background') is quite common to all prejudiced reasoning. What is important is that this kind of treatment is reserved for gypsies alone in the media.

Attitudes towards gypsies also have connections with xenophobia. In Romania it is almost unthinkable to adopt a gypsy child. The fact that many foreign individuals and organizations provided relief for gypsy abandoned children and even adopted some has been viewed as an illustration of the alliance between gypsies and foreigners against non-gypsy people and as the expression of low opinion toward them. The support international agencies and organisms provide for gypsy political, social or cultural organization is sometimes seen as a part of the international conspiracy against Romania.

Discrimination against the gypsies is not a juridical matter. There is no special legal framework for this group or legal barriers to limit their rights. It is rather a matter of every-day application in connection with the nature of interpersonal relations. Gypsies' access to education, the labour market, social services and other facilities is sometimes more difficult than for the average citizen because of the rejection they suffer. Town hall officials, medical nurses or school masters might refuse to deal with gypsies simply because of their ethnic membership. State authorities sometimes deny gypsies the assistance they are entitled to by law. When their villages were being burnt, local police officers looked on passively and did not intervene to protect them. After the process of land distribution started, Gypsy groups were most of the time overlooked, as it was argued that they don't like to work in agriculture.

The attitude of the political powers in relation to the Jews is a kind of double discourse: more democratic when it speaks outside and less democratic inside. It is like that because of the balance it is looking for in order to show to the world its democratic openness towards human rights abroad, whilst not offending the negative attitude of the majority of the population inside. This is only one of the dilemmas of a populist policy. Some gypsy political leaders consider that the Romanian state has less interest in gypsies because there is no powerful gypsy state which can ask for the fulfilment of their rights, as is the case for the Jewish or Hungarian population.

One fact that might call for an explanation is the low proportion of gypsies who declared themselves as such. Two main hypotheses seem to be the most plausible. The memory of mass deportation at the time of Antonescu and the fear of a new one are continuously present. From this point of view it is better not to be identified as a gypsy. Another hypothesis is that many gypsy individuals have internalized the stereotypes of the majority and believe that the term 'gypsy' has connotations of inferiority. They claim not to be Gypsies as far as their actual culture or skills (though not their origin) are concerned, in order to 'deserve' equal treatment. Nevertheless the claim to a gypsy cultural identity, different but not inferior, is beginning to develop. Some speak about a rising gypsy ethnic awareness. The existence of more than twenty gypsy political parties in Romania is being used as an argument. The annual meeting of the International Catholic Committee for Gypsies held in 1993 concluded that a kind of 'gypsy nationalism' was developing in the former communist countries (including Romania) after the regime changed.

The issue of the Romany minority in Romania is now an important concern and little evidence is available to point to its future.

HUNGARIANS

The Hungarian minority is clearly the most active one. The Hungarian population has also decreased through emigration in the last decades. Hungarians now represent 7.1 per cent of the total population (about 1.5 million) and have an influential political party (about seven per cent in the Parliament), churches and sometimes separate schools or sections in universities. Both positive and negative attitudes are expressed by the Romanian population towards this ethnic group. The debate on nationalism in Romania mainly concerns the question of relations between Hungarians and Romanians.

Negative attitudes are based on the fear that Hungarians would like to split the country and either join Hungary or create an autonomous area. Every act which offers more specific opportunities for Hungarians (Hungarian schools, bilingual street names, ethnic cultural organization, etc.) is being seen as a step towards the final splitting. The grounds for stereotypes about Hungarians do not stem from beliefs in cultural or biological superiority but from diffuse fears nurtured by a common historical past. Both Hungarians and Romanians are accustomed to resort sometimes to historical arguments as to determine who first arrived in the territory of Transylvania and has specific rights because of that.

Nationalist propaganda at the time of the Ceausescu regime had been directed almost exclusively at the Hungarians. The official history of that period is still influential and plays an important role in the perception of the Romanian majority. The past is painted black and the atrocities the Hungarians are considered responsible for would justify both fear and increasing vigilance. This is probably just one of many anachronistic lines of argument which disregards the evidence.

In juridical terms, the main debate now concerns the issue of individual against collective rights. The Government considers that the Constitution is the guarantor of generic individual human rights and that nothing more should be done in order to ensure collective rights as Hungarian representatives claim. Such claims are denounced as illegitimate pretensions which aim to give more rights or privileges for Hungarians. This position is sometimes held by people not involved in the political struggle. On the other hand, the impossibility of implementing institutions according to the presumed standards of a set of collective rights is perceived by the Hungarians as discrimination.

The stereotypes about Hungarians are largely present in the media and in school education. Anti-Hungarian propaganda is effective, at least to some extent. Research conducted in a village near Cluj, part of a larger CRESPO research, proved that even in the villages with mixed population where no actual tension exists, stereotypes are present. The Romanian inhabitants of the village have nothing against their Hungarian neighbours and no actual fear is present, but they still agree that, generally, Hungarians represent a significant menace. This distance from the generic, prejudiced representations to the reality of everyday co-existence might be considered as a general feature. Evidence for the fact that this reality is less tense than reflected in political debates is also the finding that about twenty per cent of the marriages in the city of Cluj are mixed, Romanian-Hungarian marriages.

Sometimes political or other Romanian groups express overt anti-nationalist attitudes, favouring better Romanian-Hungarian relations. The democratic opposition's coalition (The Democratic Convention) includes the Hungarian party in order to challenge anti-Hungarian prejudices. The price for it, according to some political analysts, has been the loss of an important amount of votes as the Romanian leaders of the Democratic Convention were accused of agreeing on the splitting plan as part of the above mentioned Jewish-Hungarian conspiracy.

There are many other aspects which should be mentioned here. One of them refers again to the double type of discourse held by the political powers. The outward discourse expresses the Government's commitment to human rights, while the inward discourse is rather ambiguous and ambivalent. A recent illustration of that is the activity of the newly created National Council for Minorities. The Council is a place where all minorities are represented. It suggests specific decisions the Government should take in relation to minority issues. The Council suggested recently, before Romania became a member of the Council of Europe, the possibility of bilingual street names, under specific conditions, and the creation of Hungarian sections of pedagogical faculties. Only the second proposal is now reality, the other being 'forgotten', probably as a result of strong nationalist protests.

GERMANS

The percentage and importance of other minority groups, with respect to the issue of prejudice and discrimination, are rather limited to local areas. Even the German community, at one time an important minority, constitutes today a very small group, the general trend for its members being emigration to Germany. Traditionally, attitudes towards the German minority are almost exclusively positive. The German minority was present in Transylvania for about seven to eight centuries and its present extinction is perceived as a loss. It might be useful to remember the post-World War II deportation or the fact that the German population in Transylvania was subject to a more severe process of 'nationalization' at the beginning of the Communist period, which meant at that time the destruction of the only modern technology existing in Romanian agriculture.

CONCLUSION

In an attempt to offer a better understanding of the present issue, both minority and majority attitudes should be considered. All that has been said so far concerns majority stereotypes. This is not because minority groups do not have theirs or because they do not play a role. It is because, to paraphrase de Tocqueville (1994), the prejudices of the majority are more dangerous than the prejudices of the minority.

The analysis of some other types of stereotypes and prejudices might prove to be useful. Tensions between religious groups (e.g. Orthodox v. Uniats) or professional groups have their specific contribution to the general *gestalt* of ethnic relations; as an example, Communist nationalism tended to overestimate the value of the national 'fidelity' and significance of workers or peasants against cosmopolitan intellectual attitudes. The strange slogan of the miners, 'We are used to work, not to think' is deeply associated with the one about selling the country.

If one is to draw a general map of the way prejudice and discrimination affect ethnic minorities in Romania then one could take into account the fact that at least three factors interact: international public opinion (including international bodies), the national State (and its institutions) and Romanian civil society. This perspective might be useful as far as it seems to prove that international pressure on Government is not a sufficient guarantee on its own to ensure a transition to a democratic society. This is firstly because civil society plays its role (not necessarily positive, however – see the miners' uprisings) and secondly because reaching compromises with even totalitarian states for geo-political reasons would not be a new practice (in view of the support Western democracies provided during a period for Ceausescu). Romanian civil society was almost completely destroyed under Ceausescu. Its present weakness and low consistency create ample space for authoritarian behaviours and for manipulation towards ethnic intolerance. Explaining street ethnic confrontations in Tg.Mures in March 1990 as the result of manipulations might not be without justification. The more 'mature' a civil society is, the more it is likely to obtain a desirable equilibrium. The political aspects in the construction of the democratic State seem to receive the greatest amount of attention as yet. But many people realize already the importance of civil society. Sometimes efforts in this direction have little effect because they fail to reach those social categories which commit themselves to other models of rationality than those which nurture the contemporary philosophy of tolerance and human rights. It is also important to mention that both the State and civil society have made important progress. Developments in the period after December 1989 provide some support for optimistic expectations. Romania's geographical position, between the former USSR and the former Yugoslavia, might offer lessons about the potential extremes of ethnic intolerance. There are now in Romania many non-governmental organizations actively involved in the promotion of human rights or in educational activities on issues such as human rights, minorities protection or ethnic and cultural pluralism.

BIBLIOGRAPHY

Bozo, K. (1993), 'Une analyse de la presse roumaine sur les tziganes', *Les Etudes Tziganes*, 1.
Kleinpenning, G. and L. Hagendoorn (1993), 'Forms of Racism and the Cumulative Dimension of Ethnic Attitudes', *Social Psychology Quarterly*, 56.
Matei, L. (1993), 'Gypsies at the Borders of the State', *Les Etudes Tzignanes*, 1.
Tocqueville, Alexis de (1994), *Democracy in America*, Edited by J.P. Mayer, London: Fontana

6 Minority Rights: Some New Intergovernmental Approaches in Europe

Alan Phillips

INTRODUCTION

With the exception of the Vatican, all countries in Europe are characterized by varying degrees of ethnic, linguistic and religious diversity. However, this diversity has only been recognized as a major European issue since the collapse of Communism in Central and Eastern Europe, and the eruption of violent conflicts involving minorities in Europe. The situation in former Yugoslavia – including Croatia, Bosnia and Serbia (with its Vojvodena and Kosovo regions) – has featured in news headlines daily. Violence continues in the Caucasus, in Moldova, while the potential for other violent conflicts is substantial. Many have been killed, and over two million people are refugees or displaced people from former Yugoslavia alone.

The history of Northern Ireland and the Basque Country shows that inter-communal tensions can develop into violent conflicts, even in Western Europe, while the growth of racism, xenophobia and intolerance has been recognized as a serious issue in joint declarations by the heads of Western governments. Nevertheless, some governments in Western Europe have been the most adamant in opposing new measures to secure minority rights in that region, denying the existence of minorities within their state, while devising language and mechanisms that will apply to minorities in Central and Eastern Europe.[1] Double standards seem to exist. The concern is not primarily for minorities and minority rights but for stability and economic development at the periphery of Western Europe.[2]

PERCEPTION

The psychology of minorities, the psychology of majorities and their different perception of the same situation is as crucial as the provision of minority rights. In Western Europe, in contrast to Central and Eastern Europe, there is little governmental understanding or support of group rights. Human rights are broadly seen as a range of individual rights that may be protected by a legal framework that includes the prohibition of ethnic or religious discrimination. The language of international standards nearly always refers to the rights of individuals.[3]

One major difficulty with the inter-state discussion on minority rights is domination by the 'democratic majority', which rarely reflects minority opinions. At the CSCE (Conference on Security and Co-operation in Europe) Expert meeting on National Minorities,[4] for example, where over 300 delegates from 35 participating states were present, only a small minority were independent 'experts' on minorities and less than half of these were from minority communities. At the United Nations and Council of Europe, representatives of minority communities are always excluded from decision making and are rarely involved in effective consultation.[5] Government delegations drawn from senior public officials rarely include members of minority communities though there have been some important exceptions. The USA and Canada noticeably have multicultural membership of their delegations while the UK, the Netherlands and the Nordic countries have included some public members, usually from non-government organizations. The lack of multicultural delegations and the lack of officials in capitals from minority communities leads to narrow perceptions of these key issues by governments. At the CSCE Review Conference (Helsinki, May 1992) MRG (Minority Rights Group) stated:

> One of the important failures of the CSCE so far has been its failure to act in a pluralist way. The conferences themselves have failed to engage and involve NGOs effectively, while decisions have been made on minority rights and duties in the absence of the very communities whose futures are being decided.[6]

An arrogant approach is shown by some Western diplomats in discussions on minorities. At a CSCE seminar on national minority issues[7] (May 1993), the rapporteur[8] of one of the two working groups was provoked into writing on the serious difficulty of discussing different situations in Europe:

> Countries with long-established democracies, with no perceived serious internal or external threats to their integrity, were asked to compare their endeavours with new democracies that are involved in building their institutions and societies in the midst of incredible economic hardship and constant threat to their integrity from inside and outside.

In plenary the seminar lacked any critical appraisal and became a celebration of 'success', much to the dismay of NGO participants.

UNDERSTANDING THE ISSUES

Since 1990 and, in particular, around the three-week 1991 Geneva CSCE Expert Meeting on National Minorities, many government officials did much to increase their understanding of minority issues and to formulate their policy towards them. MRG knows, for example, that the results of its own conference in Leningrad in 1991[9] were distributed for comment to sixteen different ministries in the UK. Elsewhere governmental policy units have concentrated attention on 'national' minority issues; there have been a continuum of conferences in Central Europe, as well as a range of research by UN bodies, academics and NGOs, many of whom had previously ignored these issues.

In September 1991 the US State Department and the Soviet Union were in accord at the Moscow CSCE Human Dimension meeting,[10] agreeing that the issue of national minorities was the gravest threat to peace and security in Europe. More recently the debate has expanded beyond examining 'ethnic conflicts' to studying the efficacy of public policies in promoting social accommodation among different ethnic groups. Important research has been undertaken by UNRISD and UNICEF.[11] Furthermore, the important three-year study by Asbjorn Eide[12] for the UN Sub-Commission provides a valuable, comprehensive overview and concludes with an impressive set of 69 recommendations. These are categorized as general recommendations, actions to be taken at the national level, at the international level, at the regional level, by UN multilateral agencies and by NGOs.

The ways of achieving rights for minorities that may be expressed individually or collectively in community with others are highly complex and remain to this day poorly understood by many government officials. Few appreciate that protecting and promoting the identity of minorities is a cardinal principle of minority rights. Understandably, some governments fear that this may be to the detriment of their own power, or of the position of other communities or of individual rights.[13] Consequently, promoting identity and promoting integration is likely to remain a source of dynamic tension and misunderstanding in all multi-ethnic states. A greater understanding of these issues is required, showing that members of minority communities that are confident and secure in their identity can strengthen the fabric of a state.

Special measures for minorities, even for limited duration as agreed under the Covenant on the Elimination of Racial Discrimination (CERD),[14] remains a controversial issue, and is often misunderstood as an exception to 'equal opportunities' and tilting the 'level playing fields'.

INTERNATIONAL STANDARDS ON MINORITY RIGHTS

The relevance of international standards on the real situation of minorities in European countries may seem obscure, especially when they may not be enforceable through domestic legislation. The CSCE and its participating states, however, have made a set of political agreements on security, economic co-operation and the human dimension since the Helsinki Final Act in 1975. This was a crucial negotiating forum between the North Atlantic Treaty Organization and the Warsaw Pact with a number of neutral intermediaries. Suggestions that a state might be in breach of a CSCE agreement was considered to be a very serious issue and all states either conformed or endeavoured to be seen as conforming. It is for this reason that some distinguished commentators[15] argued that the political regimes of the CSCE were much more effective than the legal or moral agreements of the UN or the Council of Europe. The political changes in Europe have since affected the CSCE (now called OSCE) but it still has an important security role.

Support for minority rights by the West in Eastern Europe is not governed by security issues alone, but reflects endeavours to create good government for economic development. The World Bank[16] in 1991 stated:

Investing in people, if done right, provides the firmest foundation for lasting development. And the proper economic role of government is larger than merely standing in for markets if they fail to work well. In defining and protecting property rights, providing effective legal, judicial and regulatory systems, improving the efficiency of the civil service, and probably the environment, the state forms the very core of development.

The Copenhagen CSCE meeting[17] (June 1990) included the following agreement:

(30) The participating states recognize that the questions relating to national minorities can only be satisfactorily resolved in a democratic

political framework based on the rule of law, with a functioning independent judiciary. This framework guarantees full respect for human rights and fundamental freedoms, equal rights and status for all citizens, the free expression of all their legitimate interests and aspirations, political pluralism, social tolerance and the implementation of legal rules that place effective restraints on the abuse of governmental power.

TYPES OF MINORITIES

In various standard-setting and implementation mechanisms in Europe, there have been attempts to identify two different kinds of minorities: national minorities and other minorities (ethnic, linguistic and religious minorities who are not national minorities). However, the concept of 'national' has different meanings in different countries and languages. In the English language the phrase 'nation state' is often used without any intended difference from the word 'state', while 'nationality' refers to citizenship and not historical, ethnic origins or 'mother country'.

The definition of what is a minority is a source of controversy and can be a topic of endless and often fruitless debate, with governments often wanting a restrictive definition and minority communities wanting a broad one.[18] The CSCE, in its various concluding documents (Copenhagen 1990, for example), refers to 'persons belonging to national minorities', without attempting a closer definition of either national or minority. Separate, specific references to the Roma imply that they, *inter alia*, may not be included in this category.[19]

The Council of Europe has referred to the 'national minorities, which the upheavals of history have established in Europe',[20] and quite separately refers to a 'Declaration and Plan of Action on combating racism, xenophobia, anti-Semitism and intolerance'. The distinction is being reinforced between national minorities, who are perceived as posing a security threat, and other minorities.

The United Nations Commission on Human Rights refused to define minority in the 'UN Declaration on ... Minorities' though it provides some definition by referring to national or ethnic, linguistic and religious minorities. Much earlier a definition by Capotorti for the Sub-Commission was rejected by the Commission on Human Rights.[21]

RECENT PROGRESS ON STANDARDS

Much has changed since 1989, when the question of minority rights was considered a fringe issue within human rights, which itself was a marginal political issue. The UN had kept discussions on human rights in Geneva, many thousands of kilometres away from the Secretary-General's office and the Security Council, while the draft 'UN Declaration on the rights of persons belonging to national or ethnic, linguistic and religious minorities' (UN Declaration on Minorities) had made little progress over the previous 10 years. Similarly, no substantial standards on minorities had been agreed by the CSCE or the Council of Europe.

The rapidity of the political changes in Eastern Europe in 1989 caught Western governments by surprise. A 'new world order' was a major subject for discussion, where democratic values might be cherished and human rights observed. There was a fear that the nascent democracies needed to rectify the injustices towards the minorities that had been a major flash-point for changes in Romania and Bulgaria, while Hungary and even Yugoslavia were pressing for new international agreements on minorities. Western governments recognized that minority rights were an issue, but were unprepared for the political momentum.

CSCE

The Conference on Security and Co-operation in Europe led the way in tackling these issues. It included 35 states and provided a dynamic, non-bureaucratic framework that was responsive to the collective political needs of its participating states. Its members included two key actors, the USA and the Soviet Union (unlike the Council of Europe), and was able to be effective.

The Copenhagen Human Dimension meeting (June 1990) marked a watershed. Those who were at the Copenhagen meeting will know that the issue of minority rights was nearly excluded from the agenda at the outset.[22] It was argued by some Western governments that consensus was unlikely and that consequently it would be futile to establish a working group on minority issues. The Pentagonale group of Central European States, led by Hungary, insisted on establishing a working group, and by the end of the conference, a remarkable set of agreements on national minorities was approved by consensus – a fact that a number of western governments have since regretted and attempted to limit.

The CSCE used the phrase 'National Minorities' in standard setting, where it has made a distinction between standards for the treatment of national minorities and measures to combat racism, xenophobia, anti-Semitism and intolerance.

The CSCE (Copenhagen 1990)[23] offered national minorities considerably better rights than other minorities. These included rights to express, preserve and develop their identity, the freedom to use their mother tongue, establish their own educational, cultural and religious institutions, profess and practise their religion, disseminate information in their mother tongue and to establish and maintain organizations or associations.

States had additional obligations: to protect the identity of national minorities, to create conditions and offer opportunities for the promotion of that identity, to have adequate opportunities for instruction in or of their mother tongue and its use before public authorities, to take account of the history and culture of national minorities in education establishments and to respect their right to effective participation in public affairs. At the Geneva Expert meeting (July 1991) it noted 'the efforts taken to protect and create conditions for the promotion of the ethnic, cultural, linguistic and religious identity of certain national minorities by establishing, as one of the possible means to achieve these aims, appropriate local or autonomous administrations'.

The measures agreed for other minorities were different:

The participating states clearly and unequivocally condemn totalitarianism, racial and ethnic hatred, anti-Semitism, xenophobia and discrimination against anyone, as well as persecution on religious and ideological grounds. In this context they also recognize the particular problems of Roma (Gypsies).

They also suggested legal measures, protection arrangements, the promotion of understanding and tolerance through education, culture and information and the right of individuals and groups to initiate and support complaints. These measures, valuable in themselves, do not have the empowerment characteristics afforded to national minorities and have few resource implications for established democracies.

These measures were not significantly strengthened at the CSCE expert meetings[24] (Geneva, 1991). However, Chapter II included crucial language limiting state sovereignty:

Issues concerning national minorities, as well as compliance with international obligations and commitments concerning the rights of persons belonging to them, are matters of legitimate international concern and consequently do not constitute exclusively an internal affair of the respective state.

THE UNITED NATIONS

The United Nations, through a Working Group of the Commission on Human Rights, had been discussing the wording of a declaration on minorities since 1978. Slow progress was being made, and although Yugoslavia was taking a leading role there was no sense of urgency from any of the five permanent members of the Security Council and little pressure from NGOs. The UN Charter[25] had no reference whatsoever to minorities and the issue had been deliberately neglected within the UN.

In 1990 much changed: there was considerable interest in the Declaration shown by the European states (especially Russia and Belarus), there was some effective NGO lobbying and representations and by February 1991 the first draft was completed. By December 1991 the second and final draft had been approved by the Working Group;[26] it was endorsed by the Commission on Human Rights in February 1992 and promulgated by the General Assembly on 18 December 1992.

This momentum, initiated in Europe, has taken much longer to influence attitudes in New York. The Secretary-General's 'Agenda for Peace' contains only one significant mention of minorities where it states:[27]

> Democracy within nations requires respect for human rights and fundamental freedoms, as set forth in the Charter. It requires, as well, a deeper understanding and respect for the rights of minorities and respect for the needs of the more vulnerable groups of society, especially women and children.

The UN Declaration on the rights of persons belonging to national or ethnic, linguistic and religious minorities clearly covered more than national minorities. The agreements reached included most of the provisions of the Copenhagen CSCE final statement.[28] It did have some useful additional provisions in articles 4 and 5:

> 4.5 States should consider appropriate measures so that persons belonging to minorities may participate fully in the economic progress and development in their country.

    5.1   National policies and programmes shall be planned and imple-
           mented with due regard for the legitimate interests of persons
           belonging to minorities.
    5.2   Programmes of co-operation and assistance among states should
           be planned and implemented with due regard to the legitimate
           interests of persons belonging to minorities.

Article 8(4) reminds the reader of the principles of the United Nations, including sovereign equality, territorial integrity and political
independence of states, while Article 9 obliges UN bodies and organs
to contribute to the full realization of the rights and principles in the
UN Declaration.

The specific standards that have been agreed by governments in one
forum often lead to the acceptance of similar standards in different
fora, where the impact may be different. The acceptance by the CSCE
(Copenhagen 1990) that

> The participating states will protect the ethnic, cultural, linguistic
> and religious identity of national minorities on their territory and
> create conditions for the promotion of that identity

was the only reference to national minorities without the caveat of
'persons belonging to' being written as a precursor. This precedent
was used successfully to persuade the UN to accept a Declaration on . . .
Minorities whose first article reads:

> States shall protect the existence and the national or ethnic, cultural,
> religious and linguistic identity of minorities within their respective
> territories, and shall encourage conditions for the promotion of that
> identity.

going beyond the limitations of 'national minorities'.

The UN Covenant on Civil and Political Rights (1966) is a corner-
stone of international human rights law. Article 27 stipulates:

> In those states in which ethnic, religious and linguistic minorities
> exist, persons belonging to such minorities shall not be denied the
> right, in community with other members of their group, to enjoy
> their own culture, to profess and practise their own religion, or to
> use their own language.

The Covenant has been signed by 126 States (June 1994) and therefore takes on considerable significance. The Committee on Human Rights
is the treaty-monitoring body and, in 1994, published an interpretative
statement on the definition of minorities as far as this Covenant is

concerned, though it has a wider impact throughout the United Nations. The Committee commented on the applicability of Article 27:

> Just as they need not be nationals or citizens, they need not be permanent residents. Thus, migrant workers or even visitors in a State party constituting such minorities are entitled not to be denied the exercise of those rights.

It later continued:

> The existence of an ethnic, religious or linguistic minority in a given State party does not depend upon a decision by that State party but requires to be established by objective criteria.[29]

This broad interpretation is helpful for the implementation of this Treaty although it may encourage states to be much more cautious in providing further rights to all these categories of persons. At this stage it is too early to judge.

THE COUNCIL OF EUROPE

The Council of Europe had developed a concern for minority issues over many years. It had projects for the Roma and it had been developing a convention on linguistic rights for some time. However, one of its most influential bodies, the European Court of Human Rights, could only receive individual complaints on abuses of human rights and not class actions for minority communities. It had grappled with the issue but submerged in other terminology, including the Charter on Regional or Minority Languages.[30]

Although the Secretary-General, Madame LaLumière, a former French politician from Bordeaux, was an inspired crusader for minority rights, the composition of the Council of Europe made it difficult to effect early action in establishing relevant standards. It had to wait for progress at the CSCE before it could consider any legal framework, though considerable preparatory work was undertaken by the Venice Commission.[31] The Council of Europe might have been accused of duplicating the CSCE, especially on national minority issues. However, by 1993 there was considerable pressure for the two bodies to work more closely together, drawing on the considerable expertise of the Council of Europe Secretariat in Strasbourg.

This point was emphasized at the Warsaw CSCE seminar on National Minorities in May 1993, where the Netherlands recommended that the impressive results achieved within the CSCE be co-ordinated with the work of the Council of Europe and the United Nations.

One of the two rapporteurs of this seminar was nominated by the Council of Europe and is closely associated with its work. The Council of Europe, Heads of Governments meeting in Vienna (8–9 October 1993) recorded:[32]

> We confirm our determination to implement fully the commitments concerning the protection of national minorities contained in the Copenhagen and other documents of the CSCE.

and continued:

> We intend to pursue the close co-operation engaged between the Council of Europe and the CSCE High Commissioner for [sic] National Minorities.

The Council of Europe summit was a significant breakthrough. Although it set no new standards, it reinforced the sentiment that 'the protection of national minorities is an essential element of stability and democratic security in our continent'. However, in attempting to restrict asylum seekers and migrants it noted:

> We will continue our efforts to facilitate the social integration of lawfully residing migrants and to improve the management and control of migratory flows, while preserving the freedom to travel within Europe.

It then agreed six important steps, including initiatives

– to improve the effectiveness of the European Convention on Human Rights
– to enter into political and legal commitments relating to the protection of national minorities in Europe
– to pursue a policy for combating racism, xenophobia, anti-Semitism and intolerance.

In the detailed text on national minorities, it instructs the Committee of Ministers:

– to draw up confidence-building measures aimed at increasing tolerance and understanding among peoples
– to respond to requests for assistance for the negotiation and implementation of treaties on questions concerning national minorities as well as agreements on transfrontier co-operation

- to draft with minimum delay a framework convention specifying the principles which contracting states commit themselves to respect, in order to assure the protection of national minorities; this instrument would also be open for signature by non-member states
- to begin work on drafting a protocol complementing the European Convention on Human Rights in the cultural field by provisions guaranteeing individual rights, in particular for persons belonging to national minorities.

There did not seem to be a limitation to 'persons belonging to' national minorities but refers to 'protection of national minorities'. This group dimension was critical.

The Council of Europe then went forward and developed a framework convention[33] on national minorities. The 'Framework Convention'[34] is legally binding under international law and contains principles which each Contracting Party must implement through national legislation and appropriate government policies. The Framework Convention sets out, in the form of provisions, the principles to be respected by the State Parties. They thereby undertake:

- to combat discrimination
- to promote full and effective equality
- to promote the conditions necessary to preserve and develop the culture and safeguard the identity of national minorities
- to afford persons belonging to national minorities freedom of peaceful assembly, freedom of association, freedom of expression and freedom of thought, conscience and religion
- to ensure the right of access to and use of the media
- in the field of linguistic freedoms:

  - to allow the use of the minority language in private and in public, as well as in dealings with the public authorities,
  - to recognize the right to use one's name in the minority language,
  - to recognize the right to display information of a private nature visible to the public in the minority language,
  - to make efforts to display topographical indications in the minority language.

- in the field of education:

  - to provide opportunities for learning minority languages and for receiving instruction in these languages,
  - to recognize the creation of educational and training establishments,

- not to hinder transfrontier contacts
- to foster transfrontier and international co-operation
- to encourage participation in economic, cultural and social life
- to promote participation in public affairs
- to prohibit forced assimilation.

The Declaration and Plan of Action on Combating Racism, Xenophobia, Anti-Semitism and Intolerance include important statements. The Declaration states boldly,

> Alarmed by the present resurgence of racism, xenophobia and anti-Semitism, the development of a climate of intolerance, the increase in acts of violence, notably against migrants and people of immigrant origin, and the degrading treatment and discriminatory practices accompanying them;

> Equally alarmed also by the development of aggressive nationalism and ethnocentrism which constitute new expressions of xenophobia;

> Concerned at the deterioration of the economic situation, which threatens the cohesion of European societies by generating forms of exclusion likely to foster social tensions and manifestations of xenophobia;

> Convinced that these manifestations of intolerance threaten democratic societies and their fundamental values and undermine the foundations of European construction.

The Plan of Action involves a European Youth Campaign, measures by states to combat racism, xenophobia, anti-Semitism and intolerance, mechanisms to propose further initiatives, support for seminar and research programmes, and promotion of education in the field of human rights and respect for cultural diversity *inter alia*. These represent an attractive menu of activities but the proof of the pudding will lie in the eating.

IMPLEMENTATION OF AGREEMENTS

These agreements on minority rights have been made by governments at intergovernmental meetings and it is primarily the responsibility of the same governments to ensure that social, economic and political measures are taken for their effective implementation.

CSCE

The CSCE has a plethora of monitoring mechanisms, which are essential for the verification of security agreements. Monitoring mechanisms are seen as being highly positive, not as intrusive and threatening sovereignty; their very presence is a confidence-building measure leading to greater security. These include major human dimension implementation meetings lasting three weeks, one of which has recently ended in Warsaw in October 1993. The regular meeting of the Committee of Senior Officials (CSO) receives reports from special missions, which may be *ad hoc* or more permanent, such as those in the Baltic States. The High Commissioner on National Minorities also keeps the CSO informed, while maintaining his independence.

The mandate of the new High Commissioner agreed at the Helsinki Summit[35] in July 1992 stated:

> The High Commissioner will provide 'early warning' and, as appropriate, 'early action' at the earliest possible stage in regard to tensions involving national minority issues which have not yet developed beyond an early warning stage, but, in the judgement of the High Commissioner, have the potential to develop into a conflict within the CSCE area, affecting peace, stability or relations between participating states, requiring the attention of and action by the Council [of Foreign Ministers] or the CSO [Committee of Senior Officials].

There are many words used here that do not have a precise meaning and consequently the interpretation by the first High Commissioner was crucial. The appointment of Max van der Stoel (the former Dutch Foreign Minister) was an exemplary choice and he is already working quietly and effectively in the Baltic states, in Macedonia and Albania, in Slovakia and Hungary in Moldova, and on the Roma.

Commentators[36] have pointed to the dangers of the Council of Europe and CSCE having different instruments, though the emphasis by the Council of Europe summit on CSCE commitments was important. A second problem is that some states may believe that any Council of Europe legal instruments may make the CSCE political agreements obsolete. This would be highly deleterious for minorities, since the two different 'regimes' should be, and indeed can be, complementary, and implementation mechanisms can be mutually reinforcing.

Each country has a different legal system, some are in the process of finalizing new constitutions, many face severe economic pressures at the moment and all have to respond to new political realities. It is unreasonable to judge a state's performance at a moment in time exclusively against legal norms, and more constructive to include measurements of progress or regression over time in both the legal and political fields.

The United Nations

The United Nations has long established mechanisms, with treaty bodies for supervising compliance with human rights conventions.[37] These treaty bodies are made up of a limited number (10–20) independent experts, usually lawyers, nominated by their states. There is the Human Rights Committee, the Committee on Economic and Social and Cultural Rights, the Committee on the Elimination of Racial Discrimination (CERD) and the Committee on the Rights of the Child. In 1994, for example, the Human Rights Committee completed an interpretative opinion of Article 27 which has specific relevance to minorities. Treaty bodies receive state reports, enter into dialogue with the states and publish their conclusions.[38] Unfortunately these Committees have no sanctions or benefits they can apply and their findings rarely reach 'we, the peoples' on whose behalf the UN Charter was signed.[39] The Committees monitor, interpret and comment, including providing encouragement to states or reprimanding them on their poor performance.

The 'UN Declaration on . . . Minorities', which does not have the legal force of a convention ratified by a state, may however become part of customary international law, particularly for those states who proposed the supporting resolution and may be interpreting it in the same way as a convention. This could include most of the states of Central and Eastern Europe and the Nordic states, but excludes France, the UK, Belgium, Spain and others. The challenge is to press states to treat this declaration seriously.

It had been suggested by some participants in the Working Group on the Declaration[40] that the UN Commission on Human Rights establish a working group with a mandate to review minority situations falling within the scope of the Declaration and, in so doing, to hear the views of governments, minorities, persons belonging to minorities and non governmental organizations.

COMMISSION ON HUMAN RIGHTS (FEBRUARY/MARCH 1994)

MRG was asked to convene an informal Seminar around the Commission on Human Rights on Minorities and the UN System. The meeting attracted 31 participants from UN bodies and Agencies, Delegations to the Commission on Human Rights, experts on Minorities and MRG Staff. Ambassador Halinen from Finland chaired the meeting, which included a number of ambassadors among the participation from seventeen governments.

The discussion included presentations from UN Agencies and bodies on their work in this field, dialogue on conceptual issues including definitional issues, tensions between university and diversity of regional approaches, and confidence-building measures. The Seminar looked at key implementation issues and a range of suggestions[41] were made including a Working Group of the Commission and/or Sub-Commission.

The meeting was remarkable in the interest that was generated in an NGO meeting around the Commission, where it is unusual to attract more than a handful of governments to such a generalized discussion. It indicated the political sensitivity of the subject and the depth of concern felt by a significant number of governments.

In the debate at the UN Commission on Human Rights a number of governments criticized the Sub-Commission for its failure to give sufficient attention to minority issues[42] and the inadequacy of its treatment of Professor Eide's highly acclaimed report. However, the final consensus resolution did not propose a Working Group of the Commission or any further implementation mechanisms for the UN Declaration or Professor Eide's report; it looked forward to the considerations of the Sub-Commission. One clear dissenting statement was made by Finland, who criticized the weakness of the consensus resolution.

At the subsequent Sub-Commission meeting (August 1994) there was a substantial and highly constructive debate held over two days, where most expert members of the Sub-Commission made significant and supportive interventions. The importance of the UN Declaration was recognized in the final resolution and genuine appreciation was expressed for Professor Eide's major study.[43] The Sub-Commission then adopted a unanimous resolution proposing to the Commission that the Sub-Commission should establish a Working Group on the UN Declaration . . . on Minorities.

Once again, in February 1995, MRG convened a seminar around the Commission on Human Rights and it had a similar attendance to the previous year's meeting.[44] The meeting was again chaired by Ambassador Halinen and included a general discussion around Professor Eide's report and the recommendation of the Sub-Commission to the Commission.

A wide number of proposals were discussed but the importance of establishing at least one new mechanism to promote the UN Declaration on Minorities was emphasized. It was proposed that the role of a working group of the Sub-Commission should be developed within this framework. The Working Group was not intended to become a permanent chamber of complaints, but might be established for a limited period of three years, to address the ways in which existing problems could be solved, including the effective implementation of the 'UN Declaration ... on Minorities' through establishing various mechanisms for its implementation.

Some two weeks later the Commission voted to accept a consensus resolution led by Austria and proposed by 32 other states to establish a Working Group of the Sub-Commission.[45]

The Council of Europe

The Council of Europe has a wide range of implementation procedures, including the proactive role of conferences, seminars and research. The new framework convention,[46] signed in its first week by 22 of the 33 member states, will have an implementing mechanism. The Convention includes a monitoring system for implementing these provisions, whereby the Committee of Ministers, assisted by an advisory committee, evaluates the adequacy of the Convention's implementation. The States Parties will be obliged to present, within one year of the entry into force of the Convention, a report containing full information on legislative and other measures taken to give effect to the Convention. Thereafter, each Party shall submit reports on a periodical basis and whenever the Committee of Ministers so requests.

The Framework Convention will enter into force immediately in each state party after ratification by 12 member states. Non-member States may also be invited to accede to it.

The signature of a convention by Western European democracies with a proper legal system to adjudicate claims has considerable constitutional implications, affecting internal case law interpretation and the behaviour of domestic courts. How states will choose to implement this framework Convention is not clear, and the Minority Rights Group has written to each of the signatories in an attempt to establish this.[47] At the moment in the European Human Rights Court petitions may take up to eight years to reach judgment, and the maxim 'Justice delayed is justice denied' is applicable. If we consider the monumental changes in the political map of Europe over the last four years, and the rapid way conflicts between majorities and minorities have developed, it will be crucial for the Council of Europe to ensure the speedy domestic implementation of the Convention. The immediate impact of the Framework Convention is therefore crucial.

Donors and Banks

The linkage that is being drawn between good governance and economic progress by Western governments and lending institutions such as the World Bank, International Monetary Fund and the European Bank for Reconstruction and Development (EBRD)[48] can place economic pressures on governments in Central and Eastern Europe. As yet this is not very sophisticated, though it can be expected that banks in their assessment programmes will be paying more attention to minority rights, with the serious implications for unsecured investments, than to human rights observance on its own.[49]

However, the European Community must go much further to be effective. Its larger schemes include neither equal opportunities provisions nor, at present, a sensitivity that 'National policies and programmes shall be planned and implemented with due regard for the legitimate interests of persons belonging to minorities'. It was the French Prime Minister Edouard Balladur who presented a proposal for a pact on stability to the 1993 Copenhagen summit.[50] This would be supported by 'incentives and flanking measures' that could be taken to encourage peace and stability in Europe. Balladur specifically asks:

> Economic: can the Community decide to provide specific assistance to countries taking particular care to solve their problems relating to minorities (for accompanying projects in specific regions), immigration or refugees (setting up resettlement programmes)? In the opposite case, can it also decide to cut off all co-operation ties with a country flagrantly violating the rights of minorities or calling existing borders into question? The Yugoslav experience shows that such incentives have their limits when they are not implemented in timely fashion.

The Stability Pact was signed in Paris (21 March 1995) and states in its opening declaratory paragraph:

> We undertake to combine our efforts to ensure Stability in Europe.

It continues:

> A stable Europe is one in which peoples democratically express their will, in which human rights, including those of persons belonging

to national minorities, are respected, in which equal and sovereign states co-operate across frontiers and develop among themselves good-neighbourly relations. A stable Europe is necessary for peace and international security.

The major provisions are a list of inter-state agreements, arrangements and political declarations for good neighbourly relations inter alia, including four projects in Hungary and Slovakia on minorities, and a list of 98 Phare-supported projects, a small proportion of which relate to minorities.

CONCLUSIONS

Intergovernmental fora are well aware that the fundamental political changes in Central and Eastern Europe have reduced the risk of wars between states and certainly between the NATO and the Warsaw Pact countries. However, the CSCE, in particular, has also recognized that this new Europe is accompanied by major social and economic upheavals and has increased the possibility of violent conflicts within states, often provoked by neighbours.

Experience over former Yugoslavia, in particular, has led to a much better understanding by foreign ministries of the complexity of the issues, the impotence of many external actors, the ramifications of how an interstate conflict could lead to a regional war in the Balkans and, a recognition that pressure through the media sometimes obliges Western governments to intervene. Furthermore, the combination of high costs of military support, emergency aid, and several million refugees and displaced persons on the borders of Western Europe have dismissed any complacency.

There is a new determination by Western European countries to prevent social upheaval, unplanned migration and violent conflicts by taking earlier action to place regional security above state sovereignty. A dilemma remains for some Western governments: how to limit violent conflicts between ethnic groups in Central and Eastern Europe while retaining the sovereignty of western governments to continue with their existing domestic policies on minorities.

The device of focusing on a tight definition of national minorities is gradually breaking down, as it is obvious that it is intellectually unsustainable and morally indefensible. Whilst intellectual rigour and moral imperatives have never been important considerations for foreign ministries, intergovernmental agreements necessitate political consistency and intellectual coherence so that they may be implemented equitably through political, economic and legal institutions. International Conventions, in particular, do demand clear agreements by all parties for the central mechanisms to be effective. However, the very narrow interpretation of 'National Minorities' by states may lead to the new Council of Europe Framework Convention falling into disrespect.

The work on new standards has been rapid and there has been some 'leapfrogging' by developing standards agreed in one forum in a second. In some fora, CSCE and Council of Europe, the emphasis has been on national minorities and the agreements have included aspects of group rights and measures for empowerment. The references are primarily to 'persons belonging to minorities' but not exclusively so. The notion that a person can freely choose whether to belong to a minority is cherished, but in reality identity is much more complex.

The UN Declaration on Minorities, in contrast, refers to national or ethnic, linguistic and religious minorities; it includes issues of involvement in economic development, planning and programmes of co-operation between states. Its major weakness is that it is a declaration, a contribution to customary international law; it has a political and moral impact without the security imperatives of CSCE or the legal regime that the Council of Europe is introducing. A variety of different standards in different international fora can cause confusion and all of them falling into disrepute. Hence it will be important for the new OSCE and Council of Europe to come together and for the Framework Convention to be implemented in a consistent manner.

The CSCE Human Dimension meetings in Copenhagen, Geneva and Moscow generated considerable debate and research within foreign and domestic ministries, many conferences and a new wave of research. This, together with the body of research already available, but often neglected, has led to a much better understanding of the issues by many governments. However, in this highly complex area that spans individual and group rights, social, economic and political rights, local state and international arrangements, much more needs to be done to find effective ways of achieving minority rights and peaceful co-existence. Issues such as the promotion of identity, the full participation of minorities in economic progress, the planning of national policies and programmes to take due regard of minorities deserve serious study to give practical meaning to these agreements between states.

There is a recognition that standards alone, even if adopted, are not enough and that specific implementation measures are needed in countries whether at state or local level. The work being done to look at 'models

of good practice' will undoubtedly help governments and donors identify the more successful cases of 'accommodation' between communities and the factors that are helping to pull them together as well as
apart. Some of the studies have been exercises in public relations and
the demand for more serious, objective and timely reviews is growing.

The new standards agreed in the last four years by the CSCE in
particular, but also by the United Nations and the Council of Europe,
have major implications. They balance the treatment of minorities and
the sovereignty of a state in a number of circumstances and, at least in
Central and Eastern Europe, these are being reinforced by economic
measures and new legal regimes both in constitutional arrangements
and within the additional protocol to the European Convention of Human
Rights. The large number of CSCE missions and interventions (110 by
the beginning of 1993) and the High Commissioner for National Minorities (Max van der Stoel), who by careful agreement and precedent
is extending his role covering the Roma among other disadvantaged
minorities, is having an impact. The CSCE and the Council of Europe
are now working much more closely together and are building a rapport with the financial institutions of the European Community and
the European Bank for Reconstruction and Development may, over
time, provide the pressure to conform to standards that the military
pressure from the Warsaw Pact and NATO provided five years ago.
However, much has to be done and the International Monetary Fund's
financial support of Russia, following the army's intervention in
Chechnya, requires close monitoring to ensure that democracy and liberal policies are practised. Additionally, the United Nations agencies
must give due regard to the UN Declaration on Minorities in their
mandates, when providing economic and technical assistance.

The pressures on Western European states to conform to these agreed
norms is less than those in Central and Eastern Europe, and the current divisions among European Community countries on practical
measures inside the Community make immediate progress difficult: Belgium, France, Germany, Greece, Spain and the UK are particularly
reluctant to give encouragement to their own national minorities. However, the addition of Austria, Finland, and Sweden to the European
Community in 1995, all of whom have clear and positive attitudes
towards minority rights inside and outside their countries, should shift
the balance.

The economic recession that is confronting most of Europe and the
moves towards open borders in the European Union are unlikely to
lead to any liberalization in policy towards immigrants and refugees

for some years, though demographic pressures may eventually lead to more liberal migratory policies within a decade. Nevertheless, the concern over growth of racism and xenophobia in Western Europe and the growing concern in Southern European States over North African migrants may mean more resources will be provided by the European Union in programmes to promote stability in the periphery and to combat racism within Western Europe.

Past and current trends are not easily extrapolated in future trends. The time for intergovernmental statements and agreements of principle is coming to an end. The emphasis in the future will continue to centre on conflict prevention and management, but the focus is likely to grow on longer-term measures to encourage robust multi-cultural societies that in practice are far less susceptible to volatility. However, contradictions can arise. New democracies have inherent instabilities in the short term that totalitarian regimes do not have; in the longer term the converse is true. The challenge remains to promote effective minority rights and economic development that will bridge the short and long term.

The European Union will be planning for further expansion in the next century. Consequently the emphasis is likely to be on new economic incentives to encourage stability, while stability at the periphery will attract new investments and the prospects of membership of a wider European Union. Conversely those states that are unstable with tense inter-communal relations are likely to be excluded from the new European Union, leading to further inter-group tensions.

April 1995

This paper has been written as a personal contribution, although it is based on the experience gained while I was Director of the Minority Rights Group. During the last few years it has been possible for me to attend the CSCE Human Dimension meetings, the expert meetings on National Minorities, and the major review meeting in Helsinki as an independent NGO member of the UK delegation. On a number of occasions I have attended meetings of the UN Human Rights Commission, briefing its working group on the UN Declaration on Minorities, as well as the UN Sub-Commission, and the UN World Conference on Human Rights. Contacts with the Council of Europe were more limited that with the European Commission, but practical experience forms the basis of this analysis. However, the views expressed here are not necessarily the views of the Minority Rights Group.

BIBLIOGRAPHY

Thornberry, P. and M. Amor Martin Estebanez (1994), *The Council of Europe and Minorities*, Council of Europe
Phillips, Alan and Allan Rosas (eds) (1995), *Universal Minority Rights*, Abo Akademi and Minority Rights Group, June
Eide, Asbjørn (1993), *New Approaches to Minority Protection*, Minority Rights Group, December
Bloed, Arie and Wilcode Jonge (eds) (1993), *Legal Aspects of a New European Infrastructure*, Europa Institut Netherlands Helsinki Committee
Miall, Hugh (ed.) (1994), *Minority Rights in Europe*, Pinter Publishers: London

NOTES

1. The French, Belgian, Spanish and, more recently, German governments have failed to support measures at the Council of Europe and the United Nations.
2. See Stability Pact, Paris, 21 March 1995, signed by 52 CSCE states.
3. See UN Covenant on Civil and Political Rights, 1966, which in article 27 refers to 'persons belonging to' and to 'in community with others', setting the precedent in standard setting.
4. Conference on Security and Co-operation in Europe (CSCE) Expert Meeting on national Minorities (Geneva, June 1991) was a meeting of governments.
5. The United Nations and the Council of Europe have recognition procedures for NGOs. This has often been used within the UN to ensure that NGOs recognized are international in their membership, and exclude political parties and minority communities in a state.
6. MRG Occasional Paper, *Representations at Helsinki Review Conference*, May 1992.
7. CSCE Seminar on National Minority Issues: Positive Results, Warsaw, May 1993.
8. Personal statement by Jean Pierre Worms.
9. Leningrad Conference on Minority Rights, 1–3 June 1991, convened by Minority Rights Group (Denmark) and Leningrad Association of Scientists. Published by MRG Denmark/London.
10. CSCE Human Dimension meeting (Moscow, September 1991). See written statements of Soviet Union and USA.
11. See UNRISD research project on Ethnic Diversity and work by UNICEF Innocenti Centre in Florence.
12. Eide, *Possible ways and means of Facilitating the Peaceful and Constructive Solution of Problems Involving Minorities*, 1993. Final report to the Sub-Commission.
13. See the 12 years it took to complete the first draft of UN Declaration on Minorities, and the absence of international nominative standards before 1990.

14. UN Convention on the Elimination of Racial Discrimination (1965). See regular reports of Treaty Monitoring Bodies.
15. See Arie Bloed, L. Leicht, M. Novat and A. Rosas (eds) *Monitoring Human Rights in Europe: comparing International Procedures and Mechanisms* (Dord recht/Boston and London 1993).
16. The World Bank: *The World Development Report* 1991.
17. CSCE Human Dimension meeting held in Copenhagen (June 1990) whose concluding statement was agreed by consensus by all 35 then participating states.
18. See Francisco Capotorti, *Study of the Rights of Persons Belonging to Ethnic, Religious and Linguistic Minorities*, New York, 1979, UN Sales No E 78.XIV.I.
19. Professor Thornberry points out that there is some ambiguity here. The Roma certainly constitute an ethnic and perhaps linguistic group for international law purposes, and possibly (in some cases) a 'tribal' group under ILO Convention No. 169. The Council of Europe has described them as an archetypal European Minority (see *The Council of Europe and minorities*, P. Thornberry and M. Amor Martin Estebanez. September 1994]
20. Council of Europe Summit: Vienna, October 1993. The phrase National Minority was used in Article 14 of the European Convention of Human Rights in 1950. The earlier origins are not obvious.
21. *Opus cit.*
22. The author was an NGO member of the UK delegation and was able to listen in to the early informal discussion when the detailed agenda and working groups were planned.
23. See CSCE Human Dimension concluding statements from Copenhagen (June 1990) and Moscow (October 1991).
24. See note 4.
25. UN Charter (1945) and agreed to subsequently by all new member states.
26. See Patrick Thornberry in *Universal Minority Rights*, to be published in Spring 1995 by Abo Akademi (and Minority Rights Group).
27. UN Secretary General, Agenda for Peace, September 1992, page 46.
28. See note 17.
29. See general comment adopted by the Human Rights Committee on 6 April 1994. CC PR/C/21/Rev. 1/Add.S. United Nations.
30. See P. Thornberry and M. Amor Martin Estebanez in *The Council of Europe and Minorities*, 1994.
31. The European Commission for Democracy through law, known also as the Venice Commission.
32. See note 19.
33. The Council of European Framework Convention on National Minorities was opened for signature in February 1995.
34. A valuable description of the development of the Framework Convention on National Minorities is given by Eeroo Amio in *Universal Minority Rights, opus cit.*
35. CSCE Review Conference Helsinki 1992 was concluded with a Summit of Head of Governments in July 1992 and a final document.
36. See Arie Bloed in Universal Minority Rights, *opus cit.*

37. For details of UN Treaties and treaty-monitoring bodies see UN Centre for Human Rights, *A compilation of International Instruments.*
38. For a critique of their work see the *Bulletin of International Service for Human Rights* (Geneva), biannual publication.
39. It is often forgotten in the United Nations, which is dominated by governmental representatives, that the Charter of the United Nations begins 'We the peoples of the United Nations determined'
40. MRG was able to play an active role in the Working Group, attending the meetings and presenting papers with ideas.
41. See Alan Phillips, *UN Commission on Human Rights*, Occasional Paper, published by Minority Rights Group, March 1994.
42. See presentations of Nordic Counties *inter alia* and Commission resolution 1994/23.
43. Resolution of Sub-Commission 1994/4.
44. See *UN Commission on Human Rights*, Occasional Paper by Alan Phillips, Minority Rights Group, February 1995.
45. See resolution of Commission on Human Rights proposed by Austria and 32 other states, adopted on 3 March 1995.
46. The following states signed on 1 and 2 February: Austria, Cyprus, Denmark, Estonia, Finland, Hungary, Iceland, Ireland, Italy, Liechtenstein, Lithuania, Netherlands, Norway, Poland, Portugal, Romania, Slovakia, Slovenia, Spain, Sweden, Switzerland and the United Kingdom.
47. Letter from Director of MRG. One small state has replied noting that it has no national minorities but signed this out of solidarity.
48. See mandate of European Bank for Reconstruction and Development.
49. The agreement (March 1995) by the IMF to provide conditional loans to Russia, reviewing developments monthly, may seem to contradict this following the Russian intervention in Chechnia but see The Economist, January 28 1995 and March 10 1995.
50. See note 2.

7 The Political Sociology of a Multicultural Society[1]
John Rex

Although a few right-wing Conservative spokesmen have recently challenged the notion that Britain should be a multicultural society and have received some support from intellectuals of the New Right (Honeyford, 1988), the idea that we already have a multicultural society and that this is not only inevitable but desirable is widely accepted. Unfortunately it is not at all clear what the term means exactly. Although it purports to be a sociological description, sociologists have done little to clarify the kinds of structure to which it refers. This paper will, therefore, seek to set out the basis for a political sociology of the multi-cultural society both as an ideal and as a reality and, while dealing primarily with Britain, indicate what the principal variables are, so laying the basis for a more generally applicable theory.

MULTICULTURAL AND PLURAL SOCIETIES

In the first place the notion of a multicultural society has to be distinguished from that of the plural society, on which there is considerable literature. Furnivall, who first used this concept, used it to refer to a society such as that which was to be found in colonial Indonesia, in which a number of ethnic groups encountered each other only in the market-place and in which, while each of the separate groups was tightly bound together internally by its own morality and culture, this encounter in the market-place was marked by an absence of a 'common will' such as had underpinned market relations in Europe (Furnivall, 1939). M.G. Smith, using Malinowski's notion of a society as a system of interrelated institutions, argued that in the British West Indies the various ethnic groups which constituted many of these societies each had its own separate and nearly complete institutional set, their incompleteness lying in the fact that they were bound together by a single political system based upon the domination of a ruling group (Smith, 1965). Later Smith was to refer to the *de jure* and *de facto* differential incorporation of the ethnic groups (Smith, 1974). Other writers have sought to apply the theory to African societies in a modified form (Smith and Kuper, 1969) and there has also been a Marxist critique of Smith's and Furnivall's theory which lays emphasis upon the mode and the social relations of production as the element which binds the groups together (Rex, 1986a).

What all these theories of the plural society have in common is that they emphasize the inequalities of economic and political power between the society's constituent groups. Thus the South African system popularly referred to as 'Apartheid' is seen to be a clear instance of the plural society. Obviously, therefore, when the notion of a multicultural society is discussed as an ideal in the British context, what is being suggested is something sociologically quite different from this, although it may well be the case that the widespread acceptance of the idea of the multicultural society has something to do with the fact that some of its supporters envisage a system in which minority cultures are treated as inferior and in which members of minority groups have unequal rights.

Another type of society from which the multicultural society in Britain has to be distinguished is that in which several ethnic groups or nations live together through a system of power-sharing. This does not imply inequality, but the major groups are thought of as maintaining their separate corporate existence while sharing in the exercise of political power. This is the case in Canada where the British and French 'founding nations' have shared control of the state, and in Belgium where the Flemish and Walloon populations co-exist in terms of a balance of power. It can also be argued that there is power-sharing in some colonial societies, such as Malaysia, where one group, the Malay, controls the political system and another, the Chinese, controls the world of business. Neither of these types of social and political system can be envisaged in Britain and the concept of a multicultural society clearly does not imply them.

CULTURAL DIVERSITY AND EQUALITY OF OPPORTUNITY – THE JENKINS FORMULA

The first official British response to the presence of large numbers of immigrants distinguished by their skin colour, their language, their religion and their culture was simply to declare that they must be assimilated to a unitary British culture. Thus the Commonwealth Immigrants Advisory Council, referring to educational provision, argued in 1964 that 'a national system cannot be expected to perpetuate the different values of immigrant groups' (Commonwealth Immigrants Advisory Council, 1964). This policy was very quickly abandoned, however, and in 1968 the Home Secretary, Roy Jenkins, said that what he envisaged was 'not a flattening process of uniformity, but cultural diversity, coupled with equal opportunity, in an atmosphere of mutual tolerance' (Patterson, 1968). Since these policy aims have never been formally abandoned, it may be assumed that, in some degree at least, they still influence government policy. In trying to decide what is meant in sociological terms by the concept of a multicultural society in the British case, therefore the Jenkins formula provides us with a starting point.

(a) Equality of Opportunity and the Shared Political Culture of the Public Domain

The most important point to notice about Jenkins's statement is that the notion of cultural diversity is clearly coupled to the distinct notion of equality of opportunity. If, then, it is taken as indicating the British ideal of the multicultural society, it is clear that this ideal is not satisfied in any system in which members of the society distinguished by their culture have unequal rights. Presumably, too, the notion of cultural *diversity* does not refer to a situation in which different cultures are thought of as having unequal worth, as is suggested by Honeyford (1988) when he attacks the notion of 'cultural relativism'.

It is also to be noted, however, that Jenkins speaks only of equality of opportunity and not of equality of outcome or of social rights. Given this minimal commitment, it is not surprising that the formula should have proved acceptable to his Conservative successors. More radical, though it is undoubtedly vague, is the ideal informing French policy, the long established one of 'Liberty, Equality and Fraternity'; and, even more radical is the conception of social rights which has enjoyed considerable currency in Britain since the publication of T.H. Marshall's *Citizenship and Social Class* (1950).

Marshall argued that the British working class, having previously won the legal rights of equality before the courts and the political rights which were secured through universal adult suffrage, had, in the Welfare State, now also won a bundle of social rights. For Marshall the range of these new social rights was still quite limited, but, when a Conservative government succeeded Labour in 1951 and did not reverse its social policies, it was widely thought that there was now a new consensus around certain policies, including planning for full employment, welfare benefits for the sick and unemployed, free collective bargaining over wages, and the provision of basic social benefits in the form of a free National Health Service, cheap housing for rent and primary and secondary education for all. The radical commitment which such a set of policies involved has, of course, been largely abandoned in the eighties, but it is clear that at times the notion of equal social rights for all citizens in Britain has gone well beyond the limited notion of equality of opportunity enshrined in the Jenkins formula.

The other important point in Marshall's thesis was that, with the achievement of social rights, the primary loyalty of the individual, and his or her primary form of belonging, would, in the future, be not to a class, but to the nation. Citizenship rather than class membership was to be the leading concept of Britain's future political sociology. This suggested that, whatever the culture and forms of belonging experienced by individuals as a result of their membership of communal, regional, class, religious and ethnic groups, there was now a shared political culture of the public domain embodied in the idea of citizenship. Such a culture was necessarily unitary and could not be challenged by any concept of multiculturalism. This is a notion which is implicit in the Jenkins formula when it couples cultural diversity with equality of opportunity.

(b) Cultural Diversity in the Private and Communal Domain

The fact that the Jenkins formula coupled the notion of cultural diversity with equality of opportunity should not, however, be taken to imply that it was not primarily about cultural diversity, but the coupling of these two ideals does involve an inherent difficulty. To insist upon a shared culture of the public domain which emphasizes equality does appear *prima facie* to be at odds with defending the rights of immigrants and ethnic minorities to be different, and it is interesting to notice that in France the emphazis, even in anti-racist organizations such as SOS, Racisme and France Plus, has been placed on ensuring that members of the ethnic minorities attain the rights of citizenship. Very often this has meant a fear of, or even positive hostility to, immigrant cultures, as when a Black headmaster refused to admit a group of Muslim girls to his school because they were wearing their traditional Muslim scarves, justifying this on the grounds that the French policy was one of secular schooling.

In Britain what has happened is that recognition has been given to the continuance of minority cultures in the 'private' domain of the family and community. Minority groups are thought of as having the right to speak their own languages, to practise their own religions, to have their own domestic and communal culture, and to have their own family arrangements. It has been thought that these forms of diversity can be tolerated and even encouraged, since they do not impinge upon the public sphere and also have positive value in that they provide social and psychological support for the individual in what otherwise appears as a harsh, individualist and competitive society. Some would also add that the flourishing of diverse cultures on this level actually 'enriches' British culture outside the political and economic sphere.

The doctrine of the two cultural domains was one which was widely shared in discussions of the multicultural society, including that by the present author (Rex, 1986b). The notion of equality and citizenship appeared to be saved by declaring it part of the public political domain, while that of cultural diversity was preserved as part of the private communal domain. Those who took this view therefore seemed able to get the best of both worlds. Embarrassingly, for them it was also taken up by some of those who did not accept the claims of minority cultures to equal esteem (Honeyford, 1988). For such writers however, what the 'two domains' thesis means is that, though the diverse cultures of the minorities may be inferior and even noxious, they may be tolerated so long as the public domain is insulated from them. Moreover, for them, the culture of the public domain is usually represented, not simply as the shared political culture which has been described above, but an all-inclusive British national culture.

DIFFICULTIES IN THE TWO DOMAINS THESIS

Having stated the 'two domains' thesis as a starting point for this discussion, it is now necessary to say that it is all too naive and simplistic. It involves intellectual difficulties because *prima facie* it appears to be at odds with accepted assumptions in sociological theory and it involves practical difficulties, especially when applied to education, but also in a number of substantive political ways. We should now deal with each of these difficulties in turn.

(a) The Problem of the Two Domains Thesis in Sociological Theory

The mainstream tradition in sociological theory has always been in some sense functionalist. That is to say, it has argued that the various institutions which constitute a sociocultural system are all necessarily interrelated so that each helps to sustain the others. Moreover, even the critics of functionalism, who have raised the possibility of inter-institutional or systemic contradictions, have envisaged these very contradictions as leading to systemic change (Lockwood, 1964), while those who have based their sociology on the notion of class conflict have still analyzed the internal culture and social organization of the separate classes in functionalist terms (Rex, 1961). There seems to be no place within such sociologies for the idea of two separate socio-cultural domains which have no impact or effect upon one another. The moral values inculcated by the family, for example, are looked at in terms of their functionality or dysfunctionality for performances in the political and economic spheres.

There is, however, also another tradition in sociological and historical thinking. This is that of the secularization thesis. According to this thesis, in the process of modernization, such forms of social organization and culture as the market, bureaucracy and modern technology and science have been gradually but systematically liberated from the controls previously exercised over them by religion, morality and the family. Now, if anything, the liberated institutions come to dominate others, but, at least, they are able to insulate themselves from their effect. Herein lies the basis of tolerance. What the secularization thesis does not allow for, however, is the extent to which the modernizing values of the market-place penetrate communal values, or how, on the other hand, the world of the market-place depends upon individuals being socialized within the family and community, and upon their providing a retreat from its rigours (Parsons calls this the Pattern Maintenance and Tension Management System (Parsons, 1951)).

(b) Practical Difficulties in the Education System

Schools in modern societies cannot be simply located in the two domains. On the one hand, they are part of the selective system of an industrial or post-industrial society, submitting their students to competitive testing, and having necessarily to inculcate the values of such a competitive system and of the wider society; on the other, they are concerned with moral education, transmitting the values which are necessary for the individual to become socialized at all, as well as for sustaining communal cultures.

Two kinds of debate go on within the education system. One is about equality of opportunity, with almost all groups demanding that their children should be able to acquire the skills and the qualifications necessary for them to obtain the best occupational positions in their adult lives. Such demands have been made in the past by the working class, despite their former cohesive culture induced by the process of class struggle, and they are made equally by immigrant groups, the rationale of whose immigration has been to ensure their children's advancement and increase their earning power. The other is about the preservation of communal values, which are threatened, both by the individualism inherent in the selective process and the economic system, and by the possibility of the host society's communal values being imposed.

Immigrant groups in Britain are almost always committed to the idea of equality of opportunity. Afro-Caribbean parents complain about racism and racist bias in the selective system which prevents their children from obtaining the best results, while Asian parents, even though their children, in most groups, are doing reasonably well, still usually have a highly instrumental attitude to education, and to the possibility that it raises of their children entering the professions or succeeding in business. At the same time racism expresses itself, not simply in unfair selection processes, but also in the denigration of minority values. Afro-Caribbean leaders sometimes attribute the apparently poor performance of their children to this denigration of their culture, while Asians fear that the values which are essential for maintaining the solidarity of their communities will be corrupted by the school.

Investigation of these matters in England was carried out by the Rampton and Swann Committees (Department of Education and Science 1981, 1985), but inevitably these committees were given a confused brief. They were required to deal both with the special problem of disadvantage amongst West Indian children and with the problem of potential culture conflict which affected Asian children in particular. Their surprising and somewhat convoluted conclusions were: that the poor performance of some ethnic minority children was due in the first place to disadvantage which they shared with poor white working-class children, but that they suffered a double disadvantage in that, in addition to sharing these working-class disadvantages, they also suffered from racism, both in the wider society and in the schools themselves; that the educational system could amend this situation in part at least by its own practice; and that the way to do this was, on the one hand, to eliminate all elements of racism from the curriculum and from selective processes, and using the disciplinary system to eliminate racist behaviour by teachers and students, and, on the other, to increase respect for minority cultures by introducing all children, including indigenous English children, to them.

Interestingly, much of the criticism which has been directed against the Swann Report (see Troyna, 1987; Modgil et. al., 1987; Verma, 1989; Chivers, 1987) has suggested that it failed to move beyond a multicultural to an anti-racist approach. In fact what this shows is that there was a powerful movement amongst educational theorists and sociologists in favour of greater equality of opportunity, and this movement was certainly right in claiming that the actual proposals for overcoming racism in the report were overwhelmed by the main proposal to educate all children in minority cultures. But what is usually less widely noticed is that the report had little to say about the value of education in minority cultures of those who adhered to them. This concern was displaced by the radical proposal that all children should be educated in minority as well as majority cultures and thereby equipped to live in an ill-defined multi-cultural society.

In fact, the story of the Rampton and Swann Committees is less important than it might have been for the future shape of British society, because its recommendations were not fully acceptable to government, and were at best very partially implemented. Actual policies in schools depended far more upon the statements of policy and attempts to implement these statements made by Local Education Authorities. These statements themselves, however, differ enormously in their proposals and reflect many of the confusions of the Rampton and Swann Committees as well as more besides.

The concern of this paper, however, is not to assess the findings of Rampton and Swann. What concerns us here is the role of the schools in contributing to the creation of a multicultural society. On this all that can be said is that the schools were the principal site of the conflicts inherent in the concept of the multicultural society itself, and experience shows that it is here above all that the contradictions and difficulties of the 'two domains' thesis become obvious. While it could be argued that the schools could contribute both to sustaining minority cultures as places of socialization and retreat and at the same time offering all children, regardless of race, cultural background, religion or ethnicity, equality of opportunity, this is not what has happened, and parents and children themselves have been left to work out the best balance between the two goals for themselves. Perhaps some Asian families have produced the most viable solution in combining through their own efforts the maintenance of a strong family organization and culture with a very instrumental attitude towards school education and educational success.

The Swann Committee, of course, has, in effect proposed the most radical form of social engineering by suggesting that, as distinct from learning to participate in present majority and minority cultures, all children should acquire a new culture which is an enriched amalgam of all of them. What seems to be the case where this has been tried is that it has simply produced a backlash on the part of majority parents. While it is true that British culture in its non-political aspects is subject to continuous change, it seems unlikely that a new multiculturally based British culture will be produced by social engineering in the schools.

A final word in this section should be added about Muslim children in schools. More than other groups, the more devout sections of the Muslim community have found difficulty in adapting to the school regime. The absence of provision for religious worship and instruction, the failure of the school meals service to provide *halal* food, the required exposure of their daughters' bodies in physical education and swimming lessons and the inaccessibility of single-sex education have all stood in the way of such adaptation. Where these demands have been met, Muslim parents have been prepared to regard education instrumentally as a means of material advancement, but some, in any case, have demanded more than this, and have sought, through the development of separate schools, to prepare their children for living primarily as Muslims, albeit within a secular world.

(c) Further Substantive Difficulties in the Way of Creating a Multicultural Society

(i) Host Culture, National Culture and Class and Status Cultures

The ideal of a multi-cultural society spelled out in terms of the two domains thesis sees British society as involving simply a confrontation between private familial and communal cultures, on the one hand, and the shared political culture of the public domain on the other, and, in our discussion so far, what we have had in mind in the private sphere have been principally ethnic minority cultures. In much public debate, however, the confrontation is seen as being between 'British culture' in the public domain and the culture of immigrants in the private, and this 'British culture' is not thought of in political terms at all. Rather it is thought of as itself a whole way of life which distinguishes the British from other nations.

National culture in this sense is often bound up with war and international relations as well as with international sport. It is supposed to be a focus of loyalty and patriotism. Those who feel this loyalty most strongly regard immigrant and ethnic minority culture as a threat. This was nicely expressed by the Conservative MP, Norman Tebbitt, when, in the course of expressing his doubts about the possibility of a multicultural society, he proposed what he called a 'cricket test' asking for whom immigrant groups cheered during cricket matches.

Although the national culture is thought of as involving a host of familiar cultural practices which distinguish the British from, say, the Germans and the French, such familiar practices and such a way of life are often thought of also in more restricted class terms. British culture tends to be dominated by ways of life developed amongst its upper-status groups and fostered in elite schools and universities. These status groups employ what Parkin (1979), following Weber, calls strategies of 'closure', which exclude lower-status groups from participation in their way of life. Here the contrast is not with other nations but with other status groups.

Status groups are concerned, as Weber saw, with the differential apportionment of honour (Weber, 1968), but they also come to exercise power. In the British case they exercise considerable control over the Civil Service and over Members of Parliament, and also form alliances with the business classes through which they exercise economic power. While the business classes seek legitimation of their own position through marital alliances and through sending their children to elite schools, the upper classes become members of Boards of Directors.

As against these strategies of closure and class alliance, other status groups develop their own distinct cultures. T.S. Eliot in his *Notes Towards a Definition of Culture*, (1948), which was primarily a defence of upper-class culture, noted that the working classes developed cultures of their own, often of a regional sort; Raymond Williams in his *Culture and Society* (1963) spoke of a 'common culture' distinct from the restricted culture of ruling groups; and Richard Hoggart, in his *Uses of Literacy* (1957), gave an evocative account of the cultural and moral values of working-class culture in Hunslet in Leeds.

Just as the culture of upper status groups becomes intertwined with the class culture of the business classes, however, so this popular culture becomes intertwined with the culture of the working classes, understood in a more political sense. A working-class culture emerges in the course of defensive and offensive class struggles based upon strong themes of solidarity, and this is projected onto a national stage through the Labour Party. Such a culture disputes the claim of the upper status groups and classes to being a national culture.

Finally, one should note the importance of the culture of the middle classes. Members of these classes often reject the solidarity of working-class culture and emphasize individualism and self-help, without themselves becoming incorporated into the closed culture of upper status groups and classes.

What one has in Britain, therefore, is not a unitary British culture, but rather a hierarchy of cultures, which, to some extent constitute cultural strata, but which are also based upon the political fact of class struggle. This is the culture which immigrant and ethnic minority cultures confront.

(ii) The Disputed Political Culture of the Public Domain

Earlier we spoke of a shared culture of the public domain. What we can now see is that there is a considerable degree of dispute within this culture. The upper status groups use strategies of closure; the business classes seek entry into the world of their status superiors; the working classes emphasize the virtues of solidarity and equality; and the middle classes emphasize equality of opportunity.

The shared political culture of the public domain arises out of the compromises which are made between these various tendencies. It is based upon the notion of hard-won rights centring on the notions of equality of opportunity and equality of outcome. Political parties are bound to make some reference to these ideals. However much upper-class conservatives may wish to defend their closed class culture and their class rule, the Conservative Party is bound to subscribe to the ideal of equality of opportunity, or even, recently, to the idea of a classless society. Labour, on the other hand, emphasizes equality of outcome. Sometimes one ideal gains the ascendancy, sometimes the other, but over the longer term what emerges is a new compromise based upon the idea of a minimum which is equally available to all, coupled with superior rewards for some, conceived of as a reward for effort.

The relationship of immigrant and ethnic minority cultures to this system is necessarily complex. On the one hand, they find their own cultures placed within a hierarchy of cultures, and their individual members having to face, not only the strategies of closure of the upper classes, but also those based upon what Parkin (1979) calls the strategies of usurpatory culture of the working classes. On the other, their members must make what claims they can within whatever is the going system of rights available in the public domain. They may seek to preserve their own solidary cultures while seeking in an instrumental way to benefit from equal opportunity policies, or they may come to share some of the values of the working classes, the middle classes or the business classes.

Race relations legislation in Britain complicates these problems. It is primarily designed to secure equality of opportunity for members of ethnic minority groups, but it also sometimes seems to be aiming at equality of outcome imposed by what Honeyford (1988) calls a regulatory bureaucracy. Inevitably, therefore, it produces resentment, both among the middle classes whose ideal is simply equality of opportunity, and amongst the working classes whose rights have been won, not through the interventions of a benevolent government but, much more, through hard political struggle. Thus, however much ethnic minority groups might seek participation in the shared political culture of the public domain, they find themselves faced with additional suspicions and hostility.

(iii) Religion in the Public Domain

Another questionable assumption in the ideal model of a multicultural society, which we have outlined, is that Britain is a secular state, and that religion is a private matter. There is some truth in this in that it is in no sense a theocracy, and that a variety of forms of religious belief and practice are tolerated, but the notions of secular state and secular state education are not nearly as clearly defined as they are, for instance, in France.

In fact the Anglican Church in Britain has a privileged position and even some symbolic power. The Archbishop of Canterbury actually crowns the monarch, and the Church endorses state institutions on many public occasions, especially those connected with war. Not surprisingly, the Archbishop was criticized by the Prime Minister for having failed to strike a sufficient note of triumph in his sermon at a memorial service after the successful completion of the Falklands War.

The various churches also provide supernatural recognition of individual life events, such as birth, marriage and death, and their religious functionaries provide a counselling service for many people at times of individual and family crisis; the schools provide occasions for Christian religious worship and instruction; and Church spokesmen are expected to make statements on social and political matters such as the plight of the homeless or of inner-city people generally, even though these are expected to avoid any kind of party political commitment (see, for example, *Faith in the City*, the report of the Archbishop's Committee on Urban Priority Areas (ACUPA, 1985).

None of this, of course adds up to more than the exercise of symbolic power by the churches, and in return for this symbolic power they are kept firmly in their place. Although the monarch is crowned by the Archbishop, she is also known as the Supreme Governor of his Church; the church is expected to support the interests of the nation in wartime; and, where it does make apparently political interventions, these are expected to be of a general moral kind rather than being precise political directives to legislators in Parliament.

Nonetheless the special role of the Christian churches, and the Anglican Church in particular, does have some significance for any attempt to create a multicultural society. They appear to endorse a national and nationalist culture rather than a society based upon a plurality of cultures; they have a privileged position in the schools, and they even have the protection of a law against blasphemy, which is at odds with the general commitment of the political culture of the public domain to freedom of speech.

From the point of view of immigrant and ethnic minorities this privileged position of Christianity does make their integration into British society more difficult. Though they have formally established their right to opt out of religious worship in schools and to have worship of their own, they have in fact to struggle and argue to enforce this right and, on the major question of protecting their religions against blasphemy, they have been sharply reminded, since the publication of Rushdie's *The Satanic Verses* (1988), that their religions do not enjoy the protection accorded to Christianity. As some of their more devout members see it, they are cultural and religious aliens in a Christian society, while, from the point of view of cultural equality, they face a national culture with a religious endorsement which is not available to minority cultures.

(iv) Human Rights and Minority Cultures

In Britain, in common with other advanced industrial societies, discourse within the public domain does not usually stop at the discussion of equality of opportunity or of equal social rights in the Marshallian sense. It also extends to the question of individual human rights and it is here that it brings the very foundations of ethnic minority social organization and culture into question. This is particularly true of the discourse of feminism. To many feminists the position of women in the minority cultures appears unacceptable, and they see themselves as having a concern for the liberation of wives and daughters from the domination of their menfolk. Though ethnic minority spokesmen may claim that they are concerned to protect their womenfolk from the corruption of a secular capitalist society, and that their forms of arranged marriage and extended kinship are essential strengths in their community organization, they are likely to find their cultures continually under attack from these quarters. There is a certain irony in this in that feminists often see their campaigns on questions of gender equality as paralleling campaigns for the equality of ethnic minorities

(v) Demands by Ethnic Minorities in the Public Domain
The model of the multicultural society based upon the two domains does not, however, encounter only those difficulties which arise from the British side. For some minority groups and minority religions, and particularly Islam, the division between the public and private domains appears unacceptable. For most Muslims, Islam is not merely a private matter but a whole way of life. Some, though by no means all, Muslims believe in the idea of an Islamic state; there is a widespread expectation that the state should protect religion; Islam has its own economic ethics, which are in some ways at odds with capitalism; it has its own ideas about education; and, not least, as we have seen in the previous section, its own views on the position of women and the family.

In fact, Islam has a long history and Muslims have in the past found ways of living in non-Muslim and secular societies. They do not necessarily all share the belief, to be found in the teachings like those of Maududi, the founder of Jamaat-i-Islami, in the ideal of an Islamic state; they have found ways of pursuing their banking and business in capitalist societies; they have found ways of adjusting to predominantly secular education; and, even on the question of the rights of women, their discourse is by no means as reactionary and patriarchal as many Western feminists assume. It is misleading, therefore, to suggest that anyone who practises Islam is a so-called 'fundamentalist' whose irrationality makes it impossible for him to live in a multi-cultural society.

To say this, however, is by no means to say that there are no difficulties in the way of finding a place for Islam in British society. In the immediate future it may well be that some extreme Muslims may make demands which appear unacceptable to most British people, as is evident from the recent publication of *The Muslim Manifesto* (Muslim Institute, 1990) by a relatively small and unrepresentative body called The Muslim Institute, which calls for the establishment of a Muslim Assembly, and a speech by the Institute's leader, Kalim Siddiqui (Siddiqui, 1990) calling for a special relationship between British Muslims and the state of Iran. On the other hand, the tendency to dismiss all Islam as 'fundamentalist' may make it impossible even for the more moderate to be accepted as legitimate citizens. In the immediate future, then, considerable religious and ethnic conflict seems likely, even though, in the longer run dialogue and negotiation might lead to the discovery that Muslim and Christian/British notions of the public domain are not incompatible.

Other ethnic and religious minorities have found it easier to come to terms with living in Britain than have Muslims. It still has to be noted, however, that, even though they might adapt very readily to living in Britain and taking the economic opportunities which living there offers, many of them may remain oriented in their thinking to homeland politics. Sikhs may use their British base to campaign for a separate state of Khalistan, Mirpuris may campaign for what they see as the liberation of Kashmir, and many West Indians, finding themselves rejected in what appears to them to be a racist Britain, may hunger for an African Zion. A multicultural Britain may well have to recognize that the continuance of such commitments is part of the culture of the private domain which can be tolerated, even though it prevents some ethnic minority members from becoming completely and finally British.

POSSIBLE OUTCOMES

The aim of this paper has not been one of simple advocacy. What it does, having outlined an ideal model, is to consider some of the difficulties which stand in the way of its realization. It is an exercise in political sociology, and the task of the sociologist is not simply to provide happy endings. All that they can so is to suggest possible outcomes, leaving it to activists to pursue this or that political ideal, including that of the multicultural society. It is to the task of considering realistically what these outcomes may be that we must now, finally, turn.

One important possibility which should not be neglected is that over several generations present problems and difficulties may grow less acute. Many of the descendants of immigrants may become less concerned with the perpetuation of their own cultures and more concerned with economic success in Britain. They may also find themselves affiliating to the class cultures and organizations of their indigenous peers. It would be 'optimistic' to believe that this process will occur as easily and smoothly as it has over two or three generations amongst European immigrants in America, because, at least so far as British Asian immigrants are concerned, they have great cultural and organizational strengths, based on cultures and religions in their homelands, more different from those indigenous to Britain than were the cultures of America's European immigrants from those of the United States. Nonetheless this does not mean that there will be no process of adaptation and acculturation.

The second more immediate and likely possibility is the continuance of conflict on all the levels we have discussed. Conflict will go on about the place of multiculturalism in education; British nationalism and racism are likely to continue in ways which deny ethnic minority cultures recognition and individual members of these minorities equality of opportunity; efforts to ensure equality of opportunity and equality of outcome for ethnic minority members will continue to provoke a backlash in the indigenous community; many members of the indigenous working class will continue to pursue strategies of usurpationary closure against the minorities, particularly if economic circumstances are such that their own livelihood seems threatened; ethnic minority cultures may continue to be attacked by human rights activists; and, finally, minority cultures may be slow to adapt to living in a secular multicultural society, the more so if their adherents feel that they are not fully members of that society.

If, however, societies attempting to be multicultural are likely to be societies in conflict for the foreseeable future, it should not be thought that this necessarily means everlasting riots and street demonstrations, even though there may be substantial and violent disturbances.

Just as, in earlier times, class conflicts which started in circumstances of riot and disorder gave way to processes of negotiation and compromise, so the relationship of ethnic minorities to British society will be renegotiated. This will include not merely a redefinition of the extent to which differences in the private and communal sphere are tolerated or encouraged, but also a renegotiation of the political culture of the public domain. So far as this latter is concerned, what may occur is that the political ideals of the minority, as well as their ideas about human rights, are not so different from those of the majority, Muslims, for example, being very supportive for their own religious reasons, of the idea of the Welfare State. On the other hand, British class-based cultures may be seen as matters of private preference rather than as demanding some sort of overall hegemony, while the privileged role of Christian religion might also come to be questioned in a secular state.

To recognize this third possibility does not, however, involve pointing, after all, to an inevitable happy ending. What it should do is to record the fact that, in a society which has to deal with cultural diversity, while there may be continuing conflicts, there may also be dialogue, and, arising out of such dialogue, negotiations and compromise. The actuality as opposed to the ideal of the multi-cultural society will, in fact, be found in a continuing process of both conflict and compromise.

BIBLIOGRAPHY

ACUPA, (1985), *Faith in the City – Report to the Archbishop's Committee on Urban Priority Areas*, London
Chivers, T., (1987), *Race and Culture in Education, National Foundation for Educational Research*, London
Commonwealth Immigrants Advisory Council (1964), *Third Report*, Cmnd 2458, London
Department of Education and Science (1981), *Report of the Committee of Enquiry into the Education of Children from Minority Groups – Interim Report: West Indian Children in our Schools*, (Chairman Mr Anthony Rampton), Cmnd 8273, London
Eliot, T.S., (1948), *Notes Towards a Definition of Culture*, London
Furnivall, J.S., (1939), *Netherland India – A study of a Plural Economy*, Cambridge
Hoggart, R., (1957), *The Uses of Literacy*, London
Honeyford, R. (1988), *Integration and Disintegration*, London
Lockwood, D., (1964), 'Social Integration and System Integration', in Zollschan, G.K. and Hirsch, W. (eds.) *Explorations in Social Change*, Boston
Marshall, T.H. (1950), *Citizenship and Social Class*, Cambridge
Modgil, S., Verma, G., Mallick, K. and Modgil, C., (1957), *Multi-Cultural Education – The Interminable Debate*, Brighton
Muslim Institute (1990), *The Muslim Manifesto*, London
Parkin, F. (1979), *Marxism and Class Theory: A Bourgeois Critique*, Tavistock, London
Parsons, T. (1951), *The Social System*, London
Patterson, S. (1968), *Immigrants in Industry*, London
Rex, J. (1961), *Problems of Sociological Theory*, London
Rex, J. (1986a), *Race and Ethnicity*, Milton Keynes
Rex, J. (1986b), *The Concept of a Multi-Cultural Society*, Centre for Research in Ethnic Relations, Coventry
Rushdie, S. (1988), *The Satanic Verses*, London
Siddiqui Kalim (1990), 'Generating Power without Politics', unpublished address to a Conference of the Muslim Institute, London
Smith, M.G. (1965), *The Plural Society in the British West Indies*, Berkeley
Smith, M.G. (1974), *Corporations and Society*, London
Smith, M.G. and Kuper, L. (eds) (1969), *Pluralism in Africa*, Berkeley

Troyna, B. (ed.) (1987), *Racial Inequalitiy in Education*, London
Verma, G. (ed.) (1989), *Education for All – A Landmark in Pluralism*, Brighton
Weber, M. (1967), *Economy and Society*, New York
Williams, R. (1963), *Culture and Society*, Harmondsworth

NOTE

1. Originally published in *European Journal for Intercultural Studies*, Vol. 2, No. 1 (1991).

8 Antiracist Mobilization in France and Britain in the 1970s and 1980s[1]

Cathie Lloyd

With increased racist and antiracist mobilization in Europe there has been renewed discussion about the strategies and effectiveness of antiracism. In France new organizations in the mid-1980s criticized the 'traditional' antiracists and there has been theoretical discussion about the failure of antiracism to halt the rise of racism epitomized by the Front National (FN) (Gallissot, 1985; Taguieff, 1987; Wieviorka, 1994). In Britain earlier disputes about the different priorities of opposing Fascism or racism have resurfaced in the form of arguments about representation and the purpose of mobilization.

Social movement theory has approached either the strategic or the identity aspects of popular mobilization, but lacks a combined approach (Cohen, 1985). The example of antiracist mobilization in Britain and France show that the aspects of resource mobilization and identification with particular interests are closely intertwined. Mobilizations make little headway without some organizational support, yet this carries with it a tendency to curb the disruptive edge of protest.

Social movement theory helps us to understand how antiracism could become a broad social movement and how it relates to other bodies such as the labour, women, peace, and Green movements. In this chapter I look at antiracist mobilization in Britain and France at two key recent points. In the period from the mid-1970s, local community groups worked through Rock Against Racism (RAR) and then gave way to the Anti-Nazi League (ANL) with its spectacular carnivals. I focus on a slightly later period in France, the early to mid-1980s, where we see a similar process with grass-roots movements displaced when national organizations are formed, notably *SOS-racisme*. The two mobilizations were connected through the medium of youth culture and important strategic lessons could be learnt by comparing the two experiences.

PROBLEMS OF COMPARISON

We need to bear in mind certain differences between the two countries and periods when making comparison. The 1970s differs from the 1980s. In the former there was economic crisis in Britain but restructuring was less advanced than in the 1980s. The feelings of despair and hopelessness were less crippling in the 1970s and the structures of the left and labour movement retained organizational strength. The British RAR-ANL movement took off on the back of militant industrial conflict and a self-assertive punk and 'two-tone' youth culture (Gilroy, 1987). Incendiary calls to anti-authoritarian action, linked to moral panics about black youth and law and order, were made in a new, anarchic way through punk music which called for 'White Riot' to emulate black rebellion.

The French movements of the early 1980s echo the earlier British events, borrowing directly from the British idea of RAR in the French Rock against Police (sic) and the Notting Hill Carnival. In France, the 'traditional' antiracist movement has a stable, local associational life which enables it to act as intermediary for the new groups.

In making comparisons we need also to take into account the different historical and political landscapes of the two countries (Lloyd, 1991). In France 'left' and antiracist discourses refer to Enlightenment universalism and the achievements of the French Revolution, particularly the Jewish emancipation and the abolition of slavery (Lloyd, 1993). The rhetoric about the 'right to difference' of the early 1980s operated within the constraints of republican universalism.

The British context has fewer references to a 'founding myth'. The youth rebellion of RAR ran counter to the symbols of British national identity. The monarchy was a particular target for dissident youth during the Queen's 1977 Silver Jubilee, as in the banned Sex Pistols version of 'God Save the Queen' (Gilroy, 1987:123). The myths which legitimated the ANL were more recent than the French, referring to anti-fascism of the 1930s and 40s. Anti-Fascists were the true 'patriots', not the NF which distorted patriotism by using the Union Jack. This nationalist discourse placed the anti-Fascist movement on an ambiguous terrain which may have made it less attractive to black people. It failed to present a positive aspect or to complement youth culture. The oppositional features of the British anti-Fascist movement have been commented on by a number of writers (Bonnet and Carrington, 1996 in press).

Despite these differences there are important similarities between the

1975-80 period in Britain and the 1980s in France. The movements were both established at a time of left-wing government when the left was more self-confident. In both countries antiracists faced co-option – the danger that their struggle would be taken over for other ends. Grass-roots movements began to counter the daily experience of racial harassment while the national organizations which cashed in on the popularity of antiracism were more limited in their aims.

MOBILIZING IN MID-1970S BRITAIN

There were many reasons for antiracist mobilization in mid-1970s Britain. The movement was prompted by resistance to the police at the 1976 Notting Hill Carnival, linked to grievances about police harassment of the black community. At the same time the growing electoral support for the National Front (NF) and increased racist violence called for a defensive response. Vibrant, militant punk youth culture and mobilizations around industrial disputes such as Grunwicks (see below) gave the movement considerable energy and a political context.

The rebellion by mainly African-Caribbean youth against the police presence at the 1976 Notting Hill Carnival was a formative event.[2] In the context of controversial police harassment of young black people under the 'Sus' laws (Demeuth, 1977), an expanded police presence at the Carnival was perceived as a provocation (Owusu and Ross, 1988). The Carnival was a highly symbolic event for African-Caribbean people as it symbolized memories of Africa and emancipation and slavery in the Caribbean (Dabydeen, 1988). It was founded in London by a group led by Claudia Jones, to assert the Black presence, following attacks by 'teddy boys' and fascists led by Moseley's Union Movement in 1958, which became known as the Notting Hill riots (Tulloch, 1988). Carnival has multiple meanings:

Today's carnival . . . is a symbol both of the growing self-confidence of Britain's black community and of greater inter-racial mixing. It is also a commemoration of the 1958 riots, being held each year on their anniversary, an irony which escapes most carnival goers (Pilkington, 1988:88).

As the Carnival drew ever larger crowds (100,000 by 1975) it was seen by the police 'as having the greatest potential for wide-scale disorder of any public event in London' (*Police Review* 25.9.1987). This was an important turning point: the Carnival became a crucial reference point for black and antiracist struggle in Britain and this was well-known and admired among French activists.

During the mid-1970s, resistance to racist violence had increased. In June 1976 18-year-old Gurdip Singh Chaggar was stabbed to death by a gang of white youths opposite the Dominion Cinema in Southall, a symbolic location for the Indian community. The police refused to recognize a racist motive (Sivanandan, 1982: 39). Anger at this response, coupled with the failure of the traditional community organizations to mobilize, led to the establishment of the Southall Youth Movement. It became a model for other Asian self-defence organizations in London, Manchester, Leicester and Bradford which co-operated on an *ad-hoc* basis with Afro-Caribbean youth groups. These defensive organizations became more political and formed organizations such as the Hackney Black People's Defence Organization and the Bradford United Black Youth League. They campaigned to put racist violence and state racism on the political agenda and to work among young people in schools and clubs. Women's organizations such as the Southall Black Sisters, OWAAD and AWAZ were formed to articulate their experiences (Bryan *et al*, 1985; Sivanandan, 1982).

A number of industrial disputes brought the mobilization of black communities to the attention of the 'white' left. The longest and most famous was for union recognition by Asian women at Grunwicks in 1976–77, but other disputes such as small disputes at Heathrow Airport and Imperial Typewriters in Leicester in 1974 paved the way (Sivanandan, 1982: 37, 41–2). These disputes drew attention to racism within the trade union movement, particularly its failure to support black workers' demands.

Conflict with the police at the 1976 Carnival was the point at which white youth culture began to force alliance with 'black struggles'. The extreme left's solidarity and involvement with 'immigrants' as the current terminology had it, often came under the heading of 'International' issues. *The Socialist Worker's* position statement appeared in its weekly newspaper throughout 1977 and 1978:

> We oppose everything which turns workers from one country against those from other countries. We oppose racialism and imperialism. We oppose all immigration controls. We support the right of black people and other oppressed groups to organize their own defence. We support all genuine national liberation movements.[3]

The conflict with the police on the streets of Notting Hill was a more immediate matter than international solidarity. 'White Riot', produced by the punk rock band 'The Clash', expressed admiration for the combative black youth at Carnival '76. While black workers were still seen as victims ('black workers are the worst (sic) victims, get the worst jobs, the worst houses' *Socialist Worker* 23 April 1977), there was also admiration and a feeling that they were at the forefront of a challenge to the established social order. The big battalions of the labour movement had a more mixed attitude and were more suspicious of struggles other than class (Wrench, 1987). Others saw black people as victims or believed in the revolutionary potential of black youth, inspired by Third World Liberation struggles. These different approaches guided the organizations set up in the next period and compounded misunderstandings between white antiracists and black community activists.

For many years local, labour-movement or church-based committees had existed to establish good community relations between 'immigrants' and the 'host' community. Many were incorporated into the official machinery set up through the Community Relations Council and the Commission for Racial Equality established by the 1968 and 1976 Race Relations Acts. These committees were not attractive to rebellious youth, who were still influenced by the new social movements. Neither was the Labour party, whose periodic campaigns against racism were lost in the party's bureaucratic election machinery.[4] However, there was considerable pressure from party activists to mount a more vigorous campaign (Labour Party, 1976). More dynamic structures were established under the banner of local Campaigns against Racism and Fascism (CARFs) which linked left activists, trades unionists, community relations activists and immigrant community organizations.

Rock against Racism filled an important gap, reminding people of the black soul and jazz origins of popular music. It represented the winning over of music from commercial interests and the political right. This was relevant for punk, which oscillated between aggressive affirmations of white identity and admiration of the self-assertiveness of black youth culture. One of the main aims of RAR was to save rock music from the right.

Within this context, the summer of 1977 saw a number of important mobilizations. Grunwicks entered a key phase in the spring with a series of mass pickets. There was a growing number of racist attacks. The NF attempted to hold provocative marches and meetings in sensitive areas.

Antiracist mobilizations opposed the NF, developed solidarity with black youth faced with police harassment and supported black trade unionists. On St George's Day in April 1977, a massive anti-Fascist confrontation with Fascists took place at Wood Green in North London, followed by other smaller attempts to prevent the NF from marching uncontested. The situation came to a head at Lewisham in South London on 13 August 1977 when, despite community appeals, the Labour Government allowed the NF to march through Deptford, home to many black people. There was pitched fighting by some older, more traditional antiracist groups.

In the following autumn the Anti-Nazi League (ANL) was launched, sponsored by an impressive list of left-labour MPs, trade union officials, political parties, writers and actors and actresses. Its first main task was to counter NF propaganda during the parliamentary by-election of Bournemouth East. Posters, factsheets, leaflets and stickers were distributed to schools, youth clubs and workplaces. The ANL's first goal was communication, according to Paul Holborow:

> We want firstly to inform as many people as possible what exactly the NF stands for and secondly to encourage them to take up actively campaigning against the Nazis (*Socialist Worker*, 19 November 1977).

The second aim was to counter the NF organization for the local elections of May 1978 and their attempts to push their influence in schools.

The Bournemouth action was successful: the NF gained fewer votes than in previous elections, and the ANL's first big popular mobilization took place on May Day 1978 (*Socialist Review* No. 3, June 1978). The emphasis was on exposing the NF as Nazis, and encouraging people to fight the Nazi threat from their own identity. Sections of the ANL represented different social groups, thus SKAN (School Kids against the Nazis), Football fans against the Nazis, Cable Street veterans against the Nazis, Gays, Doctors, Vegetarians, Bikes, Women and so on. This then appealed to different constituencies in different ways.[5]

The first Carnival was euphoric: floats passed through central to east London carrying the heads of Hitler, Tyndall and Webster (the latter were NF leaders) pierced by the ANL's yellow arrow. Martin Webster was depicted in bed with Margaret Thatcher with ANL supporters ('reds') under the bed. One of the slogans of the day expressed the spirit: 'We are Black, We are White, We are Dynamite'. During his set, Tom Robinson said 'We are all here for one reason, to tell the NF "Hands off our People"' (*Socialist Worker* 6 May 1978).

The NF's electoral support was reduced in the following local elections, although it remained uncomfortably high with 22 candidates in

Bradford who had in 1976 gained 9,524 votes, being reduced by 1978 to only 2,619 votes. This relative success was blighted by renewed racist violence, the murder of Altab Ali in East London in May 1978 and far-right terrorist attacks on left-wing and labour movement buildings. Even the most dedicated ANL supporters knew that NF votes had slumped because the Conservative leadership had taken an anti-immigrant position, not because the ideas had gone away. The ANL's attempts to build an organizational base were complicated by the conflicting aims of its members. There were also tactical differences: should there be more carnivals or a focus on opposition to the NF? During the second carnival in September 1978 the NF staged a provocative march through east London to clash with the celebrations. There were bitter arguments about the real motives of the different political groups involved. The Socialist Workers Party (SWP) had never hidden their aims to use the ANL's broad-based activities to recruit to their own organization.[6]

The ANL continued to mobilize during the 1979 election campaign but there were plans to downgrade its activity, first discussed after the early successes of the May 1978 local elections, and 'Paradoxically at a time when the growth of the ANL has isolated the Nazis, their racialist ideas are more influential than ever before. The Nazis will not be defeated unless the racialism of the Labour and Tory parties is challenged (Callinicos, 1978: 4). The silencing of ANL activity is eloquent testimony to this abandonment, despite evidence of an upturn of far-right activity in 1981. The ANL's organizer Pete Alexander admitted to a slump in sales and activities (Alexander, 1981). Although the league was still in existence at the time of the Brixton riots in April 1981, it gave little response to these events except to decry the 'black nationalism' of the committees set up in their wake (*Socialist Review* 19 September 1981: 4–5).

The experience of the ANL seemed to justify activists' fears of co-option and that the 'white left' was not interested in antiracism for its own sake. It encouraged the movement which had been pushing for self-representation and autonomy since the 1960s. The ANL had mobilized very different constituencies at local level, including trade unions, community groups, and most importantly, young people, the different 'interest groups' distinguished by their badges. At national level it appealed to the mainstream through trade unions, many of whom were already committed to more traditional forms of solidarity such as Liberation and Anti-Apartheid. By the 1980s the extraordinary revival of the Campaign for Nuclear Disarmament (CND) took on much of the innovative street theatre of the ANL. The League left behind a complex situation in which antiracists were increasingly distinguishing themselves from anti-fascists. There was a mounting demand from black community activists for a more prominent leadership role, which has since been articulated through Labour Party black sections and the Antiracist Alliance. There is little doubt however, that the interventions of RAR and the ANL established an antiracist hegemony in popular music.[7] It became fashionable to be antiracist.

Mobilization was at a broad level of young people, music fans, political activists and the relatively apolitical. The use of badges as a sign of defiance was an important feature of RAR-ANL campaigns. Badges and stickers were signs of belonging, enabling political mobilization in a mass society where people did not know one another. It helped to forge a feeling of solidarity in a fragmented, alienated urban society.

The main issues changed considerably during the period 1977–79. The initial issues for antiracists were set by black youth and motivated by racism and police harassment at the time of Carnival '76. As the 'white left' moved in, the focus shifted to the need to destroy the NF's electoral hopes and the move to confront them on the streets.

The relative failure of this social movement against racism can be attributed to a number of causes. Like other manifestations of youth culture, it lost its fashionable appeal as it became established. It ran out of steam as a political project as a number of key differences appeared, particularly the tension between antiracism and anti-Fascism. The movement was then co-opted by the SWP, which wanted to use it for its own ends, and this meant that other groups had no interest in supporting it. We will also see from the French experience that the problem of its survival lay in the lack of a harmonious fit between the movement and suitable intermediary organization which could drive it forward on a day-to-day basis.

Discourse also changed during this period. In the early stages it was about urban rebellion, but with the rise of the ANL references shifted to the legacy of fascism of the 1930s and the anti-Nazism of the Second World War. The struggles of the 1930s were evoked by the slogan 'They shall not pass' and references to the Spanish Civil War. Universalist appeals such as 'Black and White Unite and Fight' were coupled with an emphasis on the individual's personal commitment to anti-Fascism arising from their ethnic background, sexual orientation or musical preferences. This contradiction also characterized the French movement as we shall now see.

MOVEMENTS IN 1980s FRANCE

In France at the end of the 1970s a ground-swell of activity against Fascist groups and daily racism was taking shape. At the same time traditional antiracist organizations such as the MRAP (established in 1949) retained considerable authority. After the bombing of the rue Copernic synagogue in October 1980, some 200,000 people responded to their appeal for mobilization (*Libération* 7 October 1980).

Other rather different forms of antiracist activity were also developing. The wave of protests and rent strikes against immigrant workers' housing conditions in hostels between 1975 and 1980 mobilized traditional solidarity organizations to protest (Freeman, 1979; Miller, 1981; *Libération* 10 November 1980). Many felt that anti-colonial history was being repeated when 55 Algerian activists had to go into hiding from arrest and were threatened with deportation.[8] Relations between the rent strikers' and traditional sources of support such as the trade unions were not good, conflicting over fears that autonomous strikers' organizations might split working class unity.

Activity centred on housing and the struggles within the hastily erected 'transit cities', little better than camps of prefabricated buildings. Local residents' committees protested against the conditions in which they were living, and against police harassment and identity checks. Young people who had been brought up in France felt these problems strongly because their expectations were higher than those of their parents. In the Paris and Lyon areas, concerts were held to draw attention to racist murders and police harassment organized by the RAP network. A loose network of young people 'of immigrant origin' was given expression through publications such as *Im'média* and *Sansfrontière*.

In the months leading up to the Presidential elections of 1981, hunger strikers protested against deportations, especially the double punishment whereby young people who had not yet acquired French nationality could serve sentences for a misdemeanour and then face deportation to their parents' country of origin. They called for civic rights for immigrants. These activities launched by young people led by Christian Delorme of CIMADE[9] mobilized massive support across France. These hunger strikes introduced the central principle of non-violent action (Jazouli, 1992: 37–9). A manifesto, 'No to Apartheid France' was launched (*Le Monde* 17 April 1981; *Sansfrontière* No. 19 Avril 1981).

This moral crusade, backed by religious authorities, gained some concessions at the end of April from the Ministry of the Interior, delaying deportations under the double penalty. One of the first acts of the new Minster, Gaston Defferre, was to issue a circular (26.5.1981) announcing that no young person born in France or who came to France at an early age should be deported. The success of the hunger strikers' demands took the initiative out of the hands of the more radical activists around Rock Against Police (RAP) and Za'ama des Banlieues (ZAB) although they never really controlled suburban youth. The uprisings in Britain's inner cities of 1981 found echoes in the French suburbs. A series of racist killings and police harassment gave rise to outbreaks of lawlessness, particularly 'joy-riding' as part of a cycle of violence.

Suburban youth attempted to organize a constructive response. At the Gutenberg 'transit city' an open door festival was organized in November 1983. The *Collectif pour le développement des droits civiques*, established in the autumn of 1982, campaigned for the Socialists to implement their unkept promises of giving immigrants the right to vote, by organizing parallel, symbolic votes in the local elections of March 1983.

In the Lyon housing estate 'Les Minguettes', a spiral of police raids, confrontation with youths and violent reprisals was halted by a group of young people (mainly from North African families) and led by Christian Delorme. They aimed at transforming anger into collective action by holding a hunger strike which would force the government to pay attention to their plight. The tactics of non-violence and hunger strike effectively gained media support but failed to strike a chord with much of the French labour movement. Although the hunger strikes secured partial gains, the wounding of Toumi Djadja in a shooting incident in June 1983, followed by nine racist killings up to mid-August, made young people seriously consider the possibility of self-defence. Another group organized a non-violent march for equality and against racism which was inspired by the great civil rights marches of the 1960s in the USA and the ideas of Martin Luther King.

The March for Equality of 1983 was a founding act in the construction of collective action suburban youths of immigrant origin. It represented their rejection of current stereotypes and ignorance about their lives, by going to parts of France they did not know to discuss current problems. It stole the limelight from organizations which had been organizing at grassroots level for many years. Many of the newer organizations which proliferated in the suburbs of major French cities in the late 1970s and early 1980s were alarmed by the Minguettes initiative. The young people who initiated the march found it difficult to deal with the media and allowed the more experienced organizers from the

CIMADE to act as spokesmen. Existing organizations made an uneasy decision to support the march. Local free radio stations such as Radio Beur (in Paris), Radio Gazelle (Marseille) and publications publicized the march.

At the same time, however, a significant conflict emerged between the marchers and some of the support committees set up by more traditional antiracists to receive them in different towns. The effervescent atmosphere of total immersion in concrete action generated a strong sense of belonging among the young people who were part of the march. There was an almost inevitable clash with some of the older generation of antiracist/anti-Fascists who felt that they had 'seen it all before' and wanted to advise the new recruits.

There were three 'logics of action' in the 1983 March: firstly, networks of Christian and Third World solidarity such as CIMADE, who were committed to non-violence, and secondly the young activists who saw the march as a way of strengthening existing mobilization and their own networks of affinity (the free radios, *Sansfrontière*). Thirdly, some of the activists around the *Collectif pour les droits civiques* and *Sansfrontière* wanted to develop initiatives against violence to build on the history of earlier struggles to push the 'traditional' organizations to re-evaluate their position and support them. Their aim was to demand civic action to oppose the institutional and political blockage and discrimination which kept immigrant populations in a situation of insecurity (Jazouli, 1992: 61–3).

After a significant media build-up the March arrived in Paris. It engendered a carnival spirit, with innovative banners, slogans referring to 'trendy' youth culture using slang. At the same time it was deeply consensual, ending with an official reception at the Elysée Palace with President Mitterand, who agreed to some of the marchers' demands.[10] The official spokesmen of the march emphasized its universalism and the links to Martin Luther King. Delorme said:

> . . . the moral legitimacy of the March rests in this desire for fraternity and the wish for unanimity (in Jazouli, 1992: 65).

In significant contrast with the ANL carnivals, the march in France was experienced more as a personal and moral renaissance, rejecting the presence of organized political groups and even trade unions.

The March for Equality of 1983 was disorganized and spontaneous, gathering momentum as it reached Paris. Young people were involved in the march but their participation was marked by uncertain dealings with the media. Although the march presented a strong, positive image it lacked a coherent programme. It was an uneasy coalition of Delorme's ecumenical allies, traditional left antiracists and young people from the suburbs, some organized, many not. Suspicion of established auth -ority was widespread among the youth, many of whom had experience of left-wing opportunism. The Socialist government tried to retain connection with the new movements, supporting a MRAP initiative at Unesco, 'Assises pour l'Egalité' in March 1984, while also beginning a dialogue with the 'beurs' (youths of North African origin) and with the Elysée reception of the marchers.

There was considerable debate and controversy among youth organizations about future directions. A strong trend was for 'identity politics' backed by their roots in the autonomous movement. Another powerful current emphasized the danger of a closed identity and the need to make links with broader social forces. This trend, specifically the ascendancy of universalism over particularism, progressively gained the upper hand. During the following summer, a convention of associations in the Rhone-Alpes region expressed their reservations about the humanist inspiration of the 1983 March. They emphasized a more autonomous expression of youth activity to prevent 'the reappropriation of their rights and their words' (*Libération* 9 June 1984).

A group of young people decided to retrace the previous march using that symbol of French working-class youth, the *mobylette*. They planned to end with another antiracist march in early December in Paris (*Libération* 8 October 1984). This was intended to reinforce local campaigns which were mobilizing against FN election meetings. The continued marginalization of the *beurs* was illustrated by Toumi Djadja's exemplary sentence of 14 months' imprisonment for a series of alleged thefts.

The division in the antiracist movement became increasingly clear. In Toulouse, the marchers were amazed to be met by a traditional trade union demonstration, with what would have been their parents' generation of immigrant workers, mint tea and loudspeakers emitting the songs of Jean Ferrat (*Libération* 5 November 1984). There were other more direct disagreements according to one marcher, Mathilde, who said:

> For us it was a shock. In the hall there were all the classical antiracist organizations, MRAP, PC, PS, FASTI and all the rest. And then during the discussions we were face to face with people talking about police patrols, ethnic concentrations . . . it was frightening! We felt that they saw us as immigrants. And they separated us from the local youth (*Libération* 20 November 1984),

This then, was the 'enormous misunderstanding'. The left 'traditional antiracists' expected their credentials to be taken for granted, and the youth saw little difference, often collusion, between them and the authorities who oppressed them. They played tricks on the organizers of reception committees. One marcher pretended to be an illegal immigrant in order to provoke the 'traditionalists' to offer to help legalize his case. When the trick was revealed, the older activist referred angrily to their own credentials, as members of the Resistance and deportees to concentration camps during the war (*Libération* 2 December 1984).

Others saw the 'traditional' organizations as doing useful work in certain areas, such as literacy schemes or legal support work, but the 'youth' felt the older groups were 'out of their depth', sometimes paternalistic and obstructing the creation of new more appropriate youth structures. One key problem was that the imperatives of antiracism in the 1980s came less from immigration than the internal problems of French society. Some commentators recognized the rootlessness of the new antiracism in the problems of contemporary France. Etienne Balibar wrote about the new demand for equality:

It is said that it is utopian! It would be if the youth . . . did not recognize the relation of forces and classes which exist in France today. But in denouncing the 'false problem' of immigration and in making the straightforward demand of equality, the 'rouleurs'[11] indicate the real problems, that of racism, based in institutions before being in people's consciousness/unconsciousness and that of inequality, of wealth, employment, culture and power.

They cannot transform this situation alone. It is clear that immigrants and their children as second, third etc. generations won't win effective equality of rights (the right to live as full citizens of the community to which they contribute without feeling perpetually threatened) if their cause is not included in other social struggles and reciprocally, that these struggles will never surmount obstacles which they are encountering today if they do not make the fight against racism a priority so that they can take up the call for equality and civic rights without restrictions (*Le Monde* 1 December 1984).

By the mid-1980s, *SOS-Racisme* and *France Plus* had emerged as national leaders of the new organizations which had given rise to the antiracist movement. These two organizations were composed of young people who were already involved in 'mainstream' political parties, many members of the Socialist Party or graduates of student politics, although their initial impulse related directly to the imperatives of local associations, especially against racist violence.

The arrival of Convergence '84 in Paris was less consensual and unanimous than the march of the previous year. A smaller turn-out of 25,000 people was recorded, very young and ethnically mixed, 'like the Notting Hill Carnival' (*Libération* 3 December 1984). One of the leading marchers, Farida Belghoul, dismissed the older antiracists as unreliable and ambiguous in the support they offered:

> They hold out their hands to us . . . but it's partly because they are at a safe distance from our suffering. And the left? . . . Why don't they realize they are in the same boat as us? They are suggesting an integration which would mean the destruction of our integrity (*Libération* 3 December 1984).

The only official banner was 'Let's live together with our similarities whatever our differences'. The slogans emphasized mixing: 'France is like a mobylette, it needs a mixture to make it go'. At the final march of Convergence '84 the *SOS-racisme* badge first appeared, which was to play much the same role as the ANL badges had earlier. The slogan 'Hands off my mate' has an interesting resonance with Tom Robinson's 'Hands off our people' at the first ANL Carnival. The difference between these two statements points to the difference between the collectivism of the 1970s 'our people' compared to 'my mate' of the French youth movement of the 1980s.

The initial position of *SOS-racisme* was that of a 'moral crusade' with no political position, as Harlem Désir made clear:

> Our only ideological reference is to the Rights of Man. We have no motions or programmes or platform, not even a little charter. It would be a waste of time and an artificial way of creating divisions. Our philosophy is humanism (*Libération* 14 June 1986).

Part of the avowed aims of this new organization was mobilization to avoid politics. Instead, *SOS-racisme* organized annual mega-concerts after 1985 with government and television financial backing. They could not avoid politics, however, getting involved in opposition to changes in the Nationality code in 1987. The following year they announced a political programme focusing on the urban environment.

During the debates about the Nationality code, new attitudes emerged among young French people of North African origin about the need to engage critically with French nationality (Hargreaves, 1988; Silverman, 1988). The mainstream 'beur' associations suggested a new synthesis of universalism not restricted to French values. Arezhi Dahmani of France Plus told the Long Committee on nationality:

> Our values are those of the French revolution. Our values are secular and we support democracy completely. We support a universal system of values which today is not the sole property of France (Long, 1988: 558)

And Harlem Désir stressed:

> For us integration is primarily the rejection of exclusion, the rejection of the ghetto which includes the cultural ghetto (Long, 1988: 558).

Secondary school protests against the introduction of selective entry for university in December 1986 demonstrated the involvement of young people of immigrant origin in broader political struggle (Perotti, 1986–7). However, the massive euphoric mobilizations of the mid-1980s have proved difficult to sustain, giving way to more routine organization. The associations which took over the national scene after the second march, *Convergences '84*, tend to be more oriented towards traditional French discursive references to secularism, human rights and citizenship (Leveau and Wihtol de Wenden, 1988; Lloyd, 1993).

CONCLUSION

The achievements of the new movements were twofold. Firstly they mobilized a very youthful population. In 1989 *SOS-racisme* claimed an average membership age of between 15 and 25, with strengths among secondary school pupils (Désir, 1989). A general identification with antiracism became commonplace among young people in the 1980s. Secondly, the new movements approached antiracism in a different way, using new resources such as music, film and cartoons (Mestri, 1987). The 'second generation' have a different political approach from the earlier youth movements following 1968, motivated by equality, their orientation being to seek results in concrete actions rather than utopian dreams. Instead of opposing the system like the earlier generation in 1968, young people of the 1980s demanded that at least the system should observe its own rules.

The initial French mobilization was around violence, the police and the immediate problems of bad housing. The March for Equality in 1983 wanted to end the spiral of violence on housing estates, but by broadening its aim it lost focus. A common theme in Britain and France is the appropriation or co-option of youth antiracism. In the late 1970s mobilizations referred to the fear of Fascism through a military coup. The themes of the 1980s were urban rebellion and the intifada of the Palestinian youth. These themes were broadened to more universalist calls for equality.

The French activities were broader, more political, less oppositional than the British. This opened up their struggle. For the March for Equality it was important to liberate a symbolic public space, which was the whole territory of France. However, the success in publicity terms carried with it difficulties of co-option which are common to the two experiences. A large number of different organizations were available with which the new movements could collaborate in making positive demands.

The case of anti-racism in Britain and France seems to confirm the analysis that short-lived insurgency gives rise to organizations which tend to abandon oppositional politics and that organization building distracts from insurgency (Piven and Cloward, 1977: 11). Yet at the same time there was a role for established organizations as, for instance, they acted as reception committees during the March for Equality.

Antiracists tread a difficult line between spontaneity and incorporation. The study of the relationship between these two tendencies will continue to throw light on this difficult matter.

BIBLIOGRAPHY

Alexander, P. (1981), 'A new kind of nazi' *Socialist Review* 14 June
Balibar, E. (1984), 'La société métissée' *Le Monde* 1 Decembre
Bonnet, A. and Carrington, B. (1996), 'Constructions of Anti-racism in Britain and Canada' in *Comparative Education* (in press)
Bonnet, A. (1992), *Radicalism, anti-racism and representation*, Routledge
Bryan, B., Dadzie, S. & Scafe, S. (1985), *The Heart of the race, Black Women's Lives in Britain,* Virago
Callinicos, A. (1978), 'Making racism respectable' *Socialist Review* No. 2 May
Cohen, J.L. (1985), 'Strategy or identity: new theoretical paradigms and contemporary social movements' *Social Research* Vol. 52 No. 4 Winter
Dabydeen, D. (1988), 'Man to Pan' *New Statesman and Society* 26 August
Demeuth, C. (1977), *'Sus' a report on the Vagrancy Act 1824*, Runnymede Trust
Désir, H. (1989), 'SOS-racisme, hier et demain' entretien *Hommes et Migrations* No 1118 Janvier
Freeman, G. (1979), *Immigrant Labour and Racial Conflict in Industrial Societies,* Princeton University Press

Gallissot, R. (1985), *Misère de l'Antiracisme,* Arcantère

Gilroy, P. (1987), *There ain't no black in the Union Jack,* Hutchinson

Hargreaves, A. (1988), 'The French Nationality Code Hearings' *Modern and Contemporary France* No. 34 July

Jazouli, A. (1992), *Les Années Banlieues,* Seuil

Labour Party (1976), *Conference Report 1976*

Leveau, R. and Wihtol de Wenden, C. (1988), 'Evolution des attitudes politiques des immigrés maghrébins' *Vingtième Siècle* No. spécial 'Etranger'

Lloyd, C. (1991), 'Concepts, models and anti-racist strategies in Britain and France' *New Community* 18 (1)

Lloyd, C. (1993), 'Universalism and Difference: the Crisis of Antiracism in Britain and France' in Rattansi, A. & Westwood, S. (eds.) *On the Western Front: Studies in Racism, Modernity and Identity,* Polity

Long, M. (1988), *Etre Français aujourd'hui et demain,* Union Générale des Editions

Mestri, E. (1987), 'Une génération charnière entre marginalité et intégration' *Hommes et Migrations* No. 1104 Juin

Miller, M. (1981), *Foreign workers in Western Europe: an emerging political force,* Praeger

Owusu, K., Ross, J. (1988), *Behind the Masquerade,* Arts Media Group

Perotti (1986–7), 'La mobilisation des étudiants de France et le code de la nationalité' *Presse et Immigrés en France,* CIEMI

Pilkington, E. (1988), *Beyond the Mother Country: West Indians and the Notting Hill White Riots,* Tauris

Piven, F. & Cloward, R.A. (1977), *Poor People's Movements: Why they succeed, how they fail,* Pantheon

Silverman, M. (1988), 'Questions of Nationality and Citizenship in the 1980s' *Modern and Contemporary France* No. 34 July

Sivanandan, A. (1982), *A Different Hunger,* Pluto

Taguieff, P-A. (1987), *La Force du prejugé,* Gallimard

Tulloch, C. (1988), 'Claudia Jones, Mother of the Mas' *City Limits* 18–25 August

Wieviorka, M. (1994), 'Les paradoxes de l'anti-racisme' *Esprit* No. 205 October

Wihtol de Wenden, C. (1995), 'Ethnic minority mobilization against racism in France' in Hargreaves, A., Leaman, J. (eds.) *Racism, Ethnicity and Politics in Contemporary Europe,* Elgar

Wrench, J. (1987), 'Unequal Comrades: trade unions, equal opportunity and racism', in Jenkins, R. & Solomos, J. (eds.) *Racism and Equal Opportunity Policies in the 1980s,* Cambridge University Press

NOTES

1. Antiracism is written as one word to avoid emphasising the negative connotation.

2. *Time Out,* 3–9 September 1976.

3. *Socialist Worker* throughout 1977 and 1978.

4. At this time Labour's NEC issued two statements, one on racism on 7th June 1976 which attacked the NF and appealed to 'immigrant communities' for restraint and the second on 28 July 1976 on 'Racial tensions'.

5. The ANL's founding statement read, 'In every town in every factory in every school on every housing estate, wherever the Nazis attempt to organize, they must be countered'. They planned to focus on the organizations of the labour movement, building alongside existing antiracist committees or to establish new organizations.

6. 'Within the emphasis of building the ANL, the SWP must be clearly identifiable through the sales of *Socialist Worker*, articles in the *Socialist Worker*, the production and use of pamphlets and contributions at ANL meetings. SWP districts and branches must be geared to meet the needs and interests of the new contacts. Local activity and meetings must be designed partly to draw these contacts to us.' *Socialist Worker*, 1 July 1978.

7. David Bowie and Eric Clapton flirted with right-wing ideas and this was dealt with sharply by the music press and other leading performers, *Socialist Review* No. 3, June 1978.

8. The warrant for their arrest was annulled by the Conseil d'Etat in March 1977, but writers such as Jean-Louis Hurst saw similarities between the solidarity network for the rent strikers and the 'porteurs de valises' who had organized illegal support for Algerian nationalists during the war of liberation in the 1950s (*Libération* 10 May 1980).

9. An ecumenical welfare service.

10. These were, an end to police raids, no more prosecution of young people involved in violence which had been provoked by the police, the removal of certain police officers and the establishment of rehabilitation projects to employ young people on the estate.

11. The 'rouleurs' were the young moped riders participating in the march.

9 Connecting Ethnicity, 'Race', Gender and Class in Ethnic Relations Research

Floya Anthias

The attempt to disaggregate and deconstruct the categories of gender, race and ethnic phenomena is a characteristic feature of contemporary debates on these issues. This paper begins by examining the problem of static and reified categories, particularly in the context of multi-culturalism and its focus on ethnicity. The need to connect social categories of difference is raised in terms of providing an account of the structuration of positions. It is contended, therefore, that the deconstruction of categories needs to be supplemented by an attempt to theorize connections between them at both the general analytical level and the local and particular level. This paper will pay particular attention to the links between gender and ethnic phenomena, although the issue of race and class will also be looked at more briefly.

Britain, like many other European countries, has been following a dual trend of incorporation and inclusion of settled migrants and ethnic minorities, on the one hand, and the barring of the doors to new entrants. However, even those ethnic minorities who came to Britain in the 1950s and 1960s, as colonial migrants on British passports, have experienced the process of incorporation in a differential way, depending on country of origin and whether they are defined as Black (Afro Caribbeans and Asians) or White (Cypriots) (Anthias, 1982 and 1992a).

A primarily Black settler population from the ex-colonies has characterized the British experience of migration and settlement in the post-war period. However, waves of refugees or asylum seekers, workers on short-term contracts from the Third World, as well as undocumented workers, are a central part of the British political scene. Britain has yet to witness, in substantial numbers, the migration from the East that has been noted in countries like Germany, just as it failed to experience the Gastarbeiter phenomenon in the 1960s and 1970s. However, other European countries over the last ten years or so have seen the settlement and stabilization of migrant worker populations. New European legislation (often referred to as constructing 'Fortress Europe' (Morokvacic, 1991; Dummett, 1991)), has spread alarm concerning the implications for Black populations, given the fact that the Treaty of Rome nowhere mentions racial discrimination (Dummett, 1991).

The main focus of the next section is the way in which unitary, reified and static notions of 'race' and ethnicity inform much of the discussion prevalent in Britain in terms of academic and policy discourse. In addition, much of the literature and discussions treat migrant and ethnic minorities as ungendered. This fails to note the differential positioning of men and women from these groups in social relations.

MULTICULTURALISM AND THE FOCUS ON ETHNICITY

There is no doubt that we are now in a period of transition, both theoretically and politically. The race relations paradigm imported from the United States (Miles, 1991) had been challenged by the migrant labour problematic (see, for example, Castles and Kosack, 1973), and the culturalist and or nationalist paradigm in the 1980s (Gilroy, 1987). A more European-influenced model of race, ethnic and migrant relations has been the result of both a number of economic commonalities facing the European nations and increasingly common policies, finally to culminate with the Single European Act in December 1992. This has led in the late 1980s and now the 1990s to a greater interest in comparative European studies, marked by a number of recent International Conferences bringing together scholars and at times practitioners throughout Europe.

The interest in ethnicity and nationalism has characterized theoretically much of the discussion as opposed to older frameworks that focused on racism and colonialism, race and class or race and prejudice and discrimination. The argument is that much racist discourse is now couched in terms of cultural identity and national boundaries rather than using the idea of the biological inferiority of groups (Gilroy, 1987; Miles, 1989). The 'new racism', as it has come to be called, has been the subject of much debate (Miles, 1989 for example). The notion of the plurality of racisms as opposed to some unitary system of representations and practices has now become commonplace (Cohen and Bains, 1988) although a core of racism must lie in any definition of racisms in order for the term to be meaningful (see Anthias 1990 and

1992b). In addition, the issue of a specific European racism, at times posed as an essence of European culture and at other types posed as a unity of concrete forms, has also become current in debates on new forms of racism. Whether this form is new or not has been variously asserted or contested (see Miles, 1991). There has also been a shift away, somewhat unfortunately perhaps, from a concern with racial disadvantage to a concern with group identification and culture, with a post-modernist tendency to talk about the proliferation of identities and the growth of new ethnicities (see for example Hall, 1989).

Academics and policy-makers have often defined the problem of ethnic minorities as one of social control or what Stuart Hall has called 'policing' (Hall *et al*, 1982). The tendency has been to combine a variety of perspectives and practices relating to managing ethnic minorities through a dual process of exclusion and incorporation on the one hand and a restriction of new entrants since the 1960s, with only family reunification migrants and some categories of refugees or those on special work permits being allowed.

The perspective of assimilationism, the earliest tendency in the 'race relations industry', sought to solve the 'problem' by postulating the need for groups to abandon their distinct identity in order to acquire full status as equal members of society. Racism was largely defined as a problem of cultural difference and hostility was regarded largely as the result of ignorance. This tendency gave way in the 1960s and 1970s to policies of integrationism, which posed the problem as that of understanding between separate cultures. Common parameters for coexistence needed to be established. This meant that the legitimacy of ethnic minorities became dependent on their willingness to acquire the aptitudes, attitudes and skills of the dominant ethnic group within the state. In the late 1970s and particularly the 1980s, the shift in Britain and a number of other European countries like Sweden has been on multiculturalism and the espousal of the notion of ethnic pluralism. This is in contrast to the retention of cultural assimilation (the French Model) or exclusionary definitions of nationality (the German model). Issues of citizenship as opposed to nationality have been of paramount importance and I shall raise these in the conclusion with reference to the European framework.

Britain is currently in the multiculturist phase with regard to policies and discourses relating to ethnic minority and racialized groups. Multiculturalism treats ethnicity as merely a question of culture and identity. Ethnicity is not regarded as related to racism. Racism and disadvantage are to be fought by the celebration and provision of, and for, ethnic difference. There is in fact an assumption that to allow and foster ethnic difference and culture is coterminous with fighting racism. However, although ethnic diversity is a necessary prerequisite of a truly egalitarian and multicultural society, the fight against racism cannot focus primarily on culturalist concerns (Gilroy, 1987); racisms are ideologies and practices which produce political and economic subordination. In addition, the concern with ethnic pluralism has tended to treat ethnicity in terms of static cultural attributes rather than as dynamic and contextual.

Ethnic difference is considered chiefly as pertaining to the question of culture and identity by many of the most dominant formulations in the literature on ethnic and race relations also (for a review, see Bourne, 1980; Miles, 1982 and Omi and Winant, 1986). This finds expression in the discourse of multiculturalism. Such a culturalist perspective is unable to attend to the political dynamics of ethnic difference (Cohen, 1974; Hechter, 1987; Anthias, 1982). The links between ethnicity, nationalism, race and racism in terms of processes of group formation, and the political pursuits of collectivities so formulated or proclaimed, may never be made. The political projects attendant on the pursuit of cultural difference may fail to get addressed, and no assessment can be made concerning how they might link to anti-racism.

Equal opportunities policies which are usually co-existent with these different types of culturalisms have tended to define ethnic groups as coterminous with communities of disadvantage. Gender and 'race' have been treated as discrete bases for corrective action, leading to the construction of women as unracialized and 'race' as both de-ethnicized and ungendered (Anthias and Yuval Davis, 1992). In the equal opportunities phase culture and identity are seen as coterminous with a common experience of disadvantage which is then to be at the root of political engineering. This has failed to take into account that individuals are positioned at the crossroads of different equal opportunities categories of disadvantage (for example, Black women who come under both gender and race policies) and that there may be conflict between policies pursued on these different bases of disadvantage. In addition, the category of disadvantage that remains absent in this programme is that of structured class or economic disadvantage.

Giving validity to different cultural pursuits, with stereotyped and static notions of culture and ethnicity, also allows academics, activists and policy makers to lose sight of fundamental issues relating to the political projects of cultural difference and allows hegemonization by ethnic elites that are often both extremely traditionalist and generally male. In addition, it conflates the issue of ethnic pluralism with the struggle against racism. For example, race committees in local boroughs may fund groups on the basis of allowing them the cultural expression that a multicultural society ought to encourage, and in the process make claims to this being an anti-racist policy.

Treating categories of the population as unitary and static fails to note the dynamic and heterogeneous nature of ethnic groups and their responses and adaptation. It also has effects on ethnicizing and producing modes of struggle that focus on culture and identity, repeating for themselves the static and ahistorical nature of the racialized definitions that they are subjected to. It serves furthermore to promote forms of politics that can be divisive.

A central requirement if these problems are to be avoided is a clearer awareness of the contested and contestable nature of the categorization of groups that are the object of policy intervention. The next section looks at the difficulties posed by particular conceptions of ethnic and race categories.

ETHNIC AND 'RACE' CATEGORIES

The tendency to define ethnicity in terms of culture or identity conceived in static, reified and ungendered terms is apparent in much of the literature on ethnic relations (for a full discussion, see Miles, 1989 and Anthias, 1992a). Indeed the focus on relations between essentialized cultures and identities is one reason why anti-racist writers reject and denounce the use of ethnicity in analysing the experiences and positioning of racialized groups. Gilroy (1987) wanted to 'introduce a more sophisticated theory of culture into the political analysis of racism, by claiming the term back from "ethnicity"'.

Other writers, such as Stuart Hall (1989), see ethnicity as relating to origins, roots and traditions, constructing belonging rather than exclusion. From this point of view ethnicity need not be essentialist for it may be founded on a premise on a commonality of experience rather than origin. For example, a black ethnicity may emerge through the common experience of racism, despite encompassing diverse histories and traditions. In addition it may be forged as a mode for rejecting 'other' attributions and be a product of a politics of culture and identity emphasizing common experience rather than common ancestry.

The position taken in this paper is that racisms do not rely only on race categorization, but use the ethnic category more generally as their essential building block. The historical manifestations of racism, how-ever, are linked to a diversity of economic and political projects and do not, therefore, emanate exclusively from ethnic processes (Anthias, 1990, 1992b).

Some writers restrict racism to 'colour racism', with its denotations of physical visibility. The argument is that colour visibility makes as-similation into the hegemonic culture and structure of a society impos-sible. Racism is here usually confined to the product of colonialists discourse of 'the Other', which is seen to have ongoing effects in the present, often derived from class interests (as in the work of Rex, 1973 and Sivanandan, 1982). In some arguments this prototype is seen to predate the colonial experience and to be a product of the historical signifier of blackness (Jordan 1974, for example).

The dichotomous categories of blacks as victims, and whites as per-petrators of racism, tend to homogenize the objects of racism. These categories fail to attend to the different experience of men and women, of different social classes and ethnicities. They fail to note racism to-wards Jews, the Irish, 'Third World' workers, refugees and so on. They treat all 'white' people as racist, without paying attention to the differ-ent articulations of racism within social class and gender categories. For example, the condemnation by radical Black writers of 'White so-ciology' (Amos, Gilroy and Lawrence, 1982) does both of these things. It constructs a black identity that is present only as victim of white society. In the process it reduces racism to what white people do to black people because they are black.

Gilroy (1987), on the other hand, regards the formulation that black identity is a reaction to racism as inadequate. He stresses the existence of a black culture and organization that is not merely structured in, and through, the experience of racism. However, he assumes a homo-genous cultural and political entity. Miles (1989) extends racism be-yond colour, and indeed points out that racism is not the privileged domain of whites, and that blacks can be racist. This needs to be modified, however. Racism is not just about beliefs or statements (discourse in this narrow sense). Racism also involves the ability to impose those beliefs or world views as hegemonic, and as a basis for a denial of rights or equality. Racism is thus embedded in power relations of different types. From this point of view, although blacks may be racist in terms of believing that some groups are inherently inferior, they do not usually possess the power to effect change.

There are good reasons for rejecting a unitary subject as victim and culprit around the binary opposition of Black and White:

- Some groups are racialized who are not regarded as 'Black' such as the Irish, Cypriots, 'Third World' migrants and Jews. In the broader European context, a multitude of ethnic exclusions and otherness exist that bear no resemblance to Black categorization.
- Different ethnic groups experience it differently – it has different *outcomes* depending on class location, political position, forms of regulation and control exercised by the state, forms of citizenship and so on.
- Groups form their own identity and consciousness *vis-à-vis* location and experiences, i.e. they are partners in the process.
- White people are not the exclusive culprits although often mediators and practitioners – minorities are racist towards each other.

One of the reasons why the notion of Black has been held on to, despite its contradictions, is that its alternative seems to be ethnic diversity and ethnicity which are regarded as politically vacuous and identified with liberalism and pluralism. But if ethnicity is related to racialization this need not be the case (see Anthias, 1992b). There is an ethnically diverse experience of racism and it is fought in a diverse way. There is a gender diverse experience also. But as Stuart Hall (1989) says, the essentializing it entails, from a political pragmatic position, may serve as a useful rallying cry. But these have the potential to delimit progressive outcomes as in hailing a nationalist cause in the struggle against imperialism and an essential feminist individualism (as a woman's right to choose) in the struggle against sexism.

LINKING THE CATEGORIES – RACE AND CLASS

Much of the debate on 'race' and class (Anthias, 1990), takes as a starting point the economic position of black people and explains this with reference to economic processes and their link to racism. The delimitation of racism to colour racism is another common characteristic of approaches that link 'race' to economic processes or to class.

In much of the analysis that links 'race' and economic processes it is racism as an ideology that connects racialized groups with a specific economic positioning. This involves assumptions about the effects of racism on economic position that treat market mechanisms or capitalist economic processes as secondary. It is not so easy to show that economic disadvantage is the effect either of racism or that racism itself is constructed as the medium by which capital benefits from an underclass that can act either as cheap labour or a reserve army of labour (Castles and Kosack, 1973; Nikolinakos, 1975; Castells, 1975). As Miles (1989) points out, there are a range of exclusionary practices in society that are not merely coterminous with racism but are 'a component part of a wider structure of class disadvantage'.

Such a position not only gives a central causal role to racist ideology, but tends to treat it as a homogenous and systematic set of ideas and practices. It fails to attend to the different forms that are directed against different categories of the racialized population, for example Asians and African Caribbeans, and against men and women. In addition it prioritizes 'race' identification against both class and gender identification, and cannot consider the ways in which gender and race ideologies and practices intersect in producing social outcomes. The notion of a double or triple burden advanced by some writers (Phizacklea 1983, for example, or Westwood 1984), treats the divisions merely in an additive way.

The main notable position that does not focus on the effects of racism in constructing the economic position of black people within a Marxist paradigm is Migrant Labour theory (Castles and Kosack, 1973; Castles, 1975; Nikolinakos, 1975). This focuses on the economic role of migrant labour in capitalist societies and was predicated on the experiences of *Gastarbeiter* or guest workers in Western Europe. Attempts to apply this problematic to Britain by Phizacklea and Miles (1980) have tried to formulate it in relation to settler black migration. In the process the problematic has actually shifted to the whole of the black population rather than to the question of migrants and migration. The unstated assumption in these positions is a homogenous migrant labour category whose embodiment is male.

The postulate of migrants as both a reserve army of labour and cheap labour, found in most of these approaches, is theoretically problematic, however (Anthias, 1980 and 1982). Also, the use of migrants as a reserve is jeopardized by the existence of a segmented labour market or dual labour market that relegates migrants to a subordinate sphere. However, there also exists labour market fragmentation in relation to gender. The position of migrant women is therefore doubly problematized as a reserve army. Post fordism has been depicted also as separating the workforce into a small permanent core and a larger peripheral less skilled sector (Murray, 1988).

The depiction of 'black migrant' labour (Phizacklea and Miles, 1980) as a class fraction, on the other hand, under-emphasizes the heterogeneity of labour categories it presents and the distinct employment characteristics of Asians, Afro-Caribbeans and other colonial migrants (such as Cypriots) is not raised. It also takes no account of gender differentiation within the migrant category. This heterogeneity problematizes the unitary application of 'class fraction'. In addition, the migrant labour problematic fails to consider the 40 per cent of Britain's black population who are not 'migrant'. The concern to show the class bases of black migrant labour allows divisions within the black population to be under-explored. There is in fact a conflation in the problematic and categories used since migrant labour is the focus but this is equated with racialized groups.

LINKING THE CATEGORIES: RACE, ETHNICITY AND GENDER

I have argued before (Anthias, 1991a) that gender divisions are central to understanding the social placement of ethnic minority groups. This does not merely mean that men and women from ethnic minorities are positioned differently in relation to each other. It also means that the social and economic position of men and women from ethnic minorities is partially determined by the ways in which gender relations, both within the ethnically specific cultures of different groups and within the wide society, interact with one another. This interaction has implications for both the positioning of men and women from these groups on the one hand and for the whole of the migrant group on the other. There are therefore two sets of gender relations that are involved, those of the minority and those of the dominant majority. These gender relations then produce a particular class structure for different migrant and ethnic minority groups in conjunction with labour market processes and racialization.

Racialization processes, which relate differently to men and women and the class disadvantages already attendant on migrant and ethnic minority status, will affect the way in which gender relations within the groups may be dynamically constituted in the setting of a racist exclusionary society also. Therefore gender relations are not regarded as static or as predetermined as in much feminist analysis of the labour market (see, for example, Beechey, 1977).

The centrality of gender for the understanding of the patterns of settlement of migrant groups has hardly been touched upon in the available literature. Where the fact of family labour has been noted (Ward and Jenkins, 1984; Wilson and Stanworth, 1988), the implications of this in terms of the centrality of analysing gender relations have been totally missed. Phizacklea (1990) on the other hand is aware of the importance of gender but misses the double set of sexist relations that are implicated for ethnic minority women, i.e. those internal to the group and those of the dominant groups and the state.

The underlying quasi-foundationalism of feminisms – a concern with commonalities amongst women and the female or feminine condition – coexists with theoretical and political pressures to recognize, acknowledge and understand the *differences* amongst women – those of class, of historical context, of state regulation of cultural norms and practices, of ethnicity, of racialization and racism and of political perspectives. These latter raise significant problems, both theoretical and political for feminists.

Most attempts to specify patriarchy (the key conceptual category of feminisms) i.e. to present it not as *one* monolithic system but as the end result of a number of different processes unfortunately has not been very successful. From Zilah Eisenstein's collection on capitalist patriarchy (1979) (an unhappy marriage as Hartmann (1981) has noted) to Silvia Walby's attempt to locate it within a range of institutional contexts (1990) – we find the repetitive monotone of patriarchy as an inevitable outcome of modern social arrangements, as an instance of the oppression, universally of women, by men.

The Black feminist critique, as I have noted elsewhere (Anthias, 1991b) considers these approaches as ethnocentric, pathologizing black experience and making black women invisible, but the call to an Afrocentric feminism (Collins 1990, for example) reinserts the totalising black female subject of experience, thus returning to earlier forms of social theory.

Feminist theories have on the whole, however, assumed a 'generic woman' (Spelman, 1988), and paid little attention to ethnic and 'racial' differentiation, although some positions have recognized the importance of class (Khun and Wolpe, 1978; Delphy, 1977). In the last decade or so, the black feminist movement and a number of other writers turned their attention to gender, ethnicity and race.

The concept of patriarchy has been proposed as an analytical concept by many feminists (for example, Millett, 1970 and Walby, 1990). Its basic premise is the universal existence of male domination over women and it attempts to provide an analysis in terms of the specificity of the relations between men and women. The concept of patriarchy prioritizes relations between men and women and the relations of power that subordinate women *vis-à-vis* men. Such an approach is unable to consider the commonalities between men and women on the basis of racialization or other forms of minority or migrant exclusion and the relations of power women are subjected to from broader social processes. For example, the orientation of women who experience ethnic or racial exclusions to the labour market is often in terms of the economic position of the family unit and the economistic aims of the unit *vis-à-vis* migration (Anthias, 1983). The family may be a site of support (Carby, 1982). In addition the tendency to full-time economic activity is not linked to domination by men but rather to the placement of the whole migrant group within racialized social relations.

However, the sexist bases of ethnic culture, both of the minority and the dominant majority, limit the place to which women can be positioned – but in different ways for different groups. Such sexist bases, however, cannot be accounted for by patriarchy theory, nor can they account for the ways in which two different modes of sexist ideology and practice, internal and external to the group, may operate in different directions and thus intersect to produce distinct effects. For example, where the notion of women as economic dependants is primary in white working-class gender relations, this may not be the case in African-Caribbean gender relations (Phoenix, 1989). Yet the ideology of economic dependency is implicated in producing outcomes for such women in their day-to-day lives through the postulate of economic abnormality. Unlike indigenous women, ethnic minority women are not only subjected to racist exclusions: they are also subjected to two sets of sexist relations. This is central to the position of this paper.

Racist exclusions operate differently, also, on the basis of the sexist relations within ethnic and racialized groups to produce different outcomes. For example, men from such groups may use sexist rules and power in order to counteract ethnic and racialized exclusions as in the super-exploitation of women within 'ethnic economies' such as the clothing industry (Anthias, 1983). Phoenix (1989) has argued that gender relations relating to motherhood amongst young Afro-Caribbean women are not derived from a static cultural attribute but are produced in interplay with the sexist and racist nature of British society. Bhachu (1988) has argued that Sikh women in Britain are taking an important role in the development of business enterprise as a response to racist exclusions that the whole of the Sikh community faces. In other words, gender relations are not static, either, but are produced in interplay with class and racialization processes.

A Marxist analysis of race and gender has been constrained by the fact that the major conceptual categories used, like class and mode of production, are sex-and race-blind, to quote Heidi Hartmann's (1981) well-used phrase. It has usually tried to understand non-class divisions in terms of class relations or tied them more functionally to the needs of capital. The domestic labour debate failed to relate to migrant women's participation in the labour market as primarily either full-time workers (West Indian women specially (Brown, 1984)) or family labourers (Asian and Cypriot women (Anthias, 1982)). They were not constituted as outside the parameters of capitalism either in a distinct domestic mode of production (Harrison, 1973) or as merely servicing the male work force. More than any other category migrant women indicate the problems of focusing on women as housewives primarily (see Molyneaux, 1979 for a useful review of the domestic labour debate). The performance of domestic labour for migrant women was not at the root of their exploitation or oppression.

The consideration of women as a reserve army of labour, on the other hand (Beechey, 1977; Breugel, 1979) failed for other reasons to provide a satisfactory explanation of women's position in the labour market. The reserve army concept could not explain the expansion of women's employment or the existence of a dual labour market (women's jobs) and how women were recruited to this. The view that it was dependence on the male wage that allowed women to be paid less than the cost of the reproduction of their labour (Beechey, 1977) did not account for the existence of a family wage so men would be paid proportionally more (for more detailed conceptual problems see Anthias, 1980).

In relation to migrants and particularly migrant women, it is clear that women could not form a reserve army in an undifferentiated way because of the sectoral nature of their employment. They were recruited for jobs and not as a reserve or a pool of unemployed, and the jobs were those on the whole that the indigenous population did not want. For example, Filipino women were recruited as single women for specific jobs in Britain (see WING, 1985). In addition, African-Caribbean women in particular were often not dependent on the male wage and the ability of capital to pay them lower wages could not be explained through the notion either of a real or an ideological dependence on men.

Feminist theorizations of the position of women in the labour market, particularly the tendency to part-time work for married women, have relied on notions of the way in which gender divisions within the family have necessary implications for labour market participation and positioning (Beechey, 1986). This is very much problematized by the work experiences of migrant women and ethnic minority women who, in spite of patriarchal social relations, have a greater tendency to full-time work. Moreover, such economic participation, even where women have been in a better position than many racialized men in the labour market, has not unproblematically led to changes in their gender subordination (Hoel, 1982; Anthias, 1983).

The partiarchy model and the Marxist feminist political economy approach both give primacy to the separation between men and women in social relations and neither is able to account for the way in which ethnic difference and racialization intersect with gender and class to produce particular effects. In fact, most of the literature on women and work has taken the view that recruitment to work and the labour market is determined by a person's sex. Dex (1987) states that 'Women are clearly concentrated into a small number of occupations and they constitute a very large proportion of certain occupational categories. Researchers are agreed that the majority of jobs can be categorized either as stereotypically female or stereotypically male' (p. 9). Explanations of this segregation that is as high as 63 per cent for women and 80 per cent for men range from employer strategies (Beechey, 1977) to sexist attitudes held by men and women (Vogel, 1990), to exclusion practices by male-dominated trade unions (Rubery, 1978). Such approaches pay little attention to the cross-cutting of racialization.

In addition, it is important to note the intersection of ethnicity, race, gender and class. For example, a quick perusal of labour market processes in Britain as they relate to ethnic minorities acts to nullify notions of a unitary category of ethnic minorities which is positioned only through racism or the internal choices of groups (two alternative explanations adopted by writers and policy makers (Anthias, 1991a)).

Employment has to be understood empirically in the context of the internationalization of the labour market and the tendencies of firms to move to the periphery to draw on the cheap labour of women, both in the Third World and in the advanced societies. This has occurred side by side with the creation of two labour markets, one for permanent white men (a core) and an impermanent casual predominantly female one which includes part-time work (Mitter, 1986). Here segmentation of the labour market is seen as more dramatic, with white males differentiated from racialized or black males but not to such an extent as to warrant treating them in the same category as either white or black females. It appears that although there is sexual segregation, race segregation intersects with this to produce specific effects.

Ethnic minorities are over-represented in the lower echelons of the labour market and are more likely to be unemployed than whites

(Newnham, 1986). However, the ethnic and gender differences within this population serve to problematize the unitary application of racialized groups as a particular class or migrant labour category. Racism or discrimination on its own cannot account for the positioning of any one racialized group. Ethnic disadvantage in the labour market is also linked to the class and gender resources that the group possesses both at the point of entry into the labour market and as a result of the ways in which racialized groups are inserted into wider social relations in the society of migration. In addition, they can draw on familial, gender and ethnic resources in the attempt to manage the disparate structural disadvantages they face on the basis of class, ethnicity, gender and racialization (Anthias, 1991a).

Attempts to explain differences have often relied on notions of different cultural attitudes (Wallman, 1979; Ward and Jenkins, 1984) and different skills and education (Swann, 1985). As Phoenix (1989) argues 'Poor educational achievement of black children of Afro-Caribbean decent is frequently blamed on "father absence"' (p. 24). Explaining Afro-Caribbean women's greater participation in the labour market and in full-time employment with reference to culture is inadequate. As Bryan *et al.* (1985) state, it is the structural constraints faced by black women that spur them to being economically independent. This relates to racialization and class positioning of the groups. Full-time and high activity rates for black women may be accounted for in a number of ways. One of these relates to the generally lower employment status and pay of black men. Another reason relates to the different notions of women's capacities and roles *vis-à-vis* the balance between the sexual division of work in the home and in paid work, different familial structures and expectations and, for first-generation migrants, the economic aims of migration including for some groups, dependents in the country of origin and the 'myth of return' (see Dahya, 1974; Anthias, 1982 and 1992a).

The conditions of entry to the labour market are less favourable than that for white women because of racialization and ethnic exclusion. The over-representation of black women in the non-manual category compared to black men, as Bruegel has argued (1988) results from the broad nature of the non-manual category that hides the class differences within it. However, it is also true that black men, because of disadvantages in the labour market, are not able to support women economically (Hooks, 1981). They gain fewer educational qualifications than Afro-Caribbean women (Fuller, 1983) and are more likely to be unemployed than white men. Both black men and women of

Afro-Caribbean origin belie the dominant gender ideologies in Britain, which relate to the construction of women as dependent on the male breadwinner and men as powerful and able to protect their wives and children. However, although not conforming to gender stereotypes of the dominant society, they are affected by them. Such stereotypes, as many Black feminists have pointed out (Parmar, 1982, for example) have tended to pathologize them.

Some feminists (for example, Pateman, 1988) have argued that citizenship, far from being gender-neutral, constructs men and women differently. The state subject is gendered although essentially constructed as male in its capacities and needs. Such critiques have failed to see that citizenship is also an ethnicized and racialized concept. Men and women are not all constructed by the state in the same way. For example, racialized and ethnic minority women are often deprived of the rights to reproduce the citizens of the state through notions of patriality – for example, in Britain (Klug, 1989), through apartheid (Gaitskell and Unterhalter, 1989) or through religious and state legislation (Yuval Davis, 1989). Thus the state is related to men and women who are racialized in a heterogeneous way. We need to recognize the importance of ethnicity, nationality and racialization. Ethnic minority men and women, through their construction as having limited rights to citizenship and outside the proper boundaries of the nation, and through racialization, can be positioned in a particularly disadvantageous position in the state. This involves an even greater extension of Marshall's notion of formal civil and social rights, to a recognition of citizenship as properly involving rights to pursue diverse cultures and ways of life (as long as they do not obstruct universalist notions of rights of social democracy). It must incorporate rights to be free from informal controls through racism and other structural exclusions, as for example in the labour market, which function through class gender, ethnicity and racialization (Anthias, 1991a).

From this section, it is clear that any attempt to correct disadvantage must take into account not only the different ways it is constructed for different 'categories' of ethnic minorities, but to differences of class and gender. Racism is not only a question of individual prejudice and discrimination to be tackled by legislating against it (although this must be done and more vigilantly undertaken). Class and gender disadvantage needs to be addressed in tandem through a policy of wider social reforms. The discrete tackling of different disadvantages cannot achieve greater equalization on its own.

CONCLUSION

This paper has attempted to show that the unitary, reified and static categories of 'race' and ethnicity used in much ethnic relations research need to be subjected to the interrogation of a more multiplex and sophisticated analysis which recognizes the heterogeneous nature of the phenomena concerned. To abandon these categories and to deconstruct them does not lead to their greater and greater 'disappearance from view' but rather can pave the way for an investigation of the connecting threads between social categories of difference and inequality such as those between gender, 'racialization', ethnicity and class. This requires us to recognize the great diversity with which gender, race and ethnic difference and inequality manifest themselves. It also requires us to recognize that at the level of their structuration they need to be examined with reference to each other and to broader social relations. The use of the terms or concepts of ethnicity, racialization, gender and class should take place within a discourse that is aware on the one hand of their contested nature but also recognizes that they establish not only social ontologies of difference but also practices of inequality. Addressing the ways they intersect and take structure is of paramount importance if our theoretical tools and our substantive research findings are to yield more fruitful analysis in the understanding of ethnicity and racialization in the modern world.

BIBLIOGRAPHY

Amos, V., P. Gilroy and E. Lawrence (1982), 'White Sociology, Black Struggle' in D. Robbins *et al* (eds) *Rethinking Social Inequality*, Gower: Aldershot

Anthias, F. (1980), 'Women and the Reserve Army of Labour', *Capital and Class* No. 10

Anthias, F. (1982), *Ethnicity and Class among Greek Cypriot Migrants – a study in the conceptualisation of ethnicity*, Ph.D Thesis, University of London: London

Anthias, F. (1983), 'Sexual Divisions and Ethnic Adaptation: Greek-Cypriot Women in Britain' in Phizacklea, A. (ed.) *One way Ticket*, Routledge: London

Anthias, F. (1990), 'Race and Class Revisited: conceptualising Race and Racisms', *Sociological Review*, February

Anthias, F. (1991a), 'Gender, Ethnicity and Racialization in the British Labour Market' Paper given to conference on *Migrant Women in the 1990s – cross-cultural perspectives on New Trends and Issues*, Barcelona, January 26–29

Anthias, F. (1991b), 'Parameters of Difference and Identity and the problem of connections' in *International Review of Sociology, special issue on Diversity and Commonality*, Series 2, No. 2, December

Anthias, F. (1992a), *Ethnicity, Class, Gender and Migration: Greek Cypriots in Britain*, Gower: Aldershot

Anthias, F. (1992b), 'Connecting "race" and ethnic phenomena' in *Sociology*, August

Anthias, F. and N. Yuval Davis (1992), *Racialized Boundaries: 'race', gender, colour, class and the anti-racist struggle*, Routledge: London

Beechey, V. (1977), 'Some Notes on Female Wage Labour', *Capital and Class* No. 3

Beechey, V. (1986), *Unequal Work*, Pluto Press: London

Bhachu, P. (1988), 'Apni Marzi Kardhi. Home and Work: Sikh women in Britain' in Westwood, S. and P. Bhachu (eds) *Enterprising Women*, Routledge: London

Bourne, J. (1980), 'Cheerleaders and Ombudsmen: the sociology of race relations in Britain' in *Race and Class*, Vol. xxi, No. 4

Brown, C. (1984), *Black and White Britain*, Policy Studies Institute: London

Bruegel, I. (1979), 'Women as a Reserve Army of Labour', *Feminist Review*, No. 3

Bruegel, I. (1988), 'Black Women in the Labour Market', *Feminist Review*

Bryan, B., Dadzie, S. and S. Scafe (1985), *The Heart of the Race: Black women's lives in Britain*, Virago: London

Carby, H. (1982), 'White Women Listen! Black feminism and the boundaries of sisterhood' in *The Empire Strikes Back,* Centre for Contemporary Cultural Studies, Hutchinson: London

Castells, M. (1975), 'Immigrant Workers and Class Struggle in Advanced Capitalism' in *Politics and Society*, Vol. 5, No. 1

Castles, S. and G. Kosack (1973), *Immigrant Workers in the Class Structure in Western Europe*, Oxford University Press: London

Cohen, A. (1974), *Urban Ethnicity*, Tavistock: London

Cohen, P. and H. Bains (eds) (1988), *Multi-Racist Britain*, Macmillan: London

Collins, P.H. (1990), *Black Feminist Thought*, Unwin Hyman: London

Dahya, B. (1974), 'The Nature of Pakistani Ethnicity in Industrial Cities in Britain' in Cohen, A. *Urban Ethnicity, op cit.*

Delphy, C. (1977), *The Main Enemy*, WRRC: London

Dex, S. (1987), *Women's Occupational Mobility*, Macmillan: London

Dummett, A. (1991), 'Racial Equality and 1992' *Feminist Review*

Eisenstein, S. (ed) (1979), *Capitalist Patriarchy and the case for Socialist Feminism*, Monthly Review Press, New York

Fuller, M. (1983), 'Qualified criticism, critical qualifications', in L. Barton and S. Walker (eds) *Race, Class and Education*, Croom Helm: London

Gaitskell, D. and E. Unterhalter (1989), 'Mothers of the nation: a comparative analysis of the Nation, Race and Motherhood in Afrikaner Nationalism and the African National Congress' in N. Yuval Davis and F. Anthias (eds) *Woman, Nation, State*, Macmillan: London

Gilroy, P. (1987), *There Ain't no Black in the Union Jack*, Hutchinson: London

Hall, S., C. Critcher, T. Jefferson, J. Clarke, B. Roberts (1978), *Policing the Crisis: Mugging, the State and Law and Order*, Macmillan: London

Hall, S. (1989), 'New Ethnicities', *Black Film, Black Cinema*, ICA Documents

Harrison, J. (1973), 'The Political Economy of Housework' in *Bulletin of the CSE*, Winter, pp. 35–52

Hartmann, H. (1981), 'The Unhappy Marriage of Marxism and Feminism, Towards a more Progressive Union', in L. Sargent (ed.) *Women and Revolution: The Unhappy Marriage of Marxism and Feminism*, Pluto Press: London

Hechter, M. (1987), 'Nationalism as group solidarity', *Ethnic and Racial Studies*, Vol. 10, No. 4

Hoel, B. (1982), 'Contemporary Clothing Sweatshops, Asian Female Labour and Collective Organization' in J. West (ed.) *Work, Women and the Labour Market*, RKP: London

Hooks, B. (1981), *Ain't I a Woman – Black Women and Feminism*, South End Press: Boston

Jordan, W. (1974), *White over Black*, Oxford University Press: London

Klug, F. (1989), 'Oh to be in England' in Yuval Davis and Anthias (eds) *Woman, National State*, Macmillan: London

Kuhn, A. and A-M. Wolpe (1978), *Feminism and Materialism*, RKP: London

Miles, R. (1982), *Racism and Migrant Labour*, RKP: London

Miles, R. (1989), *Racism*, Routledge: London

Miles, R. (1991), 'The Articulation of Racism and Nationalism: Reflections on European History'. Paper given to Conference on *Racism and Migration in Europe in the 1990s*, Warwick, September 20–22

Millett, K. (1970), *Sexual Politics*, Hart Davis: London

Mitter, S. (1986), *Common Fate, Common Bond*, Pluto Press: London

Molyneaux, M. (1979), 'Beyond the Housework Debate', *New Left Review*, No. 116

Morokvasic, M. (1991), 'Fortress Europe and Migrant Women', *Feminist Review*

Murray, R. (1988), 'Life after Henry (Ford)' in *Marxism Today*, October

Newnham, A. (1986), *Employment, Unemployment and Black People*, Runnymede Trust: London

Nikolinakos, M. (1975), 'Notes towards a general theory of migration in late capitalism', *Race and Class*, Vol. 17, No. 1

Omi, M. and H. Winant (1986), *Racial Formation in the United States*, Routledge: London

Parmar, P. (1982), 'Gender, Race and Class: Asian Women in Resistance', *CCCS op cit.*

Pateman, C. (1988), *The Sexual Contract*, Polity Press: Cambridge

Phizacklea, A. and R. Miles (1980), *Labour and Racism*, RKP: London

Phizacklea, A. (ed.) (1983), *One Way Ticket*, RKP: London

Phizacklea, A. (1990), *Unpacking the Fashion Industry*, Routledge: London

Phoenix, A. (1989), 'Theories of Gender and Black Families' in T. Lovell (ed.) *British Feminist Thought*, Blackwell: Oxford

Rex, J. (1973), *Race, Colonialism and the City*, Weidenfeld and Nicolson: London

Rubery, J. (1978), 'Structured labour markets, worker organizations and low pay', *Cambridge Journal of Economics*, Vol. 2

Rubery, J. and R.J. Tarling (1983), *Women in the recession*, Economic Reprint No. 68, Dept. of Applied Economics, Cambridge University: Cambridge

Sivanandan, A. (1982), *A Different Hunger*, Pluto Press: London

Spelman, E. (1988), *Inessential Woman*, The Women's Press: London

Swann Report (1985), *Education for All*, HMSO: London

Vogel, C. (1990), *Segregation, Sexism and Labour Supply*, ESRC Working Paper 21

Walby, S. (1990), *Theorizing Patriarchy*, Blackwell: Oxford

Wallman, S. (ed.) (1979), *Ethnicity at Work*, Macmillan: London

Ward, F. and R. Jenkins (eds) (1984), *Ethnic Communities in Business*, Cambridge University Press: Cambridge

Westwood, S. (1984), *All Day, Every Day*, Pluto Press: London

Wilson, P. and J. Stanworth (1988), 'Growth strategies in small Asian and Caribbean businesses' in *Employment Gazette*, January, Department of Employment

WING (Women in Immigration and Nationality Group) (1985), *Worlds Apart, Women under Immigration and Nationality Law*, Pluto Press: London

Yuval Davis, N. (1989), 'National Reproduction and the Demographic Race in Israel', in Yuval Davis and Anthias, *Woman, Nation, State*, Macmillan: London

Yuval Davis, N. and F. Anthias (eds) (1989), *Woman, Nation, State*, Macmillan: London

10 Present Trends in Women's Migration: The Emergence of Social Actors

Giovanna Campani

INTRODUCTION

According to United Nations data, almost half of all international migrants in the world are women; even if official statistics, at world and national level, cannot be considered reliable (they use different sources and are not always up to date), they show a major trend in migratory movements: an increase in the movement of women and an increased number in ethnic communities. In Europe, women constitute around 45 per cent of the immigrant residents.

Women have always played a role in the processes of reproduction of an immigrant labour force in the countries from which they migrated, and migrant women have always formed part of the labour force. During the last twenty years, the growing importance of women as labour has been seen in the phase of de-industrialization and tertiarization which characterizes the passage from industrial to post-industrial society and the shift to services ('flexibility', loss of guaranteed jobs, segmentation, development of the so-called 'informal' economy) (Piore, 1979 and 1986; Reyneri, 1992).[1]

In the present context of international migrations, women cannot be considered marginal economic subjects. Their labour force demand is functional to economic production mechanisms, as well as to social needs (care for children and old people, and domestic help), which cannot be satisfied by the welfare system in the Western world and in the newly industrialized Asian countries (where industrialization is not followed by a welfare system).

As far as gender relations are concerned, migration does not necessarily mean an improvement, as a Eurocentric or Western-centred point of view could suggest, considering Western woman's status which is the model to be followed. According to this point of view, migration – meaning contact with the industrialized 'modern' society, progressive absorption of Western models in family-care and in professional life – is a factor of 'emancipation'.[2]

In fact, through the migratory process, several factors can be considered responsible for the improvement or deterioration in women's position:[3] Tienda and Booth (1991) make a long list of these factors (family and marital obligations, productive roles in the communities of origin and destination, reasons for migration, nature of the move, cultural arrangements that give concrete meanings to social outcomes). Tienda and Booth suggest three possible outcomes of the migratory process, which are empirically interrelated: (1) improvement, (2) erosion and (3) restructured asymmetries. This third position – more difficult to evaluate – seems the most frequent: after a careful consideration of the empirical situations, few changes in women's position are so clear and linear that obvious improvement or deterioration result.

Migration means a restructuring of gender relations, but establishing how migration alters gender relations requires some means of calibrating women's position before and after moving.

Changes in gender relations are often analysed through the categories of tradition and modernity.[4] More than in terms of dichotomy, tradition and modernity should be understood in terms of hybridity and syncretism, combining customs and values.

The analysis of women's position – in order to understand how gender relations are restructured through migration – must consider family and market relations, domestic and market spheres; it must also consider the social relations immigrant women establish inside their own ethnic community, that is with the different informal and formal networks composing their own community, in the receiving society (help and assistance structures, solidarity, anti-racist or women's associations). In the social sphere, women do not limit themselves to taking part in networks and associations created and directed by men, or organized through the receiving society: they produce their own networks and their own associations.

This paper deals with the analysis of networks and associations women produce in their migratory experience: the empirical researches presented have focused informal networks and formal associations where the majority of members are women or where leadership is provided by women. Processes through which immigrant women structure networks and associations, and the emergence of women's leadership, assume a special relevance in the new migratory flows, some of which are made up by a majority of women (from the Philippines, the Cape Verde Islands, Mauritius and, more recently, from Somalia). They have left the home-country for employment, without their family, and have found a professional insertion only in traditional women's jobs (as, for example, domestic work). They have to face two specific difficulties: reproducing their domestic sphere in the receiving country is hindered by their jobs, and their position in the labour market means they have very limited contact with the receiving society.

Through networks and associations, immigrant women try to cope with the restructuring of gender relations, following their specific migratory experience: they reconstruct pieces of family of all female members (sisters, cousins, aunts); they reconsider – as women's groups – their position *vis-à-vis* the men (often in smaller number) of their own ethnic group; they act – as a group – in front of the receiving society networks. The empirical study of networks and associations reveals also different types of interaction between the sociocultural and anthropological models of the society and cultural practices; it shows how this interaction is translated in a collective action.

MACRO- AND MICRO-DIMENSIONS: THEORETICAL APPROACHES

Present sociological theories state explicitly that migrations, as a complex social phenomenon, must be considered at the world level: practically, they cannot be explained or understood from the point of view of just one local and/or national society.

Migration cannot be reduced to the movement of individuals or peoples into one country, as a consequence of economic and political macro-processes, nor can the issues of settlement/return or assimilation/integration be seen from the point of view of a single-state system. The transnationalization of the migratory flows gives to the macro-dimension a broader meaning than the former limited approach: the growing attention to the migratory links (between sending and receiving countries, between migrants and non-migrants, among migrants themselves) and to the networks immigrants produce (transnational networks, interacting with local networks in the receiving country), the interest for the notion of 'diaspora'[5] show the search of different approaches connecting the macro- and the micro-dimension, the economic processes and the social actors.

The connection between the micro- and macro-link cannot be completely understood, if the main unit of analysis which is taken is the individual migrant, or the ethnic group in a national reality. The link appears clearly if the unit of analysis is the migratory link, as a specific social relation, to be understood not only in a logical, but also in an historical and concrete sense.

Sociologically, migrations can be defined as 'social relations', not only logically, but historically and concretely, which bind migrants and non-migrants (those who stayed in the country of origin), immigrants and citizens, foreigners and natives in time and in space.

On the one hand, migratory links have a systemic character – for example, the links among states establishing migratory policies (regulation), and the concrete economic links (business, finance flows, remittances, etc.). On the other, networks (personal, family, village) and migratory chains result from series of micro-interactions.

The connection between macro- and micro-analysis appears in the study of migratory choices and migratory projects: migratory choices and migratory projects are seldom an individual matter. Very often, they are a matter of family and networks, connected with macro-systemic links (migratory policies, economic agreements between countries, transnational flows of labour and capital, etc.).

To summarize: in order to analyse the migratory phenomenon, two levels can be considered:

(a) The systemic one (macro) and the dimensions of economic functionality and institutional integration (labour markets and migratory policies) at the two poles of the movement (sending and receiving country), to explain stability and mobility of each migratory flow;

(b) The personal, family, village networks (micro-level or level of the social actors), expressing, in their internal structure, cultural and sociocultural specificities; this is also the level of identities, claims to identities, and loyalties.

As far as immigrant women are concerned, the macro-analysis shows the importance of women in migratory flows, migratory policies encouraging the migration of maids (from the Philippines and Sri Lanka), and a growing demand for a women's labour force. Even if economic insertion in services apparently reserves for women a marginal social role, their economic weight, both in the sending and receiving countries, should not be underestimated, as different indicators show; for example, the economic balance of the Philippines depends upon the remittances of Filipino maids in Rome or in Hong Kong, as it will be shown in the analysis of domestic work at world level. The macro-analysis helps to overcome a stereotyped view of the maid or of the entertainer as socially marginal characters and shows their economic weight for the sending and receiving countries. The micro-analysis considers how women react in the new context of international migrations, through their social action (through analysis of women's networks), and how gender relations can change.

INTERNATIONAL MIGRATIONS AND THE DEMAND FOR WOMEN'S LABOUR: WOMEN AS ECONOMIC SUBJECTS

There are two traditional migratory models:

- 'Settlement migrations', which mainly concern the transoceanic flows into Europe
- 'Temporary migrations', which mainly concerned Germany and Switzerland in the fifties and sixties.

In these models, women's presence has involved different economic and social roles. In the first case, entire family groups are moving; in the second one, migratory flows are mainly composed of males. In both models, however, women play a central role in the processes of labour force reproduction (in the receiving and in the sending country).

In settlement migrations, a proportion of the women enter the labour market of the receiving country, while in temporary migration, women often stay in the original country, in order to preserve rural economy.

In both models, the woman's role has gained little social recognition either by laws or by research: the central role – mainly economic – in the migratory process has always been occupied by men.

Since the seventies, times and locations of new migrations have changed, as well as their influence on deeply changing societies (Calvanese and Pugliese, 1990).

The Continuous Reporting System on Migration of the OECD (1992) describes a context of acceleration and the worldwide dimension of the flows. 'Worldwide dimension' means the extension of migratory phenomena to regions of the world which had not been or had been scarcely touched until now, both as sending and receiving countries; to give two examples, Asia has become a whole continent of migration, including countries like Japan, where immigration was erstwhile practically unknown; Eastern Europe is becoming again a region of emigration, after a long period of closed borders.

In Europe, we are now witnessing the natural growing of already established immigrant groups and the diversification of new flows, directed also to former emigration countries, such as Italy, Spain and Greece.

Different authors have tried to determine what variables are new in migratory phenomena compared to the past and what has not changed, both at the macro and the micro level. A quite dramatic analysis considers present migrations not as a traditional labour migration, but as a general population movement from South to North, following the socio-economic disaster of the Third World and, more recently, of Eastern Europe (Melotti, 1990). This approach considers immigration in the framework of North-South relations, which are marked today by conflicts, deepened poverty and worsening of economic and social differences. According to this analysis, 'push' factors are much more important than 'pull' factors, the European labour market not needing immigrants (Melotti, 1990; Sergi, 1988). That is why, in the Western World, migration co-exists with unemployment. Policies of closed borders and of drastic filters for new arrivals are the sad answer to these unwanted flows. The consequence of this is the growing importance of clandestine migrants: the only possibilities of getting into Europe are now family reunification and refugee status – and in both categories women play a growing part.

Other authors, even if they do not contradict the 'North-South approach', consider also the socio-economic changes which have taken place in the receiving societies, in the international labour market and in the national ones, because of the industrial restructuring, the increase of flexibility in productive processes, the development of informal economy, the tertiarization, and the segmentation of the labour markets (Palidda, 1992; Reyneri, 1992; Venturini, 1989).

Venturini (1989) writes that migration flows are no longer attracted by an overall quantitative imbalance in the labour markets of receiving countries, but rather by sectorial imbalances which may even arise in situation of unemployment where they are the result of the 'segmentation' process in labour markets and apply mainly to jobs at the lowest or higher rungs of the occupational ladder. In other words, in spite of high unemployment in local populations, there are areas in the labour markets of the European countries (and also in the United States), where there is a demand for an immigrant labour force.

The specificity of this demand particularly concerns a female labour force: the importance of women in the new flows relates to changes in the labour market. The number of active women, migrating alone, for employment purposes, is increasing as a result of:

- the slackening in the international demand for male manpower (Lim, 1990; Weinert, 1991) and the growing demand in traditionally female jobs (maids, nurses and entertainers) (Lim, 1990)
- the processes of informalization, loss of social security benefits and of 'guaranteed' jobs, which create new spaces for the employment of immigrant women in labour-intensive sectors (mainly in the textile and garment industry) (Sassen-Koob, 1984; Morokvasic, 1988) and of tertiarization (including development of services to private persons) (Weinert, 1991).

The employment of immigrant women in the European and international labour market reveals one of the main aspects of the new migratory processes: the change in the economic integration of immigrants, from the industrial sector mainly to the service sector (including services to private persons) and the informal economy.

This change corresponds to the passage from the industrial to the post-industrial society – in economic terms, from the Fordist-Taylorist model to the flexibility and the heterogeneous segmentation of society (Reyneri, 1992). Consequently, immigrant women are a central economic subject in present economic trends, revealing also the migratory link between sending and receiving countries.

The increase in women migrants is also a consequence of the changes in their original countries, which have affected selection processes of migration and the composition of flows. There are now more women, more students and more middle-class migrants; migrants' social and professional origins have also changed: there is an increase in immigrants with high school education and those coming from urban areas.

In the Third World countries, social and cultural changes – destructuring of traditional family structures, 'anticipatory socialization' (Alberoni and Baglioni, 1965) through mass media and, more generally, the diffusion of Western models through consumption models and life-styles, and Urbanization – are destroying social and cultural barriers to emigration.

According to Giannini (1994), the model of work in the society of origin is conditioning the choice of migration and its forms. Women who migrate have already interiorized the possibility that women can obtain an independent role as workers. The micro-approach reveals the importance of 'emancipatory' motivations – influenced by an idealized Western model – among the reasons for departure, particularly for women (Cruz and Paganoni, 1989).

EMPLOYMENT FOR IMMIGRANT WOMEN

Domestic work has traditionally recruited immigrant women in the past; in the present situation, two phenomena should be noted:

- The worldwide dimension of the flows is in no way influenced by factors such as proximity and/or traditional boundaries between sending and receiving countries (there are, for example, maids from the Philippines in Kuwait, and maids from Peru in Italy). The flow of maids also goes to western European countries (especially the southern European countries of Italy, Spain and Greece), the rich industrial Asian countries (Hong Kong and Singapore), the so-called 'oil-monarchies' (Saudi Arabia, Kuwait, United Arab Emirates, Bahrain and Oman), and Latin America, the continent which has the highest percentage of household employees (including national and non-national women).
- A revival of services to private persons, after a period of decline (female domestic staff, gardeners, chauffeurs, etc.) is one of the categories of migrant workers which has recently grown more in various parts of the world; this means the revival of jobs, which had dropped, at least in the European industrial countries, since the postwar years (Bohning, 1991).

Migrant maids have a range of national origins. Women of some national origins are 'more migratory' than others and more 'specialized' than others in services to private persons (from the Philippines, for example, Sri Lanka, Eritrea, Cap Vert, Mauritius or Salvador). This is due both to economic and cultural factors and to the migratory policies of the countries of origin.

Women currently comprise half of the Filipino 'overseas contract workers' labour force, going all over the world as maids, nurses and entertainers; data for legal immigration in the period 1988–86 shows an increase in the annual flow of 36 per cent women in 1980 to 46 per cent in 1986. In Asia (Hong Kong, Singapore and Japan), 90 per cent of Filipino workers are women (maids, nurses or entertainers) (Lim, 1991). But Filipino maids are also in the Gulf countries, in Saudi Arabia, and in Europe. The migration movement of the Filipino women has to do both with the processes of change in women's status in the Philippines (improvements in women's schooling, which mean that many cleaning women have college degrees, and women's pressure on the labour market, where there is little possibility of finding a job because of high unemployment or of being well paid, women's wages being still lower than men's wages, together with interiorization of a Western consumption model), and with the policy of the Filipino government encouraging emigration to earn foreign currency: 'Worldwide, 3.2 million Filipinos' labour abroad send home about $3 billion – no mean sum' (*The Nation*, 5.10.92).

The policy of encouraging migration concerns other countries in Asia: Sri Lanka has developed women's migration to the Middle East through official government bureaux for the placement of domestic workers abroad. There is a great pressure (in the mass media, official speeches and so on) on women to leave, even if their experience in the Middle East is often not very favourable.

Thailand has also become a country of emigration, exporting maids and entertainers, mainly to Hong Kong, Singapore and Japan, but also to Western Europe and the Middle East; the authorities in Bangkok are starting to be worried about a shortage of housemaids for the rich Thai families (the reasons of migration are clear: maids are better paid in Hong Kong than in Bangkok).

As far as African countries are concerned, the Mauritius Islands have a long tradition of exporting maids to Europe. The Cap Verde islands have since the seventies supplied rich families in Italy with maids. The Catholic Church, and especially the Capucin Fathers, have played an important role in channelling this immigration. Cap Verde women work as maids also in Spain. In Portugal, Cap Verde immigration concerns both men and women: still, women are often maids, having taken the place rural Portuguese women held in the past. Portuguese women are still domestic helpers in France and in Great Britain, but they are seldom live-in maids.

Eritreans have provided domestic help since the sixties to rich Italian families and a more recent flow of Somalian women, working mainly as maids, has arrived in Italy, following the tragic events of the civil war.

Latin-American women migrate not only to other countries of the continent (from Colombia to Venezuela, or from Bolivia to Argentina), but also to Western Europe. Since the seventies, there have been in Italy maids from Salvador and now there is an important flow from Peru.

From Islamic countries, women do not generally migrate alone, but there are more and more exceptions – for example, Egyptian women going to the Middle East as nurses, teachers and maids (Saleh, 1988), Indonesian women going to Singapore as maids and also Sri Lankan women, some of whom are Muslim (Dias, 1987). The stereotype of the Islamic woman as passive and forbidden to work because of family constraints does not help us to understand a much more complex and differentiated reality. In most of our researches on Islamic women in Italy, I have interviewed quite a few Moroccan women, who have come alone to be maids: they are mainly widows or women with grown-up children. This trend – coming mainly from the big cities – is definitely growing and should be followed by researchers, because it reveals interesting changes in the migratory flows from North Africa.

The working conditions of maids vary largely from one country to another, but the general situation is far from attractive:

> The general picture emerging from the literature, research work and newspaper reports, is that foreign female domestic workers are highly exploited both in the developed and in the developing countries. (Weinert, 1991, p. 2)

There are some observations to make on domestic work: we are not only witnessing the substitution of national women labour force, now refusing to do a job which presents too many disadvantages as live-in domestic work, but we are also witnessing the revival of this job in the same industrial countries, where it had dropped in the post-war years and where, nowadays, there is a broadening of social groups asking for maids.

> The increasing phenomenon of migrant women working as domestic servants can equally be attributed to the growing wealth of the rich countries, enabling families to pay for households; a demand that cannot be met by the national workforce owing to the work's low social status, low pay and precarious working conditions. (Weinert, 1991).

In fact, the phenomenon is complex and can be attributed to different factors. One of these factors is the development of professional activity and mobility among Italian women, which is not matched by adequate social services. The connection between the lack of social services (particularly for children and old people) for working women and the increase of the demand for immigrant maids has been made by different researchers in Southern Europe, particularly in Italy and in Greece (Pugliese and Macioti, 1991; Emke Poulopoulos, 1990), where, by the way, women had, for a long time, low labour rates.

But this connection is also recognized by the policies of different governments, giving, in spite of the closed borders, entry visas to immigrants coming on domestic work contracts (as Italy did until 1990). The government of Singapore recognizes this connection openly:

... hiring foreign maids helps to encourage our women, especially those with marketable skills and qualifications, to continue working and raise families. (*Straits Times*, 20/12/1989).

To understand the phenomenon of domestic work, the Italian researcher Enrico Pugliese adds another element:

On one hand, the use of maids is a necessity, determined by the lack of social services in our country: families with just one parent or with both parents working are forced to look for this type of service. On the other hand, the preference for the archaic relationship with the maid, available all day long, expresses a certain type of mentality or the will to reaffirm old habits which, with the civil development of our country during the sixties, seemed largely outdated. (Pugliese and Macioti, 1991, p. 57).

Even if concerned only with the Italian case, the considerations of Pugliese can be applied to other countries too, particularly in Southern Europe.

The mentality which prefers the archaic relationship with the maid (the servant-master relationship), can be seen as the survival of old habits, but it is also the product of an over-fast 'modernization', without the progressive interiorization of the values expressed by what we could call the 'social democratic' model of the industrial society (it is not by chance that in Sweden or Denmark, live-in domestic work has practically disappeared, whereas the Italian middle and small bourgeoisie, recently promoted to a higher standard of living, considers the maid as a sort of status symbol).

Paradoxically, this mentality combines old and new: it corresponds in fact to the new 'modern' ideologies (which, by the way, are beginning to be questioned), glorifying together the free market, privatization and individualism. The present policies encouraging privatization, the dismantling of public services, the reduction of State expenses, which have been introduced all over the world, including social services for children and old people, and which could allow women to work, have indirectly favoured the development of private services to privileged people. Immigrant women thus answer important social needs.

The recourse to immigrant maids by the women of the 'rich' world brings into question the relation between gender, race and class. We have in fact the example of how women of rich countries, belonging to the middle-upper classes and enjoying the possibility of having an interesting professional life, contribute to the oppression of women of poor countries. We may also wonder if the present economic phase (wild liberalism, the cutting of welfare programs) doesn't risk bringing a polarization between white women, whose number at a high professional level is increasing – and 'ethnic' women at the bottom (Phizacklea, 1992).

This contradiction appears in fact in the relations which immigrant and non-immigrant women establish in associations and networks.

SOUTH EUROPE AND IMMIGRANT WOMEN: THE CASE OF ITALY

In the European Community there are six million immigrant women (out of around thirteen million immigrants); of these, four million come from non-EEC countries. Minority women number many more, considering the naturalized (those who have taken on the nationality of the receiving country). Immigrant women living in the European Community have different experiences; we can try to define four types or typologies:

- immigrant women already settled, belonging to settled groups, who came generally through family reunification
- their daughters, the so-called second generation
- the women who arrived with the new flows for employment purposes
- the women arriving in Southern Europe through family reunion.

In Southern European countries, it is the last two typologies of immigrant women who are common. This is the case in Italy, too.

Italy was an emigration country until the end of the sixties, the flows being mainly directed, at this time, from Southern Italy to Germany and Switzerland. During the seventies, a few flows of immigrants started to arrive: political refugees from Latin America, Vietnam and Eritrea and 'border immigrants', Tunisians in Sicily working on fish boats and in agriculture, and Yugoslavs in Frioul and Trieste, working mainly in construction (Frioul had been destroyed by an earthquake in 1976).

Women were among the first immigrants, coming as maids from the Cape Verde islands, Eritrea, Mauritius, Salvador and, later, the Philippines and Sri Lanka (maids were given a special resident's permit, not having the possibility of changing their job). Women's flows were among the first ones which arrived to Italy, and women always constituted an important part of immigration, because of the high demand for maids. At the end of the eighties, when the first regularization law was passed, women represented 45 per cent of the immigrant population. They are presently 42 per cent of the immigrant population, but in some areas, such as Florence, where the sector of services is important, they are more than 50 per cent.

In the labour market,[6] the majority of the women who came alone are still mainly employed in the domestic sector, such as maids (live-in domestic helpers). This concerns particularly some national groups, such as the Filipino or the Cap Verdian, where the men:women ratio is very unbalanced, women being 70–90 per cent.

There has been a passage from live-in domestic work to domestic help, but even this small professional promotion has been limited, because of the difficulties of finding a house (which is a problem not only for the immigrants, but also for the Italians). It must also be considered that the possibilities of savings are reduced if live-in work is abandoned. Consequently, the change is not always profitable for immigrant women.

One possibility could be employment as nurses in the hospitals (some, especially Filipinos, work already in private clinics). But conditions of entry to the Italian nursing schools are very strict, and, because of the employment crisis, this possibility has been delayed.

In spite of the absence of professional perspectives, women's immigration to Italy is beginning to be more and more diversified: Maghrebian women are coming for family reunification, Chinese women in family migration come to work in the Chinese small enterprises, and Eastern European women present a great variety of professional activities.

Unlike active women coming alone, who have been in Italy for twenty years, migration through family reunification is recent, dating back to Laws 943 of 1988 and 39 of 1990, and still limited, because of the precarious integration of male immigrants, not being able to guarantee a stable job and a house. This migration concerns mainly women from the Maghreb – Morocco and Tunisia, who rarely enter the labour market, even if their schooling and qualification level is much higher than that of their mothers' generation, who had migrated to France in the sixties. The Maghrebian women, who are, as we will see, practically absent from the life of associations, are very active in their private life. They have developed attitudes towards their family and towards work quite different from the ones developed by immigrant women who went to France in the sixties, to whom researchers and social workers had attributed the stereotype of the 'passive Maghrebian woman'. They are active, they do not hesitate to approach social workers if their husbands are too authoritarian, to divorce if necessary and to continue life on their own. Changes in gender structures do not concern only immigrant women; they are taking place on both sides of the Mediterranean (Giannini, 1994).

Another case of immigrant woman in Italy is that of the Chinese, coming from the People's Republic of China, the province of Zehjang. They are either self-employed (restaurants and leather and handicraft) or employed inside the community (by Chinese employers). The Chinese have succeeded in reproducing in Italy the model of economic-family organization of their world diaspora: women are a necessary component of this organization (Campani *et al.*, 1994).

We have pointed out that the possibilities of mobility for immigrant women are very scarce: still, other pieces of research carried out in Italy point out their ability to realize a migratory project, their strategies in front of the family of origin and their initiatives to improve their situation in spite of the constraints induced by the migratory situation: abilities, strategies and initiatives which seem in contradiction with their working position.

In fact, the specific characteristics of the new migratory flows generate contradictions: just to give an example, let us consider the fact that many immigrant women have a high level of education and are of middle class social origin (for example, the majority of the Filipinos and the majority of women from Eastern Europe) and are forced to accept jobs as maids. However, it is precisely because of these abilities, and their class origin, that immigrant women manage to develop social relations among themselves, and a collective action, ending up in an associative life.

The next part of this paper will present two different research projects on immigrant women's social life: the first one concerns an informal network of Filipino women in Florence, the second one concerns formal women's associations in Florence and elsewhere in Italy. They analyse the specific developments in networking and associative life in women-dominated groups, in comparison with groups where the men:women ratio is more balanced. The Filipino group[7] is a prime example, being mainly composed of women (60–70 per cent), married and unmarried, who came alone to Italy, for employment purposes.

The research on immigrant women's associations was carried out under the auspices of the Women's Lobby, an association of Socialist Women established in London. The Women's Lobby mainly aimed to understand the scarce interest of European structures for black, migrant and refugee women and verify the absence of pressure groups of immigrant women. Yet, if the goals of the Women's Lobby were mainly practical, we could develop other issues, through the research. While Florence has been the place where the majority of the interviews have been done, this research has tried to give a general view of women's associations in Italy through interviews in Rome and Bologna with associations' leaders and experts.

In the choice of associations, it was impossible to be limited to women's associations, or associations where the leadership is controlled by women. Mono-ethnic associations[8] of immigrant women are rare (Cape-Verdians, Somalians, Nigerians and Arabs). However, immigrant women are also active in multi-ethnic associations and in Italian associations, national and local, engaged in anti-racism, feminism or voluntary work.

The research has chosen the following types of associations:

- foreigners' mono-ethnic
- foreigners' multi-ethnic
- foreigners' cultural, mono-ethnic and multi-ethnic
- mixed Italians-foreigners, anti-racist
- Italian anti-racist
- Italian feminist.

Beyond the two research projects in Italy, I am presently developing comparative research in Italy and in Portugal, concerning the associative life of women from Cape Verde: this research shows the difference in the migratory trajectories of Cape Verde women coming alone as maids (as in the case of Italy), or through family reunification (in the case of Portugal).

The three research projects are part of a more general project on immigrant women, whose issues are changes in gender structures – from the countries of origin to the host countries – through the migratory process. Immigrant women are not marginal social actors, being able to cope with contradictory situations: the breaking-up of traditional family structures, while men are still dominating in immigrant communities, ambitious migratory projects and the impossibility of getting out of domestic work, class origin not corresponding to the social and professional position in the receiving country, and difficulty in combining work for the family with work for the market.

AN INFORMAL NETWORK OF FILIPINO WOMEN IN FLORENCE

This research examined an informal network of six Filipino women, coming from the town of San Pablo in Luzon Island. The six women are between 20 and 42 years old: four of them are married, all with children; two are not married and one of them is a single mother. Among them, they have kinship or neighbourhood relationships. They all come from the same 'barrio' (district). They belong to the social class which could be defined 'Filipino petty bourgeoisie'. In the country of origin, they were primary school teachers, secretaries, employees, daughters and wives of small employees, functionaries or tradesmen. They all speak Tagalog, the language of the majority of the Filipinos.

In Florence, they are all live-in maids, living in the employers' houses. Just one of them lives in a flat with her child and the old man of whom she is taking care.

The 'leader' of the network is A, 36 years old, who has been in Italy for five years. In the Philippines she was a secretary, married to a policeman. She has three children: when she left, the older one was eleven years old, the second child was seven and the third little girl not yet two. A had decided to leave with her sister for Italy, seeing the economic success other people from San Pablo had attained in Italy.

A had to leave first, alone, because her sister had no money to pay for the air-ticket. A promised her sister she would send her the air-ticket from Italy, when she had earned enough. Inside the family, the decision to migrate was taken by the women, and by the women alone; they spoke with their husbands and, although the latter were not particularly keen on this choice, they accepted it as the only possible way to ensure a good life for the children. A asserts she migrated because she wanted their children to study, a dream which would have never become true with the wages she and her husband could get in the Philippines. There were no conflicts between her husband and herself – on the contrary, the relationship was good: the economic conditions have pushed A to leave her family.

A arrived in Italy through a San Pablo agency, together with another Filipino woman. In Italy she had the address of a person coming from the same 'barrio'. The agency sent A to work in Ancona, a town on the Adriatic coast, but A felt isolated and decided to get in touch with the friend whose address she had in Milan. The friend found her work with a family of actors. For two years, A longed for her sister, wishing to have at least 'a small piece of family' with her. Through another friend, coming from the same 'barrio' of San Pablo, she found a job as a maid in Florence, where there was an important concentration of people from San Pablo. After working for two years in Italy, A had saved enough money to send for her sister. B, the older sister of A (she is 38 years old) came to Italy two years ago, leaving six children. She arrived in Italy through the same agency her sister had used.

C, cousin of A and B, is 24 years old and married to a bank employee; she has two small children (one is just a baby, one year old) and came six months after B (she had enough money to pay her trip), with the purpose of buying a house back home. In fact, the family was forced to live with her husband's parents and she could not bear it.

Later, an aunt of A, B, and C came: D is 42 years old, was a teacher in the Philippines, and came to make it possible for her three children to study.

A has also helped a neighbour, E, who is only 20 years old, to come: she has been pushed by her mother to migrate. E is taking care of an old man. She does not want to stay in Italy, but she has progressively adapted herself to the situation and is protected by the small network. She is in love with a man from Sri Lanka and she has introduced in the network a girlfriend, F, who had a child from another man from Sri Lanka. This girl is the only one in the network coming from Manila and not from San Pablo. She is an unusual case, having migrated not for economic reasons, but for 'adventure' and 'desire to know the world', as she says. She would like to stay in Italy and to set up a family with the man from Sri Lanka, the father of her child, who, apparently, is not ready to do it.

A and B have helped a girlfriend from San Pablo to leave Saudi Arabia, where she was being 'exploited excessively'. She came to Italy where she has found a better position. G has been part of the network for a while, while working in Florence, but now she has followed her employer to Milan.

Presently the network is made up of A, B, C, D, E, F.

The function of A is that of a 'leader': she has played a major role organizing the migratory chain of relatives and neighbours, she has provided the money necessary to migrate and has found jobs for her relatives and friends.

If the migration of B was already foreseen from the beginning, that of C and D was not. The reciprocal borrowing of money among the girls of the network seems a usual practice, not limited to the moment of departure. This practice leads to mutual duties and mutual dependence; up to now, the dependence has been accepted, the solidarity is very strong and no conflicts have appeared.

A is recognized as leader of the small group because of her greater experience: she helps to find jobs, gives advice on the way to behave in Italy, on the best way to save money and to invest it in the Philippines, on the way to handle the husbands and the children; she knows the Italian social workers or the nuns who can help in case of need, the cheap Italian doctors, the stewards of Philippines Airlines, who can take remittances home, illegally, in order to avoid paying taxes. During the group interviews, it was always A who answered more than the other members of the network. Still, A needs the other women, the 'small piece of family' – as she calls it – she has been able to reconstruct in the immigration country.

The six girls call each other by telephone almost every day (the employers allow it) and meet twice a week in a Florentine square, Piazza Santa Maria Novella, one of the meeting points of immigrants (not only Filipinos). In fact, because of the high percentage of live-in maids, the lack of personal flats, the absence of immigrant districts, because of the scattering in cheap hotels, hostels (both religious or communal), in all the Italian towns, 'meeting points' have become the central place for the social life of the immigrants.

In Santa Maria Novella, the girls can talk, eat Filipino food sold by other Filipinos who have an apartment and are able to cook, meet other Filipinos and exchange information on the situation in the home country or the problems of immigrants in Italy. They also meet some male friends (they normally choose friends from Sri Lanka, to avoid gossip inside the Filipino community).

The network takes part in some activities of the formal associations, such as mass, parties, dinners and religious feasts, the most important one being the feast of the Santacruzan in May.[9] They take part in these activities, but they are not individually members of any association.

The San Pablo network is an interesting example of a family migratory chain composed and directed wholly by women: men seem to be quite absent in all the processes of decision-making concerning migration and the use of remittances; all the investments (to buy a 'jeepney',[10] to buy a house, to change the furniture) are decided by the women who earn the money. The family of origin is a large one, composed not only of the parents and the children, but also of the grandparents, the aunts and the uncles. But this large family does not seem to have a 'decision-centre': the husband, the father and the grandfather do not seem to have more authority than the women. A states, however, that the position of women has changed compared to the time of her mother and that now, men and women decide together, and collaborate in raising the children, etc. Migration seems to have reinforced the position of women (at least, that is the immigrant women's point of view).

Migration has meant increased availability of money for immigrant women, whose opportunity to take decisions inside the family has grown, including decisions concerning the husband (such as buying a jeepney for the husband). The autonomy obtained through the migration – and also in the family decision making – is probably one of the reasons why the moment to go back is constantly postponed by all the six women. There are of course other reasons for it: the important gains in Italy and the difficulty in finding an interesting investment in the Philippines, which would allow the big families to live well, for example.

The suffering imposed by the separation from husband and children seems to find a sort of compensation in a new autonomy, a new role women can play in the family. Another compensation can come from the pleasures of the consumption society, which women can taste in Italy. The consumption model has been in fact strongly internalized by the Filipinos, because of the influence of the American culture in the islands. It is not by chance that Filipinos are called 'brown Americans'. To taste even the crumbs of Western consumption society is heaven for the Filipino women, who consider that the most pleasant moment of their migration experience is when they buy things to bring or to send home (Cruz and Paganoni, 1989).

INFORMAL AND FORMAL FILIPINO NETWORKS

Informal networks, like the one we have described, are numerous inside the Filipino group: these networks gather themselves inside the formal associations and take part in their activities. The Filipino group in general combines a strong solidarity from the ethno-cultural point of view and a political division between the left-oriented associations and the ones which depend on the Catholic church. This division exists at the national and local level (in Florence there are two associations, one left-wing-oriented and one supported by the Catholic Church).

The formal associations have different functions of help, solidarity, information, mediation with Italian social forces (trade unions, etc.) and Italian authorities. The left-oriented associations try to put their members in contact with the trade unions and to make their members aware of political questions.

All the associations try to maintain the Filipino cultural identity through activities such as folklore groups, religious feasts, masses in the language of origin, the great feast of the Santacruzan once a year, and as preparation, involving all the Filipino communities in Italy.

Women are dominant not only as members of the associations but also as leaders. The two Filipino associations in Florence have both women as president and vice-president. The four national Filipino associations (Life, Kamapi, Kampi and Afli)[11] are directed by women. The women's leadership has emerged mainly through the 'legitimization' from the base, inside the small informal networks, and the progressive contacts among them to create a formal association. In the Catholic-oriented associations, the 'legitimization' has often come from Filipino priests, who have been in Italy for many years, collaborating with different associations.

WOMEN'S LEADERSHIP AND ASSOCIATIONS

This research on formal associations has collected fifteen in-depth interviews with immigrant women leaders. Thirteen interviews have been done in Florence and two at the national level. We do not have national data on women's associations or women leaders. The last research of the Iref[12] on 212 associations promoted by immigrants (mono-ethnic and multi-ethnic) does not take the gender variable as a criterion of classification (Iref, 1993).

What emerges from the interviews, the field observation and the data collected in the associations?

It is much easier for immigrant women to develop informal networks than to create formal associations having an official status; it is as if immigrant women were frightened by bureaucratic practices and the fact of facing the 'public life'.

The mono-ethnic associations directed by women are not numerous at the national level: there are only those of immigrant women from the Philippines, from Cape Verde, from Somalia and Nigerian women.

At local level there are multi-ethnic women's associations. For example, in Florence, there is Bystress, an association of African women from Ghana, Senegal, Cameroon and Gambia, which has developed new kinds of solidarity, social and cultural activities in spite of the cultural and religious differences. Associations of 'Arab' women, gathering Maghrebians and Egyptians, exist in different Italian towns (Florence, for example, and Bologna). Islamic women are sometimes leaders of associations. In Florence there are cultural associations – Iranian and the Iraqi – directed by women.

If the general picture is not very encouraging, it must not be forgotten that, in a situation of recent immigration such as the Italian one, the women's associative movement is already quite developed and is developing further. The involvement of immigrant women in associative life cannot be limited to the ethnic – mono-ethnic or multi-ethnic – associations: they take part in Italian associations engaged on issues such as racism and anti-racism, both national and local; in feminist associations, where there are often interesting discussions on ambiguous notions such as emancipation, tradition, modernity, etc.; and in mixed associations of Italians and immigrants inspired by the principles of voluntary work and solidarity.

The main points which have emerged through this research are:

- The class origin, or the level of education, is an important factor which encourages or allows the women's leadership; still, in some groups, as for example, the one of Cape Verde women, promotion through study has been done starting from the lower instruction level (at least for the generation of the Revolution);

- The relationship with the Italian feminist movement is not always easy, the attempt to develop specific 'emancipatory' models being quite common among all the ethnic groups. Immigrant women often criticize the models Italian women propose and seek to combine different values and cultural characteristics. This research on a 'third way' for women between a 'tradition' which is criticized and is going through a destructuration process in the country of origin, and a Western model, is particularly strong among Islamic women, who perceive that it is precisely around Islam that the strongest point of conflict exists between Western society and the other.

- The activities women develop in associations are mainly of solidarity and self-help. The cultural activities are female-oriented: talking together in the Western feminist tradition is an important element, but there are also dances, folklore activities, care of the body (it is very important for all the immigrant women to get the beauty products of their country of origin through frequent trips home), particularly for the African women. In the cultural groups, art activities such as painting and poetry are important opportunities for joining together. The observation of these activities has suggested the possibility of theorizing a sort of 'female ethnicity', combining cultural tradition and modernity, the traditional forms of being together with the feminist model of talking together. This point would, of course be better analysed with more field observation.

- Women's associations are still quite absent from the political scene. They take part in anti-racist demonstrations, immigrant meetings and other types of activities, but they seldom take the political initiative.

They are always dominated by the men's leadership in relation to the local authorities, in the possibility of getting financing and support, with the exception of Filipinos and Cape Verdians.

Immigrant women find it difficult to express themselves in the public sphere (the relationship of private/public in the action of immigrant women must be deeply analysed), even if some of the official representatives of immigrants are women (on television, a woman from Cape Verde, directs the only programme for immigrants and the main Italian Trade Union, the CGIL, has a Filipino woman responsible for the immigration sector).

CONCLUSION

The empirical analysis of women's networks and associations at microlevel, mainly limited to the town of Florence, cannot be understood if the general background – economic, social and cultural – against which women's migrations take place is not taken into account.

The micro-analysis confirms that immigrant women are not marginal economic subjects, even if they are confined to the work of live-in maids. This job – and the differential earnings compared to the country of origin – gives immigrant women power in relationship to their family of origin and the possibility of decision making, as the San Pablo women show.

Migration does not mean an improvement in status, but it means a restructuring of gender relations. Women's role in associative life traditionally dominated by men is changing. Women – including Islamic women – can be leaders of associations and try to develop a sort of 'ethnicity' in a women's perspective. If the class origin is quite important in the capacity of assuming a formal life of association, the high presence of qualified immigrant women in almost all the ethnic groups – a peculiar character of the new flows – makes this capacity possible.

The development of networks and of associations takes place in a country – Italy – where, in contrast with Northern Europe, women do not belong to settled migrations, but to the most recent flows. This means the acceleration of the processes of change in gender structures, at the world level: on these changes migration acts as catalyst.

It is difficult to say which direction the changes in gender structures will take. It seems that immigrant women are looking for specific ways, different from the Western models of gender relations, even if the dream of something is covered with mist.

BIBLIOGRAPHY

Alberoni, F., Baglioni, C. (1965), *L'integrazione dell'immigrato nella società industriale* (*The integration of the immigrant in the industrial society*), Bologna, Il Mulino

Andezian, S., Streiff-Fenart, J. (1981), *Les réseaux sociaux des femmes maghrébines immigrées, en Provence-Côte d'Azur*, Thèse de Doctorat de Ille- cycle, Université de Nice

Anthias, F. (1989), Gendered Ethnicities and Labour Market Processes in Britain, paper presented at the Conference 'Transitions', Science Center for Social Research/Labour Market and Employment Unit, May 13/14 Berlin, p. 44

Anthias, F. and Yuval Davis, (1992), *Racialized Boundaries, Race, Nation, Gender, Colour and Class and the Anti-Racist Struggle*, London and New York, Routledge

Balibar, E. and Wallerstein, I. (1990), *Race, nation, classe, les identités ambigües*, Paris, Editions la Découverte

Bhachu, P.K. (1985), *Twice Migrants*, London, Tavistock

Bohning (1991), Introduction to Weinert, *op. cit.*

Boumedienne, T.H. (1988), 'Work and Associative life amongst North African Women in France', paper presented to the Conference, Women in International Migration, Social, Cultural and Occupational Issues, Berlin Technische Universitat and UNESCO, October

Boyd, M. (1990), 'Migration Regulations and Sex Selective Outcomes in Settlement and European countries', paper presented at the United Nations Conference, International Migration Policies and the Status of Female Migrants, San Miniato, 27–30 March

Brah, A. (1985), 'Les femmes du Sud-Est asiatique en Grande-Bretagne: questions concernant l'emploi, l'éducation et la culture', in *Conseil de l'Europe*, DECS/ EGT

Calvanese, F. and Pugliese, E. (1990), 'I tempi e gli spazi della nuova immigrazione in Europa' in *Inchiesta*, October–December

Campani, G. (1988), 'Le politiche di stop' in Sergi, N. (ed.) *L'immigrazione straniera in Italia*, Edizioni Lavoro, Rome

Campani, G. (1993), 'I reticoli sociali delle donne immigrate in Italia' in Delle Donne, M., Melotti, U., Petiffi, S. (ed.) *Immigrazione straniera in Italia Solidarietà e conflitto*, CEDISS, Rome

Campani, G. (1989), 'Du Tiers Monde à l'Italie: une nouvelle migration féminine', *Revue Européenne des Migrations Internationales* (Poitiers), vol. 5, n. 2, pp. 29–47

Campani, G. (1991), 'Donne immigrate' (Immigrant women), in Cocchi, C. (ed.) *Stranieri in Italia*, Bologna, Istituto Cattaneo

Campani, G., Carchedi F., Tassinari, A. (1994), *L'immigrazione silenziosa. Le Comunità cinesi in Italia*, Fondazione Giovanni Agnelli, Turin

Chan Kwok Bun, (1994), 'Migrazioni, dispersione e identità: il nuovo cinese d'oltremare', in Campani, Carchedi, *Tassinari, op. cit.*

Cruz, V., Paganoni, A. (1989), *Filipinas in migration, big bills and small change*, New Manila, Quezon City, SMC Scalabrini Migration Center

De Troy, C. (1988), *Femmes migrantes et emploi*, CEE, Direction Générale de l'Emploi, des Affaires Sociales et de l'Education, Seminaire Communautaire,

Bruxelles, 17–18 Septembre 1987

Dias, M. (1987), *Female Overseas Contract Workers*, Sri Lanka, Colombo, CENWOR

Do Ceu Esteves, M. (1991), *Portugal, Pais de Imigraçao*, (Portugal, country of Immigration), Lisboa, Istituto de Estudlo para o Desenvolvimento, Caderno 22

Dominelli, L. (1988), *Anti-racist Social Work*, Macmillan Education LDT Houndmills

Emke-Poulopoulos, I. (1990), 'Metanastes xai prosfughes sten Ellada 1970–1990' (Immigrants and Refugees in Greece 1970–1990), in *Exloghe*, (Athenes) April–June 1990, June–September, 1990, 85/86

Eurostat (1992), *Indagine sulle forze lavoro*, Statistical Institute of the European Community

Giannini M. (1994), 'Donne del Sud', in Vicarelli, G. (ed.), *Le mani invisibili, La vita e il lavoro delle donne immigrate*, EDIESSE, Rome

Gimetz, A. Wilpert, C. (1987), 'A micro-society or an ethnic community? Social organization and ethnicity among Turkish migrants in Berlin', in J. Rex, D. Joly and C. Wilpert, (eds.) *Immigrant Associations in Europe*, Aldershot, Gower & ESF

International Migration Review, Special issue, Women in Migration, 68, vol. 18, Winter 1984

Labos, (ed.) (1991), *Politiche sociale e bisogni degli immigrati*, Rome, TER

Liauzu, C. (1993), 'Les migrations dans l'enseignement de l'histoire en France' in Campani, G. (ed.), *Educazione interculturale una prospettiva internazionale*, Tecnodid, Rome (in print)

Lim, L.L. (1990), 'The Status of Women in International Migration: background paper for the meeting on International Migration Policies and the Status of female Migrants', *United Nations*, 27–30 March, San Miniato

Melotti, U. (1990), 'L'immigrazione straniera in Italia: da caso anomalo a caso' esemplare (Foreign Immigration to Italy: from anomaly to model). In Cocchi C. (ed.) *Stranieri in Italia*, Bologna, Istituto Cattaneo, pp. 31–44

Morokvasic, M. (1988), *Entreprendre au féminin en Europe: cas des immigrées et des minorités en France, Grande Bretagne, en Italie, au Portugal et en République Fédérale d'Allemagne. Motivations, situations et recommandations pour Actions*, Commission des Communautés Européennes, Direction Générale de l'Emploi, des Affaires Générales et de l'Education

Morokvasic, M. (1993), Emerging Trends and Major Issues in Migration and Ethnic Relations in Western and Eastern Europe, paper presented at the International Seminar organized by UNESCO-CRER, Radcliffe House, 5–8 November 1993, pp. 460–483

OECD, OCDE, SOPEMI, (1992), *Tendances des migrations internationales*, Paris, p. 164

Palidda, S. (1992), 'Eurocentrisme et réalités effectives des migrations', *Migrations Sociétes*, Paris, vol. 4, no. 24, Nov.–Dec.

Piore M.J. (1979), *Birds of passage: Migrant Labour and Industrial Societies*, New York, Cambridge University Press

Piore M.J. (1986), The Shifting Grounds for Immigration, in Annals Aaps

Phizacklea, A. (1992), A Single or Segregated Market?: Gendered and Radicalized Divisions, BSA Conference 1992 University of Kent at Canterbury, April 8th, p. 14

Pugliese, E., Macioti, M.I. (1991), *Gli Immigrati in Italia*, Roma-Bari Laterza

Reyneri, E. (1992), 'L'innovazione produttiva nella rete delle relazioni sociali', in *Stato e Mercato*, no.23, August, pp. 147–176

Saleh, S. (1988), Egyptian Women in Oil Countries, paper presented at the UNESCO Conference on Migrant Women, Berlin, October

Sassen-Koob, S. (1984), Notes on the incorporation of Third World women into wage labour through immigration and off-shore production, in *International Migration Review*, n. 4

Schwartz-Seller, M. (1981), *Immigrant Women*, Philadelphia, Temple University Press, p. 347

Sergi, N. (ed.) (1988), *L'immigrazione straniera in Italia*, Editizioni Lavoro, Rome

Simon, J.J. (1989), *The Consequences of Immigration*, Oxford, Basil Blackwell

Taboada-Leonetti, I. (1983), 'Le rôle des femmes migrantes dans le mantien ou la destruction des cultures nationales du groupe migrant', in *Studi Emigrazione* n. 70

Tienda, M. and Booth, K. (1991), Gender, Migration and Social Change, in *International Sociology*, vol. 6, N. 1, pp. 51–72

United Nations Population Division, (1990), Department of International Economic and Social Affairs, Measuring the Extent of Female International Migration. Paper prepared for the United nations Expert Group meeting on International Migration Policies and the Status of Female Migrations, San Miniato, Italy, 27–30 March

Venturini, A. (1989), 'Emigrazione e Immigrazione' (Emigration and Immigration) in Ministero del Lavoro, *Occupazione e politiche del lavoro. Rapporto 1989*. Rome

Venturini, A. (1990), 'Un'interpretazione economica delle migrazioni mediterranee', in Maccheroni C., Mauri, A. (eds.) *Le migrazioni dall'Africa mediterranea verso l'Italia*, Milan, Giuffre

Vicarelli, G. (1993), 'Il lavoro per il mercato e il lavoro per la famiglia', paper presented at the Conference, *Cittadine del Mondo Le donne migranti tra identità e mutamento*, Ancone, 20/21

Weinert, P. (1991), *Foreign Female Domestic Workers: HELP Wanted* International Labour Office, Geneva, March

NOTES

1. The notions of post-industrialism, and, even more, of post-modernism, are still at the centre of the epistemological, philosophical, sociological and economic debate. Some of the analysis dedicated to these subjects concerns mainly the institutional changes (we are passing from a system based on the production of material goods to one producing information). The philosophical approach of Jean-François Lyotard considers post-modernity as the loss of the perspective of founding an epistemology and of the faith in a progress controlled by men.

2. The word 'emancipation' is in fact a very ambiguous one, indicating the liberation of the slave by the will of the master (through the symbolic act

of the imposing hand). Feminist movements criticize this notion: they do not want simply to obtain the same rights as men, the same opportunities, they want to create something new, through women's difference.

3. According to Tienda and Booth (1991), 'Although gender inequities are often defined in status terms, this approach is too restrictive for assessing sex roles in the course of social change, because 'status' typically is defined without reference to the embeddedness of gender in a web of culturally and socially circumscribed obligations and expectations.' (p. 53). They give as an example the difficulty of establishing if the entry of women in the labour market means an improvement of their position *vis-à-vis* men, if the social foundations of the sexual division of labour in the family are not considered. The term 'position' in reference to gender inequities seems more convenient to allow a consideration of contradictory outcomes within various domains of gender relations.

4. If we consider the tradition as a connection between the past and the future, modernity unifies past and present in a way of thinking oriented towards the future. In fact, the analysis of immigrants' trajectories, strategies, etc. shows dialectic processes between ways of thinking oriented towards the past, the present and the future (Chan Kwok Bun, 1994).

5. The notion of diaspora has entered the sociology of migration to describe processes which concern the different expatriated communities dispersed all over the world and keeping transnational boundaries among them.

6. In comparison with other European countries, Italy has a particularly large sector of the so-called informal economy and a stronger segmentation of the labour market. In Italy, immigrants have found an integration mainly in specific sectors, taking places Italians have abandoned, or creating new jobs for themselves (as is the case of street-vendors). The occupational areas which attract foreign immigrants are the tertiary sector (hawking, domestic work, small cleaning enterprises, conciergerie, catering) and the primary sector – fisheries and some agricultural activities. Recently, the industrial sector has started to absorb immigrants, but the process is limited to some regions (Lombardy, Emilia-Romagna), to some sectors (for example, foundries), and mainly to small industry.

7. We prefer to use the term 'group' to the one community, the Filipinos not being able to structure a community in Italy, because of the unbalanced men:women ratio, the type of professional insertion, etc.

8. The distinction in mono-ethnic, multi-ethnic and mixed associations has been made by F. Carchedi in Labos, 1991.

9. It is one of the most important feasts in the Philippines, during the month of May, dedicated to the Virgin Mary and to Saint Helena, mother of Constantine. In fact it is a feast celebrating women through the 'sagalas', different characters of the Bible and of history.

10. The jeepney is a sort of a big taxi.

11. LIFE – League Italo-Filipino of Filipino emigrants; Kampi, Organization of Filipino workers in Italy; Kamapi, Organization of Filipino Workers in Italy; Afli, Association of Filipino Leagues in Italy.

12. IREF: Istituto di ricerche educative e formative, Institute of Education and Training Research.

11 Circe or Penelope? An Analysis of the *Problematique* of Latin-American Women in Exile

Angela Xavier de Brito
and Ana Vasquez

This paper deals with the experience of exiled women and the analysis of the processes they experience over time while living away from their home country. Indeed, in the exile situation, men and women do certainly undergo similar experiences, but we argue that the specific gender experience can attribute a different meaning to these common processes. We cannot grasp the complexity of exile without analysing the specific way by which women live this process. The meaning which women, as a social group, give to the exile experience is far from being the same as men, even if both share the same social imaginaire. Nevertheless, even in their specificity, women are far from being a homogeneous group: we must also analyse the differences in the way different groups of women interpret exile. This article proposes to show, at the same time, the universal elements which characterize women's experience in exile, the feminine specificity in the transculturation process and the diversity of the feminine paths in exile.

The analysis of the lives and experience of exiled women we intend to present here is founded on fieldwork developed between 1975 and 1990 with a population of Latin-American males and females coming from Argentina, Brazil, Chile and Uruguay, and living in Europe, chiefly in France.

Designed originally to provide psychological help to these people, this work was later organized as a research programme. An ethnographic approach was adopted, which was founded on participant observation of individuals and groups, mainly through the institutions organized by the exile community. One of the main interests of this work is that the observation was done in real time, that is to say, while events were happening, while situations were created and modified. We have also conducted sequences of personal interviews, some of them with a therapeutic aim, over several years, which allowed us an access to the meaning these actors give to their own experience. Finally, our work has also been discussed and analysed together with many groups and individuals belonging to this community.

THE DIACHRONIC PERSPECTIVE: THE STAGES

The theoretical framework we used led us to a diachronic conception of exile. In our research, exile and exiled people's experience is conceived as it happens, allowing us to take into account the way individuals and groups change through time. We believe we cannot define exile only at the moment of arrival in the host country – however much it is filled with tragedy and anguish – or only taking into account the situation exiles are in after some years in the host country. We must follow them throughout the time they stay in the host society as political refugees and observe the changes they undergo, for these facts weigh on the individual and collective memory, thus influencing the way exiles perceive themselves while they are away from their own society. In other words, a definition of exile must take into account the succession of these moments and how individuals react to the new social and cultural patterns as time goes by. All these situations must be considered as a whole in a comprehensive conception of the exile situation.

Analysed throughout time, we have noted significant changes in day-to-day life experience and in the way the exiled men and women interpret their personal situation and, in a more general way, the exile situation. We have thus distinguished different stages in the exile experience, whose characteristics are as follows.

The First Stage

This involves the departure from the home country and the arrival in the host country. This stage is characterized by traumatisms due to the violence of forced departure and the effects of sudden and unwilling transplantation, and the elaboration of the profound rupture caused by the prohibition to return. The moral and physical sufferings which accompany departure are heightened by a very complex feeling of culpability.

Exiles are thus forced to employ all sorts of defence mechanisms, the most important being a refusal to live in the present, accompanied by an idealization of their home country and of their past experience. Exiles go through this first stage by refusing contact with the host country, and by living among themselves in a kind of confinement which leads them to consider the time they spend in exile as a provisional life. Together with many other authors (Amati, 1977; Barudy, 1977; Muñoz, 1980; Vignar, 1983), we think that this stage is also characterized by a mourning process which includes the loss of parents and friends as well as the loss of a lifestyle. The experiences exiles undergo in this first stage are so inherent to the exile situation that we can say they permeate the whole of exile experience.

The Second Stage

This is characterized by the transculturation process and cannot be summarized only as the learning of a new culture. As a matter of fact, it is a very painful process permeated by the contradictions between the original culture, in which individuals have been socialized and made into persons, and the new one. Exiles have the feeling that they are neglecting or even abandoning their cultural roots, which is not easily done. As they face the new context, they change, little by little, their codes of social relations. This process, which begins as an instrumental practice, involves some profound changes which call into question not only the cultural values and ways of being but the psychological structure of the individual as well, as we will see later.

The Third Stage

This stage develops as time goes by, as the enhancement of the transculturation process shakes the myths around which the exiled group is constituted. The sudden loss of commitments and self-representations which maintained the cohesion of the exiled group carries along the questioning of individual identities, provoking a kind of permanent crisis. In the case of Latin-American exiles, this crisis calls into question their own role, if a situation of political change ever allows them to return to the home country.

Most exiles go through these stages, with individual variations. We intend to highlight, above all, the differences in how men and women experience them.

ULYSSES: THE EXILE'S MYTH

All human groups have the need to create myths, so as to legitimize their existence and to maintain cohesion between their members (De Preez, 1984). Sometimes, as Jankelevitch (1974) puts it, men retain the strong ideas and features of certain legends which they feel can represent their profound wishes and their images of themselves, transforming them into their own myths.

Jankelevitch proposes the myth of Ulysses as symbol and as a synthesis of the personal experience of exile. He retains above all two of its features: the punishment and the prohibition to return. Exile is thus presented as punishment for an unspecified fault, which can partially explain why exile is lived, at the subconscious level, with a feeling of culpability.

The prohibition of return turns the home country into an ideal object, a sort of paradise lost. Feeding on nostalgia, Ulysses does not try to come back only to a certain geographical space: he is willing to return to a mythical Ithaca, where he was king, where he was recognized, respected and perhaps even loved. In this perspective, the myth provides also the means to analyse the ambivalence of exiles towards their living in a foreign country. The return dream mingles with the unconscious desire to find 'their time', even 'their youth'. Time and distance melt in the unconscious desire: the opposition between 'the present' and 'the past' is superimposed with the 'here' and 'there'. Thus, unconsciously, the will to return possessed by exiles concerns not only the recovering of a lost space but also the will to rewind the clock of history (Vasquez and Xavier de Brito, 1993).

Most exiles identify themselves with this hero who, banished from his kingdom, always maintains his wish to return during his travelling around the world, in which he discovers certainly its risks, but also its charms. When he finally comes back, he is able to recover his power, his social status and even his wife, who awaits him patiently and faithfully.

Most of the research works on exile present this phenomenon as if there were no differences between the way both sexes live it, or even as if the way women live it should be subjected to the masculine way, considered to be universal. Exile's founding myth – that of Ulysses – assigns a higher importance to the masculine hero, almost neglecting women's place.

In the most common way of interpreting the Ulysses myth, the feminine characters are, if not entirely forgotten, always placed in a secondary position or as playing a secondary role. Most of them are situated in islands. None of them dares follow him on this adventurous journey: their role is limited to protecting him (Athena), waiting for him (Penelope), seducing him to stay away (Calypso) or even transforming his nature (Circe). In their devotion to him, they help him fulfil his desire of going back to his country and re-conquering his realm, in spite of their own desires.

In this way, the myth which Jankelevitch proposes as being representative of the profound desires of all exiles is, at the same time, a gender-marked myth which excludes women from the exile journey, a journey which symbolizes an opening to the world, the acquisition of lore and inner development. The question is then to discover if women – who make up a high proportion of Latin-American exiles – can feel themselves interpreted by the myth of Ulysses.

THE FIRST STAGE: ADHERENCE TO THE MYTH AS PART OF THE UNIVERSAL DIMENSION

During the first stage, at the imaginary level, women and men interpret exile in the very same way. The identity feeling of both sexes is linked to the solidarity with ideals shared by the whole of the exile community (Erikson, 1972). Women feel as guilty as men, they are explicitly willing to return, and they dream of going back to their own country, about which they too develop an idealistic representation. They surely share this collective imaginaire as they form a part of the exiles' community, whose organization is woven around the forbidden country.

> Could I have stayed in Brazil? The more I thought about it, the more the feeling of culpability grew, lessening the happiness of having a job, of knowing new people, of doing things. Each time the news about the death or the imprisonment of a comrade arrived, beside the revolt, there was the guilt . . . I was here, in security . . . (Interview with a Brazilian political activist, Da Costa *et al.*, 1980)

However, from the beginning, women feel they do not fit the myth, because they cannot identify themselves as the feminine complement of the hero. Some of them tended to identify themselves with the hero himself – for they were militants – or with Circe, in the sense they used to control their lives and to have a certain degree of autonomy in relation to the opposite sex. Unlike Penelope, many a Latin-American woman did not stay home waiting for her man to come back (Silva, 1981; Xavier de Brito, 1986; Kay, 1987). On the contrary, they did share their journey, since they either followed the 'acknowledged hero' (whether husband, son or father) or they were themselves expelled from their country because of an autonomous political and social activity.

So, exiled women really share with their male comrades, at least in the first stage, the essential characteristics of exile: the feeling of a provisional life, the entrapment in a national community, the mourning, the moral commitment towards the forbidden country. For us, it is in the social *imaginaire* and the everyday lives of these women that the key which explains the very specific ways women have of appropriating the collective *imaginaire* can be found.

Unity and Discord Among Women Exiles

These women, be they political activists themselves, wives or companions, mothers or daughters of exiled men, share a common characteristic: the double workday, even a treble one, when they add to their domestic and professional chores the participation in a political party or organization.

Women – above all, those who are themselves political activists – were unanimous, in their interviews, in speaking about the lesser consideration they received from society. The hero's image mentioned earlier is above all attributed to men. As the 'head of the family', men's status helps them obtain the best jobs from the solidarity networks and the highest prestige, as political activists and intellectuals (Vasquez, 1982). These social conditions enable men to recreate in exile their own political activities, while women are reduced to undertake the same 'feminine' chores for which they had been socialized – to feed, to dress, to look after, to raise children – even inside the political organizations. Quite a few of them say that the exile period meant 'turning back ten years in my life' (interview with a Brazilian political activist, Da Costa *et al.*, 1980), as they are led to reproduce very old patterns they thought they had definitely left behind. Women's first reaction in front of the host society was to preserve the same values within which they were trained in the home society: they value the familial structure, they accept a secondary role where their work is concerned – it being always valued as a minor activity – and they neglect their personal projects for the benefit of the family ones. Married women maintain the subordinate status they used to have. Interviews with women who used to be political activists in their home country reveal a disowning of their prior political status, and an impossibility of developing themselves in the host country because of their married status (Da Costa *et al.*, 1980).

Women belong roughly to two big groups: those who used to have an autonomous political activity in the home country and those who have no other reason for being in exile except for following their husbands. The governmental bureaucracy treats them equally, denying both of them their legal rights, such as the right to hold a passport. The split is mostly established by the exiled women themselves, the political activists looking down on those who did not participate in the political struggle.

Militant women adhere more easily to the group's myth. We should not forget that almost all exiles belonged either to extreme-left or left organizations, whose theoretical instruments and political practice did not allow, at this time – in the seventies – an analysis of the feminine condition. Women's specificity is not taken into account in this context, it is even considered as an element of division of the working class. This fact does not prevent militant women's identification with the masculine image initially – even if they continue to accomplish the double workday, being all of them suddenly deprived of the family network and, for those belonging to the middle classes, also of the maids they used to hire in Latin America (Kay, 1987). As they did not have their own identity references nor those which are socially attributed to men, identity crisis is more frequent in these women.

> In Brazil, I used to spend 24 hours a day on political work. All of a sudden, I came to a foreign country, I wondered, what will I do? How can I begin anew my career? I've lived through an identity problem, which was a very slow process. These last seven years have been years of a permanent questioning in my life. (Interview with a Brazilian political activist, Da Costa *et al.*, 1980)

Albeit sharing the whole of the exile's experience, that is to say, the same trauma, the mourning of exile, the defence mechanisms, the culpability feeling and the impression that life in a foreign country is always provisional, these women's lives are not structured in the same way as men's. Their tasks force them to assume everyday life in another culture, under unknown conditions. Being deprived of their prior status, having at the same time a kind of clear-headedness about what is going on around them, they take refuge in the most traditional values of their own culture and their psychological withdrawal is more marked than men's.

SECOND STAGE: THE TRANSCULTURATION PROCESS INCREASES THE DIFFERENCES

Paradoxically, it is the very exercise of these everyday and common-place chores – shopping, domestic tasks, the rearing and schooling of children – which sets off or accelerates women's calling into question their feminine identity.

This process is developed in a subtle way, which begins with a comparison between their home country and the new one. In the beginning, the group's mythology leads them to devalue as a whole the new country's customs and habits. But their motherly role favours more frequent contacts with other adults – from teachers and other children's parents to other foreigners who share with them the same situation. They can compare their way of living and see that there are other ways of being a woman. As the transculturation process goes on, they begin to understand the relativity of cultural codes.

As a matter of fact, men follow the same route but their evolution is slower: there is a gap between men and women in the way they perceive the culture of the host country and, above all, in the way they take a critical look at their own values. This can be explained by the fact that the positions of power which men hold inside the exile group help them to bear better exile conditions such as loss of professional status and political practice, and social isolation. It is also explained by the perception the host society has of men, identifying and valuing them as symbols of the deprived hero: they are seen as ambassadors of the victims of torture and of resistance movements against dictatorships. The exercise of this role justifies, in some way, their underestimation of everyday life and their lack of interest about the host society, including the learning of the new language and the making of new friends.

The more modest expectations women have give them more opportunities to acquire, albeit with an instrumental purpose, the intellectual and economic instruments available in the new society (Camilleri, 1983). They discover they are able to conceive their own projects, for example, going to university or finding a job. Others discover new values, such as autonomy, which allows them to endeavour to alter the traditional relation between genders inside marriage. Some of them learn they can even earn more money than their husband, which provokes in the Latin-American male a feeling of devaluation, a narcissistic wound difficult to bear.

> I've done so many things here in France: I've changed the orienta-
> tion of my studies, I've finished them, I've separated from my hus-
> band, I've had a child . . . But the most important thing I've discovered
> in exile is the discovery of being a woman . . . (Interview with a
> young Argentinian woman, Vasquez and Araujo, 1990)

The Role of the Feminist Movement in the Transculturation Process

We must bear in mind that the analysis of these Latin-American communities in exile is done, above all, in France. Between 1973 and 1980,
there existed in this country a very active feminist movement whose
after-effects are still relevant in the French society as a whole, in a
diffuse way. The ideological and cultural frame the exile communities
used to have led them to mistrust European feminist movements. They
were regarded as leading to a diversion in the class struggle, and
answering to other interests different from those raised by the Latin-
American context. That is why, initially, women rejected the feminist
movement as a whole, partly out of fear, and partly out of the habit of
bending to the dominant norms of the exiled community.

> In the beginning, I used to think that the feminist movement was, in
> a way, a foolish thing, that it had nothing to do with real life and
> was composed of alienated women. I had a very critical representa-
> tion of this movement, I thought the important task was to do what
> we did in Brazil, that is to say, to incorporate women to the politi-
> cal struggle, in a socialist perspective (Interview with a Brazilian
> political activist, Da Costa *et al.*, 1980)

Adherence to the feminist movement by some exiled women, at a
later stage, presents a double characteristic: it is done above all in the
second stage of exile, as a signal of the deepening of the transculturation
process; it is also done, for those who belonged to political organizations, within their ideological framework, inside which they fight to
conquer a certain margin of autonomy leading to the recognition of
their specificity.

The recognition of feminine individuality is not an easy task. It requires a certain amount of struggle and it is a process involving many
contradictions. To be accomplished, this process of consciousness-raising
requires their being in exile in societies where the social conditions
favours its emergence, such as France. The contact with other women
who asserted their differences and their collective identity made those

exiled women wonder about their own perception of the world and of themselves. It allowed them to substitute an identity founded on the global myths of the group – which were, as we have said, essentially masculine – for other identity marks linked to the collective aspects of the feminist struggle.

The feminist movement's role is certainly very important. Adherence to feminist groups is made in different ways, depending on whether women participate or not in a political organization, and on the characteristics of those organizations. The Communist Party's members, such as Zuleika, stuck to the 'feminine work' for a long time, thus recognising the minor role of women in the revolutionary struggle. For the activists of this party, the changing from 'feminine work' to 'feminist work' is done later and is almost always linked to a traumatic event in their personal lives such as divorce.

More recently created political organizations, with a minor tradition of working class struggle and mostly composed of middle-class intellectuals, were more willing to integrate feminine specificity in the frame of oppressed minorities' struggle. They created a 'feminist' sector with a relative autonomy, where women could partake of a certain degree of leadership – as is the case within some Brazilian and Chilean organizations. Thus, some of them could define themselves as 'feminists' inside the Latin-American community and claim a certain amount of autonomy which was denied before. They start to reflect on their everyday lives, on the artificial separation between their public and their private lives, on power relations among genders in society and on the roots of the patriarchal society within which they have been raised (Xavier de Brito, 1986). Those practices have an echo among all exiled women, thus increasing their recognition and making feminist women accepted as full political partners by the whole of the exiled community.

The objectives they defined at the beginning were very much linked to the political situation of their own country: information about the oppression of women in their countries, political campaigns for the liberation of imprisoned women and so on. But the movement's own dynamics led them to establish more and more contacts within the French feminist movement (neighbourhood groups of women, family planning and so on), contributing to their progressive adoption of other kinds of practice, to the constitution of consciousness-raising groups where they mix with other women who were not necessarily exiled, coming from different generations, horizons and training routes.

Our personal experience and some of our reading allows us to say that the process other exiled women coming from other geographical and ideological horizons underwent coincides, in some ways, with the process of the Latin-American ones. However, this process seems to be slower inside those communities which are structured in a more authoritarian way.

Unfortunately, we lack data which would allow us to compare the influence of the French feminist movement over Latin-American women and women from other origins, so we are reluctant to extend our intent to generalize.

Similarities of the General Process but Diversity of Individual Routes

In spite of being under the same influences in the new society, not all women took the same routes. So, it is in the synthesis of the biographical data with the double historical context of the home as well of the host society that we can find the keys to understanding these different feminine routes (Vasquez, 1990).

Exile brought, for certain, as a direct consequence, a weakening of marriage links. With the raising of the political veil, some militant couples see each other, for the first time, face to face. Quite a few of them cannot face this trial. Some women who economically supported a husband entirely dedicated to the revolutionary cause, and who found that this situation was normal 'because he was the political activist', begin to wonder about its legitimacy when the same situation is reproduced in the host country. For men, as we have said, did not have the least wish to participate in a more active way in everyday responsibilities, being mostly dedicated to revolutionary practice and to the preservation of their old image. A number of exiled women, partly as a result of the direct or the diffuse influence of the feminist movement, began to call into question the traditional division of labour inside the home, particularly when both members of the couple do professional and political work. Some of them decide to rebuild their lives on new lines, establishing a new relationship with their husbands in marriage – whether he be the same one they have followed in exile or a new partner from the same or from a different nationality they have married when in exile. Finally, seldom do people resist the transculturation process: its action on men is also important, making them change.

> It is funny how everything changes . . . nowadays, my husband does not wish to be perceived as an old-fashioned 'macho', he shares a lot more at home . . . The paramount change concerns the children,

he has learned to like the contact with Nicolas and Claudia . . . he has even begun to develop new links of tenderness, complicity and love . . . Before, he would never dare to express them so in the open . . . (Interview with an Argentinean political activist, Vasquez and Araujo, 1990).

Some other women have put into practice, in a happy mood, different projects they would never dare to realize in Latin America: reconciling motherhood and career, living without a permanent partner and having no inferiority feeling about it, or assuming alien sexual options, for instance.

It all depends, in a way, on the balance they achieve in the exile period. Women assess this period in different ways. Some of them, like one Brazilian woman, state that 'exile has been more positive than negative', for it has allowed her 'to fulfil my life with another world', to acquire new values, to give a different education to their children (Da Costa *et al.*, 1980). An Argentinian political activist has said that exile has been for her 'a second birth, where I could rediscover, even discover, pleasure' (Vasquez and Araujo, 1990). Even those who have a more negative vision of exile are led to recognize the positive side of it. Another Brazilian woman said, for instance, that even if 'exile has been the worst punishment', for it 'did destroy individuals', 'I have learned and matured a lot, even in what concerns Brazil, from which I have a much more critical vision nowadays' (Da Costa *et al.*, 1980).

Very few women failed to question their lives in exile. They are those who, like men, had a very strong and permanent feeling of exile as a provisional life, who refused to take advantage of local resources and to change their lives at any level, who confined themselves to the exiled community and who accepted in a passive way the secondary status this same community attributed to them. We have observed the case of a Chilean political activist for whom the refusal of assuming her feminine identity followed different strategies (Vasquez, 1990): from an aggressive struggle to impose herself as the men's equal inside the political organization to the only and giving exclusive importance to the intellect, which led her to neglect her physical appearance – which makes it harder for her to find a job in France. As Reed (1979) and Rowbotham (1980) have put it, for her, the acceptance of the feminine criteria common in French society would imply 'an acceptance of dependence and a loss of power'.

But women's journeys are not limited to a questioning process of objective social facts. Quite a few of them begin to call into question their own individual values, their capacity to assume the role of full individuals in society. Some of them begin to recognize their own capacity in organizing everyday life, in managing tasks at home – which they already exercised without even being conscious of it.

> During years, while he studied sociology at the university and while he went to political meetings four days a week, it was me who struggled to earn the money and me who took care of our daughter. Enough of all this hypocrisy! I had really enough of it. I felt myself able to live alone and to rear my daughter alone. As a matter of fact, I did it already . . . (Interview with a Uruguayan woman, Vasquez and Araujo, 1990).

Some others allow themselves a degree of autonomy as individuals, which they have always denied or feared to assume. Thus, they begin to change not only their relations as a couple but also the relation they established with the extended family, this overpowering institution in Latin-American society.

THIRD STAGE: CERTAINTIES ARE SHAKEN, THE RETURN TO THE HOME COUNTRY BECOMES A CHOICE

As times goes by, as the exile period becomes longer, exiled men and women become progressively integrated in the host country and its values, even if sometimes against their own will. A larger proportion of them marry people of this new country, children grow and are socialized in the host language and culture. The imaginary boundaries of the home country begin to blur. In the case of Latin-American exiles, this period coincides with the shaking of the foundations of 'real socialism', which also shakes their ideological certainties. This process affects also their personal projects, even as important a project as the return to the home country. Nevertheless, we must not forget that the sojourn in exile for each national community has a different span of time. Almost all Brazilian exiles returned after the political amnesty was proclaimed in 1979; Argentinians begin to return a little later. The other communities have not made so clear a choice: if there is a common tendency to return, each individual can make his/her own decision, prolonging thus the transculturation process they are under. There is, nevertheless, a distance between the moralising discourse they held about the need to return and the effective choice of returning. Here also, women maintain their own specificity and behave differently from men.

Women's discourse speaks of a kind of loyalty to the national community: they dream, as do men, of going back to their home country. But even when conceived as a dream, the decision to return is not an easy one, nor is it an isolated point in a destiny: it is a process woven in the whole of a trajectory (Xavier de Brito, 1991). Women's doubts concerning return raise questions which men do not raise.

The key word of the feminine discourse is 'fear'. What do these women fear, and why? First of all, they fear the overpowering influence of the extended family. Being accustomed in Europe to an autonomous way of life, they fear the struggle they will have to fight to preserve their present lifestyle.

I have a very good relation with my family, but I think I will not live with them anymore . . . and I know they are expecting it. They say: 'The house is all ready, waiting for you'. This has me wondering, I don't want to hurt them . . . (Interview with a Brazilian woman, Da Costa *et al.*, 1980).

Some of them speak out about their fear of not finding their place in the home society, either on a material or on a symbolic level. They wonder if they will be able to find jobs according to their competencies, they fear the social control. They are conscious of the limits imposed either by the dependence links woven by the extended family or by society as a whole, as they dare defy social norms and live as a divorced woman or homosexual. The balance one Brazilian woman draws up, after six months spent in her host country, is a cruel one:

How could I fool myself so, idealize so many things? I've discovered there's no place for me in Brazil . . . You want to live in your home country but you feel that your country is not the one which really exists (interview with a Brazilian woman, Da Costa *et al.*, 1980)

Some others fear that returning may mean the end of the political, material or moral stability they had to fight so hard to conquer. Last but not least, women are conscious of the extension of their changing process; they wonder if people in their home country have evolved in a similar way. To return and not be able to find their place in their home society will be as if exile has begun anew and, this time, in their own country.

I am afraid of not recognizing people there. I have changed a lot, I don't know if my friends have also changed, I fear they won't understand me. Ah, I'm so very much afraid . . . and I feel also a

kind of nostalgia ... as if something belonged to the past, which I
could never recall ... (Interview with a Brazilian woman, Da Costa
et al., 1980).

Nevertheless, the choice of staying is a very hard one to make. Those
who have decided to stay emphasize the temporary nature of this decision and try to justify it with all sorts of arguments. Finally, a few of
them are always coming and going between the home and the host
society for more or less extended periods. They may or may not have
institutional links, they may or may not be married to partners belonging to the host country: these coming and goings show, above all, the
difficulty of making a real choice between the two societies. It is interesting to observe that this behaviour is scarcely found among men.

Men also show fewer doubts or fears concerning social refusal or
the extended family's control. Even if they have also changed, men
are more sure about the solidity of their social status, more concerned
about their professional and political reinsertion. The interviews conducted both with men and women who returned show that the former
have a better reinsertion in their home society, although this does not
prevent them from suffering the effects of the cultural distance which
exile years have developed between them and their own country.

CONCLUSION

In this article, we have endeavoured to grasp the complexity of the
phenomenon of exile through the analysis of women's experiences.
The stages we propose as a theoretical model, though common to the
bulk of the exile population, are lived differently according to the characteristics of individuals, and gender plays a major role here. We hope
we have shown that life experience in exile has changed both women
and men, but that the intensity of change and the way change is woven
into their life journeys are not the same. Yet, women as individual or
collective actors cannot be isolated from the more global frame of
society's norms, which includes not only comparison with men, but
with other social groups as well.

Two questions at least remain, which concern above all the transculturation process which Latin-American women in exile have under-
gone. The first one is linked to the changes they underwent when in
exile, in personality, representations, attitudes and practice. How can
they pursue, or even simply maintain these, in societies which are still
largely marked by some sort of 'machismo'? Will these new influences

be somehow permanent, will they be able to transmit them to other women, even to their children? The second one focuses on the new structures and practice which they can create in this context. What room will they have to manoeuvre? What mythological character will be more suitable to analyse their present practice? We have said that they are not Penelopes, for they have followed their male partners in exile and shared with them the very same reality. Can they be comparable to Circe, that is to say, females whose practice and power are bound to alter the very nature of the men they are close to, of those they interact with? In other words, to what extent will they be able to alter the social trends of these Latin-American societies?

BIBLIOGRAPHY

Amati, S., (1977), 'Quelques réflexions sur la torture pour introduire une discussion psychanalytique', *IPSO Newsletter* No. 2

Barudy, J., (1977), 'Salud mental y exilio politico'. *COLAT* (Brussels)

Camilleri, C., (1983), 'Images de l'identité et ajustements culturels au Mahgreb', *Peuples Méditerranéens* No. 24

Da Costa, A. *et al.* (1980), *Memórias das mulheres do exfio*, Rio de Janeiro, Paz e Terra

De Preez, P., (1984), 'Myths and social individuals', Paper to the *International Conference on Self and Identity*, Cardiff

Erikson, E.H., (1972), *Adolescence et crise: la quête d'une identité*, Paris, Flammarion

Homère, (1982), *Odyssée*, Le livre de Poche

Jankelevitch, V., (1974), *L'irréversible et la nostalgie*, Paris, Flammarion

Kay, D., (1987), *Chileans in exile. Private strategies, public lives*. Basingstoke: Macmillan

Lewis, O., (1965), *Los hijos de Sanchez*, Mexico, Mortiz

Morin, E., (1990), *Introduction à la pensée complexe*, Paris, ESF

Muñoz, L., (1980), 'Exile as bereavement: social and psychological manifestations of Chilean exiles in Great Britain', *British Journal of Medical Psychology* No. 53, pp. 227–232

Reed, E., (1979), *Féminisme et anthropologie*, Paris, Denoël/Gonthier

Rowbotham, S., (1980), *Féminisme et révolution*, Paris, Payot

Silva, M., (1981), 'Estudio de mujeres exiliadas chilenas entre 17 y 45 años', *Chile-América* No. 74 (Rome)

Vasquez, A., (1982), 'Des troubles d'identité chez les exilés', *Amériques Latines* No. 12

Vasquez, A. & Araujo, A.M., (1990), *Exils latino-américains. La malédiction d'Ulysse*, Paris, L'Harmattan

Vasquez, A., (1990), 'Les mécanismes des stratégies identitaires: une perspective diachronique', Camilleri *et al*, *Stratégies identitaires*, Paris, PUF, pp. 143–171

Vasquez, A. and Xavier De Brito, (1993), La situation d'exil: essai de généralisation fondé sur l'exemple des réfugiés latino-américains', *Intercultures* No. 21, No. spécial sur Stratégies d'adaptation, April, pp. 51–66

Vignar, M.N., (1983), 'L'étranger'. Actes du Colloque 'L'étranger, Crise-Représentation', vol. 1. Paris, Collectif *Evénements Psychanalis*, pp. 204–214

Xavier De Brito, A., (1986), 'Brazilian women in exile, the quest for an identity.' *Latin American Perspectives* issue 49, volume 13, number 2, spring, pp. 58–79

Xavier De Brito, A., (1991), *Construction de l'espace de formation et études à l'étranger. Stratégies et 'carrière morale' des étudiants brésiliens dans l'Université française. 1960–1986.* Ph.D thesis in Sociology, Université René Descartes/Paris V

Index

235

QM LIBRARY
(MILE END)